The Design Agenda

A Guide to Successful Design Management

Rachel Cooper
University College Salford, UK

and

Mike Press
Staffordshire University, UK

JOHN WILEY & SONS
Chichester • New York • Brisbane • Toronto • Singapore

Other Wiley Editorial Offices

John Wiley & Sons, Inc., 605 Third Avenue,
New York, NY 10158-0012, USA

Jacaranda Wiley Ltd, 33 Park Road, Milton,
Queensland 4064, Australia

John Wiley & Sons (Canada) Ltd, 22 Worcester Road,
Rexdale, Ontario M9W 1L1, Canada

John Wiley & Sons (SEA) Pte Ltd, 37 Jalan Pemimpin #05-04,
Block B, Union Industrial Building, Singapore 2057

Library of Congress Cataloging-in-Publication Data

Davies-Cooper, Rachel.
  The design agenda: a guide to successful design management/
  Rachel Cooper and Mike Press.
      p.   cm.
  Includes bibliographical references and index.
  ISBN 0-471-94106-9
  1. Design, Industrial – Management.   I. Press, Mike.   II. Title.
  TS171.4.D38   1994
  658.5'752 – dc20   94–13491
                                                                 CIP

British Library Cataloguing in Publication Data

A catalogue record for this book is available from the British Library

ISBN 0-471-94106-9

Typeset in 11/12pt Palatino by The Setting Studio, Newcastle upon Tyne.
Printed and bound in Great Britain by Biddles Ltd, Guildford and
King's Lynn.

Contents

Acknowledgements

In developing the content and argument of our book we owe much to the many students, teaching colleagues, designers and industrialists with whom we have worked. Some deserve special mention: David Walker from the Open University for his critical comments and suggestions for improvement, Danielle Ellis and Janet Sleath at Staffordshire University for their encouragement and feedback, Diana and Nigel Press for patient proof-reading and Julie Nock for valued insights on fashion design. We also wish to thank Steve Jobs for his Apple Macintosh, a constant reminder of good design, without which the whole enterprise would have been a great deal more arduous and even more consuming of paper

Special thanks go to our partners, Cary Cooper and Liz Swinburne for stimulation, criticism, sympathy, sanity and patience.

Rachel Cooper and Mike Press
Salford and Stoke-on-Trent
1994

1 Introduction

"How long will it take our industry to realise that UK Ltd is uncompetitive because its products are uglier, clumsier and less appealing to the buyer than those of our competitors".[1]

Tony Key, Corporate Head of Design, British Telecom, 1993

"Design is a political act. Every time we design a product we are making a statement about the direction the world will move in".[2]

Stefano Marzano, Philips Corporate Design, 1993

In answer to Mr Key's rhetorical question – at least 160 years. During a parliamentary debate in 1832 on the problem of Britain's declining export of textiles, Sir Robert Peel blamed poor designs. In the years following Peel, the design message has been pursued with increasing vigour by designers, enlightened industrialists and the government. When Mrs Thatcher backed the message with hard cash, in the form of grants for design consultancy, it appeared that the case for design had been won.

The 1980s has been described as the "design decade", with various events symbolising design's elevation to a prominent position in our industrial culture. Design consultancies raced each other for a listing on the stock market and expanded into Europe and North America. Sir Terence Conran built up his Storehouse design-led retailing empire and attracted sponsors for a Design Museum overlooking

---

London's Tower Bridge. The consumer boom created a market for designer goods which were often the subject of critical examination by a rising number of design journalists. The business of corporate identity transformed the once familiar faces of well-established enterprises and utilities, and a new business discipline – design management – found its way into MBA programmes.

Design's rapid ascent as a significant economic and cultural activity made its collapse all the more dramatic. Michael Peters, the foremost consultancy of the new design industry, called in the receivers; Sir Terence Conran lost control of Storehouse and saw Habitat sold to a Swedish company; the Design Museum cut back on its staffing and activities in the face of financial uncertainty; and Wally Olins redesigned British Telecom's corporate identity. The prancing piper adorning public telephone boxes was seen to be playing design's last post. Even the director general of the Design Council described it as a "trivial and irrelevant cliché".[3]

The consumer boom of the late 1980s enabled the design industry to indulge in a superficiality and hype to which it ultimately fell victim with the onset of economic recession. The 1990s poses our society with new problems and new challenges. Design must demonstrate that it remains a vital economic and cultural resource rather than a stylistic fad. To develop Stefano Marzano's point, design must reflect and contribute positively to the changing social values that underlie the future direction of the world in which we live.

Behind design's somewhat tarnished public profile is its reality as a resource of considerable benefit to management:

"Design is the process of seeking to optimize consumer satisfaction and company profitability through the creative use of major design elements (performance, quality, durability, appearance, and cost) in connection with products, environments, information, and corporate identity".[4]

As this definition indicates, design brings together the needs of consumers and the objectives of the firm in creating products and services which perform appropriately, express a commitment to quality, have positive aesthetic qualities and can be produced efficiently. It is clearly an interdisciplinary activity of some complexity.

This complexity requires that the design process is effectively managed. Like any other corporate activity, design requires monitoring and control mechanisms. Standards and policies are necessary to ensure that design is consistent and maintains a recognised degree of quality. Effective management structures are needed to ensure that design meets company objectives and integrates appropriately with other corporate activities. Overall, a strategic approach to design at board level elevates design to an innovative process with a long-term horizon.

Design management "is the application of the process of management to the processes of innovation and design".[5] There is a considerable body of research which examines the dimensions and efficacy of design management. This research has shown that effective design management, although not a general panacea for industry, is a significant contributor to success, deserving a place on the corporate agenda. Companies large and small, both manufacturing and service-based, all need a *Design Agenda*.

However, a crucial argument developed in this book is that design, in its interaction between industry and society, provides a means for organisations not only to accrue profits but also to manifest the social responsibilities increasingly demanded by the public. It must therefore be viewed from a broad perspective in order to appreciate its social, cultural, technological and commercial dimensions.

Background to the Design Agenda

This introduction to design management arises from our teaching and research, both jointly and independently, over several years. At the Universities of Salford and Staffordshire we have taught a range of design students ranging from fashion and graphics to glass and industrial design, and more particularly have developed undergraduate and postgraduate programmes on design management, which have been geared to both design and business students. We have also been involved in design awareness training for managers in industry. Through this work we identified a need for an introductory text that wove together theory and practice, and a guide to the growing literature and other sources of information in the field. *The Design Agenda* aims to meet this need.

Perhaps this book also has a hidden agenda – the commitment of its authors. Our writing and work is rooted in the belief that rekindling a passion for things – things that work, things that communicate, things that evoke meaning and emotion, things that solve urgent problems – is essential in both generating wealth and improving the quality of life. The Japanese clothing designer Issey Miyake described how "we dreamed between two worlds".[6] As a description of what designers do, Miyake's phrase has much to its credit. Design lies between the worlds of culture and commerce, between passion and profit. Design is indeed a passion for things, offering methods that enable them to come into being. It follows that design should also aspire to a passion for the people who use these things, for their quality of life and their aspirations: a passion for betterment. The management of design is about fostering that passion and linking it to the fulfilment of corporate goals and profitability. *The Design Agenda* explains why it is necessary and how it can be done. More so than other books on design management, *The Design Agenda* considers some of the cultural dimensions that are essential to an understanding of design on the part of those who manage it.

This book distils and synthesises our perspectives and arguments on design management, which derive from two different starting points in the field. Rachel Cooper was educated as a graphic designer. Through the practice of design she developed research activities on its management, which currently co-exist with teaching on marketing and design courses. Mike Press was formerly a research consultant for industry and local government on economic development and innovation, whose interests developed towards the role of design in these issues. With backgrounds and interests that span a range of practices, the authors' intentions were to exploit this diversity in a multidisciplinary introduction to design management.

Using *The Design Agenda*

This book is an introductory text designed for students studying design management at undergraduate and post-graduate levels, together with practising managers who wish to develop an interest in the field. It is not a "how to" book but a "what you need to think about before you do and where to get more detailed information about it" book. In detailing the relationship between design and management it aims to make business students and managers more design aware, and design students more business aware. It is an agenda of issues and possibilities that through further study and the practice of design management will lead to an agenda of action.

The Design Agenda combines contextual analysis, reference to research findings and other literature, relevant exemplars and summaries of practical methods and techniques that enable design to be managed effectively. The book falls into two parts: Chapters 2, 3 and 4 provide a theoretical discussion of design and its influences, while Chapters 5, 6 and 7 look at the practical issues of design and the organisation. Although the book is very much a joint effort, the overall responsibility for the first part was taken by Mike Press and that for the second part by Rachel Cooper. Each of the six main chapters is structured to enable a rapid grasp of the issues covered, provide contemporary illustration of its arguments and promote further study. Chapters start with a graphic "map" of their content and themes, and end with a summary of conclusions and implications.

Going beyond the usual bibliography of most texts, *The Design Agenda* concludes with a Resource Guide, which comprises an annotated selected bibliography organised by subject, a listing of periodicals and journals for those wishing to maintain an up to date understanding of the field, a listing of organisations that support and encourage design management, and details of the main educational and research bodies involved.

Structure of Content

The Book Map indicates the themes covered by each chapter, and a summary of the main arguments that are drawn from them.

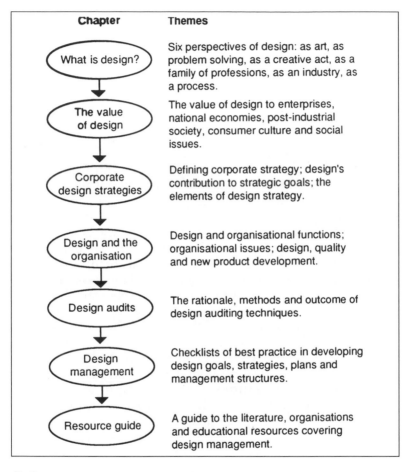

Chapter	Themes
What is design?	Six perspectives of design: as art, as problem solving, as a creative act, as a family of professions, as an industry, as a process.
The value of design	The value of design to enterprises, national economies, post-industrial society, consumer culture and social issues.
Corporate design strategies	Defining corporate strategy; design's contribution to strategic goals; the elements of design strategy.
Design and the organisation	Design and organisational functions; organisational issues; design, quality and new product development.
Design audits	The rationale, methods and outcome of design auditing techniques.
Design management	Checklists of best practice in developing design goals, strategies, plans and management structures.
Resource guide	A guide to the literature, organisations and educational resources covering design management.

References

1 Letter to *Design Week*, 30 July 1993, p.11.
2 *Design Week*, 24 September 1993, p.22.
3 Owen, Ivor (1991) Comment, *Design*, March, p.9.
4 Kotler, P. and Rath, G.A. (1984) Design: a powerful but neglected strategic tool, *Journal of Business Strategy*, **5**(2).
5 Heap, J. (1989) *The Management of Innovation and Design*, Cassell, London, p.5.
6 Penn, Irving (1988) *Issey Miyake*, Little, Brown, Boston, Mass., p.19.

2 What is Design?

There is a Sufi parable about the desert city whose citizens were all blind. One day a king arrived riding a mighty elephant and camped close to the city. Curious as to what this strange animal was, a group was sent from the city to learn about it. Each of those sent out gathered information on the animal by touching some part of it. When they returned to the city a crowd assembled around them to learn the truth about the elephant. "What shape is it?" they asked.

The man who had felt the ear said, "it is a large, flat, rough thing, like a carpet."

"Rubbish", said the man who had handled the trunk, "it is a long, bendy hollow pipe."

"Don't you believe it", exclaimed the one whose arms had embraced the legs, "it is mighty, firm and strong, like a pillar."

Knowledge, the parable concludes, is not the companion of the blind.

Design is a broad field covering many different disciplines. It can be viewed as a discrete activity, as a total process or in terms of its tangible outcome. Design can be viewed as a management function, a cultural phenomenon and as an industry in its own right. It is a means of adding value and a vehicle for social or political change. Design is defined differently in different countries with our understanding of it changing over time. As in the case of the Sufi parable, these various interpretations are not necessarily mutually exclusive, but they are partial views of a complex set of related activities.

Given management's prosaic concerns, the philosophy of knowledge may not appear the most useful starting point for an introduction to design management. The design professions have spent considerable effort ridding themselves of the more esoteric baggage which has in the past accompanied them, to present themselves as practical and valuable servants to industry. Philosophical discourses are fine in their place, but that place is far from the boardrooms or design studios, where issues and decisions are concerned with designing and making things that accrue profit. Management is the science of pragmatism and British management especially so. The British, according to the historian R.H. Tawney, "are incurious as to theory, take fundamentals for granted, and are more interested in the state of the roads than in their place on the map".[1]

Much of this book is concerned with the state of the roads and how they can be improved, but some notion of where we are now and the changing contours over which these roads will travel is first necessary. Different perspectives or definitions of design will help to reveal the broad nature and various functions of design in industry and society. This chapter is therefore structured around different ways of perceiving design, as shown in the Chapter Map.

Design as Art

"Industrial designers are really the folk artists of our civilisation."

Lionel Tiger, Professor of Anthropology, Rutgers University

Wedged between an article on sex therapy and an interview with David Bowie, a recent issue of the men's lifestyle magazine *Arena* carried a feature on Mazda's design philosophy. It quoted the Japanese car maker's chief designer asserting, "We are finished with industrial design. We want to make emotional cars".[2] The marketing of cars as fashion accessories is not particularly new. Elevating a particular design philosophy to a lifestyle trend which is discussed alongside safe sex and the new Bowie CD is perhaps just a sign of the times.

Chapter Map

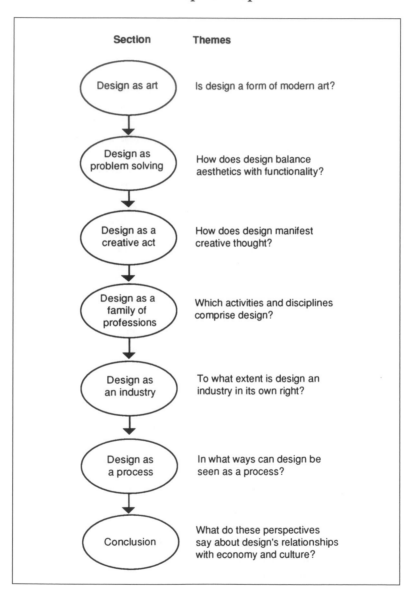

When *Business Week* ran an article on the changing face of American industrial design, the story centred on the flamboyant and highly individual character of Hartmut Esslinger, founder of the consultancy "frogdesign" and responsible for the design of products which grossed $15 billion in sales during 1989. Esslinger described his styling of the NeXT computer, conceived by Steven Jobs, formerly of Apple Computers, as "an expression of revenge to a company that killed its founder".[3] The NeXT project is a declaration of Esslinger's design credo *form follows emotion*.

According to Lionel Tiger, the higher profile of individual designers and their emotional agenda is evidence that they have become the artists of the postmodern age. Design, in his view, has joined with art in expressing popular ideals and aspirations.[4] Consumers look to design, not to manifest function, but to communicate values. Few wearers of Levi 501s are employed in the stevedore or mining industries, for whom the riveted denims were originally designed. Russian youths will offer several months' salary for a pair, not because of their proletarian utility, but because they are expressions of rebellion and freedom. The concerns of design to express lifestyle have always been paramount in the fashion industry. The difference now is that this principle is being extended into other fields of design such as cars and electronic consumer goods. Japanese manufacturers are using the term "humanware" to describe design which injects lifestyle into products and bases differentiation more upon image and user requirements rather than function, as we will see in more detail in Chapter 3.

Some of the latest Japanese products are among the exhibits in London's Design Museum. The four recently established museums of design throughout the world are a measure of design's increasing cultural significance. Stephen Bayley, former director of the Design Museum, is among those to argue that design has become the art of the twentieth century.[5] As painting and sculpture left the concerns of the general public behind and sought refuge within the art gallery and world of the collector, so popular aesthetic pleasure was sought increasingly from the products of consumer society. The phenomena of "design icons" and contemporary crafts, which blur the distinction between art, craft and design illustrate this tendency.

Of all the icons that characterise the design decade of the 1980s, perhaps the most notable is a conical stainless steel kettle with a small brightly coloured plastic bird on the spout – the Alessi kettle. Michael Graves, the kettle's British designer, was responsible for the best selling product in the Italian company's 70-year history. From its factory on the shores of Lake Maggiore, Alessi exports to 70 countries,

Figure 2.1 – The Alessi Kettle

The Alessi kettle, designed by Michael Graves, is one of the best known examples of Alessi's products, which aim to present innovations in form, style and methods of manufacture, unconstrained by the usual limits of industrial mass production

supporting a workforce of over 300 people. Building upon the success and exclusive reputation of its metal tableware products, the company is broadening its interests into time-pieces, porcelain and furniture. If any one company characterises design as art, Alessi is it.

Alessi's mission is to "bring poetry to the people". Alberto Alessi claims that his firm's products are in keeping with the spirit of the age: "on the one hand people are looking for more amusement and on the other they are bored by the consumerist culture of the seventies and eighties; they have a desire for truth. We are in the midst of galloping cultural growth, and increasingly people want beautiful things which are outside the parameters of the old marketing-led approach".[6] The company commissions artists, architects and designers to develop product ideas, which are realised in its craft workshops. Alessi presents itself as drawing together art, craft and advanced technology with the aim of providing a visual poetry appropriate to contemporary concerns and aesthetics.

Jasper Morrison is a British furniture designer who claims that "design contains its own art, a part of which is close to sculpture and another part which is not".[7] He is one of a new generation of designer–makers or contemporary craft makers whose experiments in form and decoration take function as a starting point rather than a destination. One-off chairs, ceramic vessels and even radios sometimes present themselves in the vocabulary of sculpture and have stimulated a whole infrastructure of craft galleries, exhibitions and critical theory. Like artists, these designers are seeking to challenge perception. In doing so, design claims a role for itself as a primarily expressive medium. As art and design historian Edward Lucie-Smith has argued, "While the frontier between fine art and design is permeable, it is also movable. Design seems to be moving into the territory the fine arts have scornfully abandoned".[8]

Although the new crafts reside mainly in the exclusive domain of galleries and collectors, they are gaining a wider audience as designer–makers are increasingly commissioned to produce "public art" for city centres, garden festivals and other environments. John Thackara has suggested that their techniques may have application in industry: "Imagine a washing machine with its bland steel panels made more interesting by the metal finishing techniques developed by craft jewellers; think of furniture with the qualities of a one-off, produced in quantity; even car interiors could be improved by the use of more original textile designs".[9]

How are we to interpret this apparent elevation of design to the realm of art? From one perspective it is symptomatic of design's vulnerability to the manipulative powers of marketing and the cultural vacuousness of the *nouveaux riches* yuppy consumers. Peter Dormer is a design critic who has been dismissive of design's pretentions to art in terms of both "design icons" and contemporary crafts. In his book *The Meanings of Modern Design*, Dormer examines the cultural packaging of expensive household goods as art, concluding that "it just happens that one of the tactics of modern marketing is to seek to elevate such objects into art by comparing them with art and, of course, converting them into the full currency of culture by having them displayed in museums".[10] *Design as art* as a marketing strategy is perhaps less modern than Dormer suggests. Over 200 years ago Josiah Wedgwood employed fine artists such as John Flaxman and George Stubbs to decorate ceramic ware as part of a marketing strategy to raise the profile and broaden the market of his company.

Dormer reserves most of his entertaining vitriol for the makers and consumers of art–craft. Craft makers who disguise their lack of skill by the shroud of artistic intent are patronised by rich collectors wanting in cultural knowledge: "Nothing in art or design or architecture or craft is more foolish than the sight of modest ideas ballooning and buffeting on the thermals of rich ignorance. ... The function of craft in this stage of the twentieth century ought not be the silly caperings after exaggerated effects of quasi-art funded by the ignorance of the nouveaux riches anxious to become collectors".[11] Dormer's criticism is an attempt to retain some of the alleged universal values of design such as skill, quality and integrity, in the face of what he considers to be culturally degrading consumerism.

Upholding similar values in the design of mass market goods is Dieter Rams, the designer behind the elegant simplicity of Braun's domestic appliances. Rams believes that products should manifest their purpose and that "good design means as little design as possible". The designer who claims that any colour can be used in industrial design as long as it is black, white or grey is trenchant against "design which cynically exploits human weaknesses; design which is superficial, random, and only out to steal the show". Rams is firm in his view that "products are not living beings nor, in my opinion, even works of art".[12]

Another perspective seeks to understand the changing nature of design in the context of broader cultural transformations associated with the current stage of capitalist development, exercising less judgement than Dormer and Rams on its desirability. Sociologists and cultural theorists have developed the concept of *postmodernism* to describe the nature of contemporary culture in advanced industrial economies. It is a concept immune to easy definition, but the debates surrounding it provide important insight on the role and nature of design.

Mike Featherstone, in *Consumer Culture and Postmodernism*, discusses the idea that a central feature of contemporary culture is now the process of consumption.[13] Replacing social class as a determinant of identity is the notion of lifestyle, where the choices and values made by people in their lives are expressed or stylised through their choice of clothes, leisure interests and consumer goods. According to Featherstone, the consumer culture this creates involves the aestheticisation of everyday life, which, in general terms, means that the boundaries between art and mass consumer culture become eroded. On one level this involves artists using consumer goods as legitimate subject matter, such as Andy Warhol's images of Campbell soup cans. It also involves artists and film makers bringing the language of surrealism into advertisements for cigarettes and car tyres. On another level it means that the shopping mall or department store must provide aesthetic pleasure and challenge.

Most significantly for this discussion, consumer culture changes the role and nature of the objects that people buy.

Consumer society was built upon the notion that status was reflected through the act of consuming more and higher priced goods and services. The use-value of products (functionality) became less significant than their exchange-value (price). Greater and more widespread affluence brought with it a need for differentiation and the concept of lifestyle. Exchange-value became superseded by symbolic-value: the product as a package of symbols and messages which could be enjoyed and used to communicate differentiation to others. Stephen Bayley has quoted an advertising executive as arguing, "In the 1960s and 1970s, possession alone was sufficient. But nowadays the concept of ideal homes stuffed with material goods doesn't work. Now that most people have a full pantry of electronic wonders, people are working for meaning beyond the fact of possession".[14] Design is therefore required to express individuality, playfulness and symbolism.

Design can therefore be viewed from a cultural perspective as a visual barometer of changing times. Products express the evolving values and aspirations of the society which consumes them. The history of design can therefore provide an important and unique insight into social change through understanding the dynamics by which "design turns ideas about the world and social relations into the form of physical objects".[15] Presenting design as art can certainly be a marketing strategy, but objectively the nature of design is changing as the boundary between art and everyday life erodes, as consumers look to goods increasingly to symbolise meaning and values, and as new markets open up for exclusive items. The cultural definitions of art, design, craft and commodity are all changing. It has been argued, in differentiating between art and design, that an artist's responsibility is "to the truth of his (or her) own vision", whereas a designer works with and for other people.[16] In the postmodern age such a distinction is less clear. However, it is still claimed that one distinguishing feature of design is that it is an activity concerned with solving problems and researching information to develop a solution. It is to this perspective that we now turn.

Design as Problem Solving

"Design: a goal directed problem-solving activity."

Bruce Archer, Royal College of Art[17]

The comedian Ben Elton has a routine in which he suggests the existence of a *Ministry of Bad Design*. What else, he argues, would account for so many poorly designed objects, such as metal cafeteria teapots with handles apparently made of a perfect conductive material, milk cartons that spray out their contents on opening and paper towels that spread liquid around rather than absorb it. His audiences' reaction suggests that this is well-observed comedy. Ben Elton prefers a conspiracy theory to account for why so many products simply do not do their job very well. Donald Norman is a psychologist who puts the problem down to a more complex interplay of factors that include who designers are, their insular culture and the negative impact of marketing, as we will examine later.[18]

Norman's starting point is that design is the process that makes the world usable – or not. The designer of a video cassette recorder should combine his or her understanding of the machine's technology with an understanding of how people view, and interact with technology, to conceive a product that is easy to use and performs the functions that users require. That so many people over the age of 10 appear to have great difficulty in using their VCR (including the authors of this book) suggests that something is going awry within the design process.

Most accounts of design refer, at least in passing, to the fact that design is about conceiving things which meet specific needs. These needs may be purely functional, as in the case of a door handle, or may be decorative, as in the case of a household ornament. But even a decorative object meets a need: the need of a particular lifestyle group for an object which enhances their decor. Because the products of design fulfil a specified function, then design is an activity concerned, at least in part, with problem solving.

Any design problem will include balancing a range of requirements determined by technology and materials, production constraints, market considerations and human factors – the physical and psychological characteristics of users. It is an understanding of human factors that will determine how easy or difficult a product is to use. For some products it is essential that they are difficult to use by some potential users, such as child-proof medicine containers, but in most other cases products should be easy to use and adaptable for different people. There are many examples of design that succeeds in balancing these factors to create products, messages and environments that are functional, flexible, affordable, well made and elegant. The question is, why are there not more of them? Furthermore, as more symbolic and emotive demands are placed on design, is there a trade-off between function and aesthetics?

The challenge for design stems from the increasing complexity of our industrial culture. Technology becomes more complex, offers new possibilities and is accessible by more people than ever before. Little more than a decade ago video machines were cumbersome devices used by broadcasters. Today they are found in the majority of households, using microelectronics to offer new functions, made of recently developed materials with new properties, and used by an ageing population whose familiarity with technology and physical dexterity differs from that of broadcasting technicians. The nature of the design problem has been compounded by changes in technology and cultural use.

Donald Norman argues that design often fails to meet its obligations as a functional problem solving activity for three main reasons. Firstly, the design community appears to put aesthetics first when awarding design prizes and according status to designers. Norman cites various examples of functionally poor design in layout and signage at London's Design Centre, but he is not the first commentator to suggest the cultural insularity of the design profession. Linked to this is Norman's second argument, that designers design predominantly for themselves. They assume that their familiarity with technology, their dexterity and aesthetic taste is general to all users, which patently is not the case.

Often they fail to understand the context of the product's use and the tasks that it will be put to. The fact that many product designers are young white men suggests an acute need for them to appreciate issues beyond their own experience, such as ageing, the requirements and perspective of women and cultural diversity. Norman's third point is that designers suffer from working for a client who is usually not the end user. Manufacturers are less concerned with functionality than the people who buy their products. Companies add functions and complexities to products in order to make them distinctive in the market and often compromise functional design with cost constraints. This argument is also developed by architect and designer David Pye, who explains how designers are often under pressure to design products that just look different from the previous model: "the best designs have always resulted from an evolutionary process, by making successive slight modifications over a long period of time, not through feverish insistence on making frequent obvious changes for the sake of offering something which looks really new and different. Innovation often hinders improvement".[19]

However, a crucial point made by Norman is that "most design is not done by designers, it is done by engineers, programmers and managers".[20] This accords with empirical research showing that in British manufacturing a considerable amount of design work is undertaken by people who have no design training or even aptitude. This has been described as "silent design".[21] It is perhaps, then, not so much a problem of designers not doing their jobs properly, but more one of other people doing it for them.

The argument that design represents a self-serving community that designs for itself is very much overstated. All professions have their own culture and criteria for professional recognition that do not accord with those of the wider public. It is for this reason, for example, that the Booker Prize is not awarded to Jeffrey Archer or Jackie Collins, although their work is "usable" by more people than that of Salman Rushdie. While there are many examples of self-indulgent or poorly considered design, designers are increasingly aware of human factors and through their professional organisations are seeking to address issues such as the ergonomic challenges of an ageing population. Failure to solve problems adequately in the design process has perhaps more to do with the pressures of marketing and cost saving imposed by clients and the slow recognition by many companies that design is a complex activity that should be undertaken by professionals.

Finally in this discussion of design as problem solving, is there a trade-off between function and aesthetics? The principle that *form follows function* suggests perhaps that there is. In a lucid and visionary discussion on the nature of design, David Pye argues otherwise: "The form of designed things is decided by choice or else by chance; but it is never actually entailed by anything whatsoever. ... Whenever humans design and make a useful thing they invariably expend a good deal of unnecessary and easily avoidable work on it which contributes nothing to its usefulness. ... If we did not behave after this pattern our life would be poor, nasty and brutish".[22] Pye identifies six requirements of good design, of which four concern use, one concerns the economics of manufacture, and the sixth concerns acceptable appearance. He is critical of any attempt to pose design in terms of "either problem solving or art"; it manifestly embraces both. For Pye, the challenge of design is the sensitive and creative balance between the two modes of thought that this entails. The view of design as a creative act is our next focus.

Design as a Creative Act

"It's possible to analyse the creative process up to the moment when it turns from being quite a useful, sensible but dull object into something that really has got a great deal of style, charm, zip and fizz about it. ... Design is 98% common sense and 2% that mystical ingredient that you might call creativity. But it's that thing that makes a perfectly decent object into something really special, really desirable that people want as much as they might want a Picasso on the wall."[23]

Sir Terence Conran

If design itself is a somewhat unwieldy beast for the purposes of definition, creativity is even more so. It has been said that creativity is easier to detect than it is to define. We can admire the Apple Macintosh computer as a creative solution to personal computing or an Issey Miyake coat as a creative application of polyester, but the products of design are merely manifestations of creativity. To understand what the concept is we need to look at the people and processes involved.

As Terence Conran suggests above, creativity is a concept with an almost mystic aura surrounding it. Our culture suggests that creativity is a gift of God, or even the direct product of the Divine Creator. There is the view that Mozart, who allegedly wrote entire symphonies without correction as he heard them in his head, was taking dictation from God. Along with such popular views is the notion that creativity is restricted to certain fields of endeavour such as art, music and indeed design. Designers have perhaps helped to perpetuate this view by describing themselves as "creatives" and having professional journals with titles such as *Creative Review.*

The scientific evidence, however, suggests that creativity comprises the application of a set of skills which can be learnt and developed and can be seen at work in all activities. Perhaps the clearest definition is provided by Arthur Koestler: "The creative act consists in combining previously unrelated structures so that you get more out of the emergent whole than you put in".[24]

Designers certainly do not have monopoly over the creative act, but unlike many other professions they are trained to develop creative skills. Design education encourages students to draw upon wide inspiration, to experiment with ideas, to solve problems and – significantly – to run the risk of failure. Idea generation is, after all, a risky business. Design educators assess the process behind a student's work as much as the end product of their labours. Their concern is with the creative thinking which led to the design solution. Figure 2.2 explains the distinctive nature of design education together with the skills, knowledge and understanding that it provides to students.

Figure 2.2 – Design education

Design students have a distinctive education based on the traditional craft "learn by doing" method. Most of their time is spent on project work based around a specific design problem or brief. A typical design project could last from four to six weeks. Very often practising designers are brought in as tutors to expose students to current practice and professional aspects of design. At the end of the project students will be assessed both in terms of the design solution – whether it meets the requirements of the brief – and the process which led to the solution. Projects are vehicles for acquiring knowledge, developing skills and understanding context.

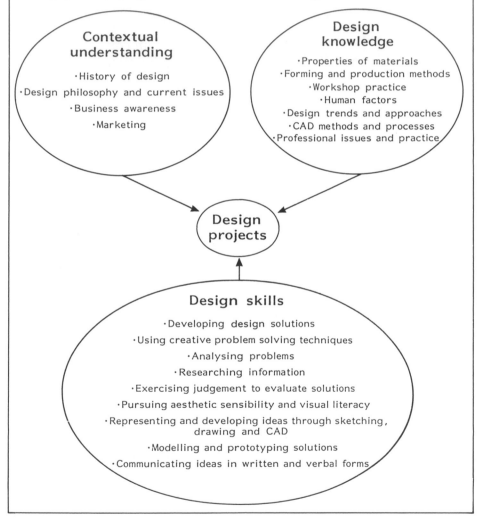

Contextual understanding
· History of design
· Design philosophy and current issues
· Business awareness
· Marketing

Design knowledge
· Properties of materials
· Forming and production methods
· Workshop practice
· Human factors
· Design trends and approaches
· CAD methods and processes
· Professional issues and practice

Design projects

Design skills
· Developing design solutions
· Using creative problem solving techniques
· Analysing problems
· Researching information
· Exercising judgement to evaluate solutions
· Pursuing aesthetic sensibility and visual literacy
· Representing and developing ideas through sketching, drawing and CAD
· Modelling and prototyping solutions
· Communicating ideas in written and verbal forms

What is Design?

However, is there anything distinctive about creative thinking in design as opposed to any other discipline? Bryan Lawson has explored this question in his book *How Designers Think.*[25] Thinking is usually categorised in two ways. On the one hand is reasoning, rational or convergent thinking, and on the other is imaginative, intuitive or divergent thinking. The former is logical, purposeful and concerned with outward directed problem solving, while the latter is unstructured, at times aimless and more inwardly directed. As Lawson argues, controlling and combining these two modes of thought is one of the most important design skills, and clearly differentiates design from art: "The designer must consciously direct his thought processes towards a particular specified end, although he may deliberately use undirected thought at times. The artist however, is quite able to follow the natural direction of his mind or to control and change the direction of his thinking as he sees fit".[26]

As we will see later, not all design problems are the same and thus some design tasks require more convergent thought than others. Different stages of a design project also involve different balances of these modes of thought. But the skill of the designer as a problem solver and synthesiser of concepts rests upon his or her ability to think appropriately and enable new creative insights into problems to occur.

Table 2.1 – The five stages in the creative process of design

Stage		Description
1	First insight	Formulating the problem
2	Preparation	Understanding the problem
3	Incubation	Relaxation to allow subconscious thought
4	Illumination	Emergence of the idea
5	Verification	Idea development and testing

Lawson has identified five stages in the creative process of design, summarised in Table 2.1. Formulating the problem is by no means a purely analytical task and usually requires an imaginative insight into its interpretation. As Lawson explains, this stage can last from hours to years. Considerable conscious thought is then required for the designers to immerse themselves in the knowledge required to enable a solution. This may involve going back and redefining the problem in hand. Then the designers put their feet up: "The secret of inventiveness is to fill the mind and the imagination with the context of the problem and then relax and think of something else for a change. ... If you are lucky your subconscious will hand up into your conscious mind, your imagination, a picture of that the solution might be. It will probably come in a flash, almost certainly when you are not expecting it".[27] If the "Eureka" moment proves elusive, there is no shortage of techniques to help force through an idea. Papanek has identified eight groups of problem solving methods, including the most well-known technique of brainstorming.[28] Once the stage of illumination is reached, it is followed by a careful and conscious development and testing of the concept.

Terence Conran has emphasised the importance of preparation, of understanding all aspects of the user: "You find out what people want by observing them: their life-styles; where they go on holiday; what they read; what music they listen to; what they eat. You're thinking about their lives. It's often imagining what they might want before they actually get it. Sometimes you go too far and its a commercial flop. It's got to be one or two steps ahead, not a cricket pitch ahead".[29]

As professionals trained in such creative thinking, designers clearly have a great deal to contribute to the corporate environment. Ideally, their talents are an appropriate complement to those of management. As Walker has observed, "Managers are good at dissection, cutting through irrelevancies, getting to hard facts and the basic structure of problems. They are very problem oriented. Designers by contrast are good at assembling, bringing unlikely things together. They work by leaping to detailed end results. They are solution led".[30]

However, productive complementarity can too often be overshadowed by misunderstanding. A number of accounts of design's role in industry express the problems posed by the two differing cultures of design and management. Designers and managers have different educations, different attitudes and different styles of thought, which can cause problems of communication. This is at least in part due to the emphasis of most non-design education, which is predominantly analytical in focus. John Heap, chairman of the Institute of Management Services, argues that "the educational system generally is unhappy with creativity. It is difficult to teach in a structured way and with predictable results. What characterises our schooling is the desire to get the right answer".[31] The requirement, therefore, is for managers to recognise the unique contribution that design can make as a creative process in industry and perhaps to accept Stephen Bayley's assertion that "Design covers those creative aspects of business which conventional education (and therefore conventional managers) tend to ignore".[32]

For management this means creating the appropriate environment to encourage creative thought. This can involve adapting new management practices. Alvin Toffler has argued that as our economic system becomes knowledge based, so the generation of ideas becomes the lifeblood of business: "But free workers tend to be more creative than those who work under tightly supervised, totalitarian conditions. Thus the need for innovation encourages worker autonomy. It also implies a totally different power relationship between employer and employee. It means for one thing that intelligent error needs to be tolerated".[33] A similar argument is made by leading British designer James Pilditch: "Corporate systems militate against the creative process. A chaotic, inconsequential, untidy affair, creativity is unlikely to flower in the tightly run, well-organised business".[34] This certainly does not mean that creativity is inconsistent with the objectives of management, rather that management needs to ensure that the fostering of creativity is one of its specific goals. Design management is indeed one of the methods used to attain this.

Design as a Family of Professions

"Design includes the work of people from a wide range of disciplines."[35]

Peter Gorb, Senior Fellow in Design Management, London Business School

So, design is about the function, nature and appearance of "things". Furthermore, it is a creative activity concerned with problem solving and, in its broadest sense, communication. But these "things" that designers create are more than just products. Design is certainly concerned with objects or products, but it is an activity which, as Peter Gorb rightly explains, embraces a range of other disciplines, some of which run not the slightest risk of being confused with art. Designers design the spark plug, the car in which it is used, the showroom where it is sold, the advertising which attracts the consumer and the power-dressing suit of the persuasive salesperson. In other words, design determines all elements of the human-made world.

Although Leonardo da Vinci grappled with problems ranging from how to capture the rather odd mood of one of his sitters through to the complex principles of aeronautical engineering, designers today tend to be more specialised in their skills and areas of work. How, then, are they to be classified?

Most attempts to classify design begin with the distinction between engineering design and "art-based" design. The former designer, with an engineering education, is equipped with skills to solve complex technical problems, whereas the latter – often termed an "industrial designer" – uses an art and craft derived education to design the visual elements of new products. Put in crude and somewhat questionable terms, the engineer makes the product work, while the industrial designer makes it sell.

Sir William Barlow, former chairman of the Design Council, has explained how virtually every product requires an appropriate balance of these design skills.[36] The design of a textile may require some engineering input in terms of solving technical problems such as fire retardancy, but it is a problem which lies almost wholly within the domain of art-based design. At the other extreme, the design of an electronic component falls exclusively within engineering design. Between the two, Barlow provides the example of the telephone. The engineering designer ensures that the electronic components are configured to perform their task appropriately, while the industrial designer gives the product both visual appeal and effective ergonomic qualities.

As Barlow admits, the engineering/industrial distinction is a crude one. He prefers to conceptualise the range of design disciplines as a spectrum of increasing technical sophistication which ranges at one end from pure aesthetics through ergonomics, human factors and structures, to mechanical engineering, electronics and eventually advanced systems. So, for example, we could envisage a spectrum of design professions which run in terms of technical complexity from fashion and textiles, through to graphics and packaging, then furniture and product design, to architecture and eventually mechanical and electronic engineering.

David Walker has developed this linear model of design specialisms into one which includes some sense of historical development, and is perhaps more useful for understanding the full scope and interrelationships between design disciplines: the design family tree.[37] With its roots in traditional craft skills and methods, such as drawing, modelling and simulation, design has grown ever more specialised. It ranges from disciplines such as graphics and fashion, which rely on artistic sensibilities, to engineering and electronics, which are science-based. Between these are branches which combine art and science to varying degrees. At the uppermost reaches of the tree are new specialisms, such as CAD, which – despite their technological sophistication – are derived from traditional craft methods. As Walker explains, some designers can span two or three main branches, and most have a sense of community with those inhabiting adjoining branches, but generally professional specialisation dominates.

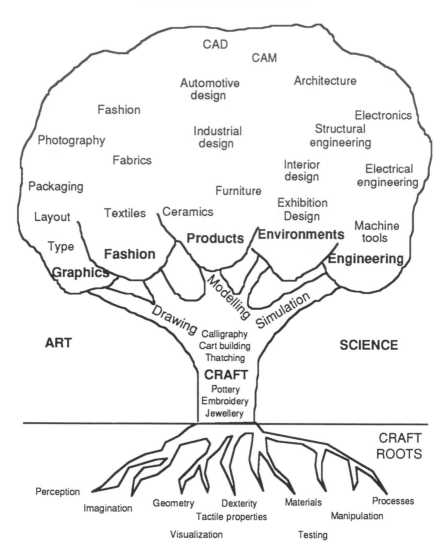

Figure 2.3 – The design family tree.
Source: David Walker (1989)

Walker's tree helps us to understand design's diversity, interrelationships and development. However, while design may be rightly perceived as a family of professions, it is far from being "one big happy one". According to former Design Council director Ivor Owen, "I strongly believe that the schism between engineering design and industrial design has been one of the most damaging issues in manufacturing industry imaginable".[38] Deep rooted tribal hostilities between engineering and industrial designers derive from different educations, modes of thought and aptitudes, manifested in a departmental separation within most companies. Studies of the electrical and capital goods industries in Britain, traditional domains of engineering, have suggested that lack of competitiveness derives in part at least from a reluctance to embrace industrial design. The challenge for industry is to recognise how the two "tribes" of design are related and perform interdependent functions.

In terms of the prosaic requirements of management, it is necessary to identify the key fields of design that contribute to a company's activities. Peter Gorb has identified four:[39]

1   Product design

2   Environmental design

3   Information design

4   Corporate identity design

Product design concerns the conceiving, styling, ergonomics, structure, function and economic manufacture of products. It is clearly a process which involves the skills of both industrial and engineering designers. Product design ranges from realising wholly new product concepts, through to restyling existing concepts for enhanced differentiation in the market.

Environmental design, which includes architecture, interiors and landscape design, is of particular relevance to service industries. The growth of retail, financial and leisure industries has been accompanied by rising investment in the design of the environments where customers consume these services. The design of a shop interior differentiates one retailer from another in the market, in the same way that product design differentiates one brand of audio equipment from another.

Information design covers a range of specialisms concerned with designing forms of communication. Companies need to communicate information in many different ways to many different people. They advertise themselves, package their products and provide them with user instructions, supply retailers with point-of-sale material, publish annual reports on their activities for shareholders and update their employees on new developments. All of these communications must be designed. Graphic design is a shorthand term for much information design, although, as in the case of packaging, designers must understand the use of different materials, and other skills such as photography and video are made use of.

Corporate identity, while derived from information design, integrates product, environmental and information design. Far more than just a logo or letterhead, corporate identity aims to project an appropriate and consistent image of a company. The identity expresses its function, its character and its aims. According to Wally Olins, a leading specialist in the field, "the most significant way in which this can be done is by making everything in and around the company – its products, building and communications – consistent in purpose and performance and, where this is appropriate, in appearance too".[40]

By viewing design as a generic term covering a range of specialised disciplines, we obtain a clearer idea of what different types of designers do and how they can contribute to a company's activities. Product, environmental, information and corporate identity design are the main professions that comprise "the design industry".

Design as an Industry

"Design in England has become a commodity"[41]

Neville Brody, Graphic Designer

The design education described earlier has secured Britain an international reputation for the quality of its designers, not to mention the quantity produced. There are currently over 50 000 students of design in this country enrolled on over 1000 courses.[42] This is one major factor accounting for London's status as the design capital of the world.

Design has evolved as an industry in its own right. While the use of design expertise by companies grew significantly during the 1980s, they were far more reliant upon the use of designers as external consultants than employing them as in-house designers. This brought advantages for both users and providers of design skills, created business opportunities for the rising numbers of design college graduates and gave rise to a vibrant design industry. But some have argued that it also engendered a superficial view of design and an immature industry that was highly vulnerable to recession. The dizzy rise and sudden fall of Britain's design industry provides important lessons for how design is viewed and its likely future contribution to the economy.

The role of the designer as consultant rather than employee was defined by the pioneering American industrial designers of the 1930s, such as Raymond Lowey and Walter Dorwin Teague. Coming largely from the world of advertising, such designers interpreted their function as market-driven jobbing stylists. As design's contribution became more recognised by American industry, employers began to establish in-house design teams, usually based within engineering departments. This was a trend emulated in post-war Japan.

The British design profession also had its origins in graphic design and illustration. But its post-war evolution has been determined more by state policy, popular culture and close ties with the retail industry than by the requirements of manufacturing. Some of the key events in this evolution are shown graphically in Figure 2.4.

The graphic designers who founded the Society of Industrial Arts in 1930 soon attracted great demand for their talents, as a result of the onset of war and the need for propaganda. The team assembled at the Ministry of Information gave rise to Britain's first modern consultancy, the Design Research Unit, specialising in packaging and exhibitions.

Figure 2.4 – The rise and fall of the UK design industry

	1930s	1940s	1950s	1960s	1970s	1980s	1990s
The design industry	1930 Society of Industrial Arts founded	1943 First consultancy: Design Research Unit founded	1954 Ogle Design founded; 1955 Conran Design founded; 1959 AID founded	1962 Design and Art Directors Association founded; 1965 Olins founded; 1966 OMK founded; 1969 Moggridge founded	1970 Michael Peters founded; 1972 Pentagram founded	1980 AID: First design group launched on stock exchange; 1986 Design Business Association founded; 1988 UK Design Industry turnover: £2 billion; 1989 Design Museum opens	1990 Conran Design sold to French company; 1990 Michael Peters insolvent; 1990-1992 Design employment halved
Consumer culture			1955 Mary Quant opens boutique	1962 First Beatles hit; 1964 Habitat opens	1976 The Sex Pistols	1980 *The Face* Launched; 1982 Next opens; 1983 Habitat and Mothercare merged in Storehouse; Recession	1992 Habitat sold to IKEA
State policy	1939 Ministry of Information formed	1944 Council for Industrial Design (CID) formed; 1946 "Britain Can Make It" Exhibition	1951 Festival of Britain		1972 CID renamed The Design Council	1982 Mrs Thatcher's "Design Summit"; 1988 State funding for design tops £25 million	1994 Design Council restructured

The role of industrial design as a competitive factor was recognised more by government than by industry. The creation of the Council for Industrial Design in 1944 and two major exhibitions – Britain Can Make It and the Festival of Britain – had the aim of promoting design in British industry. As we will see in later chapters, these seeds of design promotion fell largely on stony ground.

If Hitler had been the catalyst for professionalising British design, it was Napoleon who had correctly observed the factor which was to begin its propulsion into a golden age. As "a nation of shopkeepers", Britain's emergence from post-war austerity found more expression in the field of shopfitting than shopfloor innovation.

The changing fortunes of one individual designer act as a microcosm for the British design industry. Terence Conran founded his consultancy in 1955, driven by a mission to bring good design to the public. With few allies in the retail world, Conran established his own chain of outlets. Habitat brought a similar style to household furnishings that a whole new generation of boutiques had given to clothing from Mary Quant onwards. The wailing harmonica which opens The Beatles' first hit in 1962 also heralded the dawn of a new age of popular culture, in which Britain became synonymous with fashionable style.

Throughout the 1960s, the design profession grew steadily as many of the consultancies which later became 1980s success stories emerged on the scene and benefited from this country's new status as the world's fashion capital. The strength of these new design outfits lay within retail design and corporate identity. This market orientation was a further reason why British designers were in demand throughout the world. By the mid-1970s consultancies such as Conran, Olins and AID earned half their turnover outside Britain.[43] The Conran Design Group continued to play a leading role in the emergent British design industry. Not only did it spawn other groups, such as Fitch, but with clients including Miss Selfridge, Marks & Spencer and Top Shop, Conran was the driving force behind the refurbishment of Britain's high streets.

While the Conran generation of professional designers grew in scale, the mid-1970s ushered in a new phase of popular culture which was to transform design further. Dressed by Vivienne Westwood and packaged by Jamie Reid, the Sex Pistols brought a new aesthetic to street style. The generation which claimed to be "pretty vacant" was certainly brimming over with new ideas in graphic and fashion design. Designers such as Reid, Neville Brody and Peter Saville, who emerged through punk, have gone on to greater things in mainstream design. The rise of the pop video and new fashion magazines such as *The Face* helped to export the new British post-punk style.

Johnny Rotten and Margaret Thatcher did much between them to turn what was still little more than a cottage industry into an adjective to describe the 1980s – *the design decade*. The former Prime Minister's design seminars for industrialists at Number 10 held in 1982 were the overture to a highly profiled state design policy. According to leading design consultant Rodney Fitch, "it is probably true that the (Thatcher) government banged the drum for design-led innovation like no other for 100 years".[44]

Grants were made available for firms to employ consultants, effectively subsidising the design industry by £25 million up to 1988.[45] The Department of Trade and Industry (DTI) and the design industry both hammered home the design message. It was a message which, while initially based more on faith than evidence, was soon advancing a well argued case for design to be taken seriously by British industry. Perhaps the most articulate member of Britain's design profession is James Pilditch, whose *Winning Ways* sought to sell product design to British industry.

Marshalling evidence on how design brings together market need and technological capability, Pilditch's book defined a positive role for the outside consultant:

"People from outside a company bring with them a new perspective. ... They want to see progress, to complete the project and move on to the next one. So they hasten the mea-

*sured tread of many companies ... at best, they may be high-
ly imaginative, able to look at opportunities in a new way"*.[46]

Pilditch's view was clearly shared by many clients during
the 1980s. As a consequence, the design industry made a
quantum leap. By the middle of the decade the industry's
annual growth rate was 30%. In 1980 Michael Peters ran a
packaging consultancy with 20 people on the payroll. Eight
years later the USM quoted Michael Peters Group owned
companies in Europe and America with a staff of 720. It was
the leading company in a design industry which was turning over more than £2 billion in 1988.[47]

While all fields of design were expanding, most of this
growth was accounted for by the retail boom. As in the
1960s, it was Terence Conran leading the way. His
Storehouse Group brought in Mothercare, British Home
Stores, Richard Shops and Heals to apply the Habitat design
mission. This group included the Conran Design Group
with its staff of over 300. Conran was also the driving force
behind London's Design Museum. A former Conran
designer, George Davies, transformed the lacklustre
Hepworth chain into the stylish symbol of 1980s retailing,
Next. And next came disaster.

Conran's Storehouse Group sold Conran Design to the
French RSCG advertising company in May 1990, which
promptly slashed its staff to 60 people. Heals was divested
in a management buy-out, and even Terence Conran himself was removed from the company. Eventually the symbol of Britain's design-led retailing, Habitat, was sold to the
Swedish retail giant IKEA.

A few months after Conran Design was sold off, the Michael
Peters Group called in the receivers. By 1992, a much
slimmed down Michael Peters Ltd was employing 31
designers, compared with 720 four years earlier.[48] Between
1990 and 1992, Britain's 100 largest design consultancies
lost over half of the 10 200 jobs they accounted for. As one
recent commentary has observed, "In five years (the design
industry) effectively grew to twice its size and then halved
again. The period of growth carried on longer but ended

faster than that of almost any other sector of the UK economy".[49]

The collapse of Britain's design industry can be accounted for largely by recession, the downturn in consumer spending and the consequent problems facing its largest client, the retail sector. But other factors have also been identified. Alice Rawsthorn has argued that structural problems within the industry hastened its decline.[50] Essentially a cottage industry, design failed to develop the strong management and effective financial control necessary to sustain a multinational industry. Furthermore, the cultural climate of the 1980s promoted a notion of design which was superficial and thus easily undertaken by external consultancies. Design became style, and style can be dispensed with easily. Rawsthorn makes the point that the relatively small number of product design consultancies is evidence that the *design decade* was more about selling goods than producing new ones. Thus, Britain's manufacturing industry largely failed to exploit the creativity of the design community. As Catherine McDermott has concluded, "the decline of our gross national product does not reflect the strength of Britain's design potential".[51]

British design in the 1980s was built upon its strengths in retailing and its close associations with advertising. Therefore, most of its business was generated in the fields of retail and corporate identity design. Its traditions as a consultancy based "cottage industry" were reinforced by a government policy that placed its emphasis on promoting design as a consultancy service. This was consistent with the stated Conservative Party policy of promoting small firms and encouraging flexibility. Jenny Lewis has described this in terms of *the distancing of design*.[52] In an argument presented before the onset of recession, Lewis suggests the possible vulnerability of a profession which is effectively distanced from the core activities of its clients.

Design as an industry thereby fosters the view of design as a buy-in commodity rather than an integrated in-house resource. The success of manufacturers in Japan, among others, stems in part at least from viewing design as a process.

Design as a Process

"Design is more than shape, colour and dimensions of products. Design is the decision-making process that deals with the manifestation of objects with consideration to economy and technical function and in answer to various consumer demands".

Ministry of International Trade and Industry, Japan[53]

Japan's influential Ministry of Industry neatly summarises the view that many Japanese firms have of design. It is not just style or clever ideas; it is not an isolated activity, but a process. Design links the needs of the consumer with the potential of the enterprise. It is a process that lies at the very heart of innovation and thus at the heart of the company itself.

The literature on design management refers to the concept of process in one of two ways; firstly, as the process involved in undertaking a design task – how designers' skills are employed in progressing a problem to its solution – and, secondly, in using "design process" to describe the strategic planning of product development. There are dangers involved in taking either interpretation to an extreme: design veers from being the job done in a back room by people in trendy clothes to being the force behind every activity in a firm down to making the tea. How, then, is a balanced view to be reached?

Let us begin with the task-based interpretations. The previous discussion on design as a creative act presented a five-stage model of what designers do when working on a problem, summarised in Figure 2.5.

Figure 2.5 – The internal creative process of design

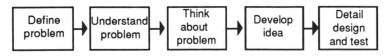

As a representation of how a designer tackles a specific problem, this model is largely adequate. This model focuses on how designers think through problems, and is therefore described as the internal creative process. In reality, though, the creative process is rarely linear. At any stage new information or insights may require designers to return to an earlier stage and amend their definition, understanding or design. However, this model does not consider the creative process of designers' work within any context. An industrial designer will work in, or for, an organisation. Problems emerge from that organisation or the environment within which it operates. The results of the designer's labours are taken up and developed further elsewhere in the organisation. A new product or a new corporate identity will be launched, having an effect on the organisation's environment and thus creating new design problems. We therefore need a model to represent this broader process which locates the act of designing within the systems of management and the environments within which they operate.

The creative process of design theorists in conceptualising the corporate design process could be the subject of a book on its own. There is no shortage of models to choose from. There is even an official model in the form of the British Standard on managing product design.[54] Walker's review of these models considers that underlying the differences of terminology and concerns with differing parts of the process is a broad consensus that design comprises four phases.[55] These are shown in Figure 2.6 and described as the external productive process of design, because this is a process concerned with the products of design activities.

Within each phase objectives are set, planning procedures established and methods of evaluation implemented. The input to the concept phase is a design brief, which defines the nature of the problem to be solved. This usually arises from market research. The output from the production phase is a product or service which meets the requirements of the brief. This is distributed and advertised, its performance evaluated, and, on the basis of further market research, a new or amended brief may be set. According to this view, then, the design process is part of a *total process* of product innovation and development, which is shown in Figure 2.7.

Figure 2.6 – External productive process of design

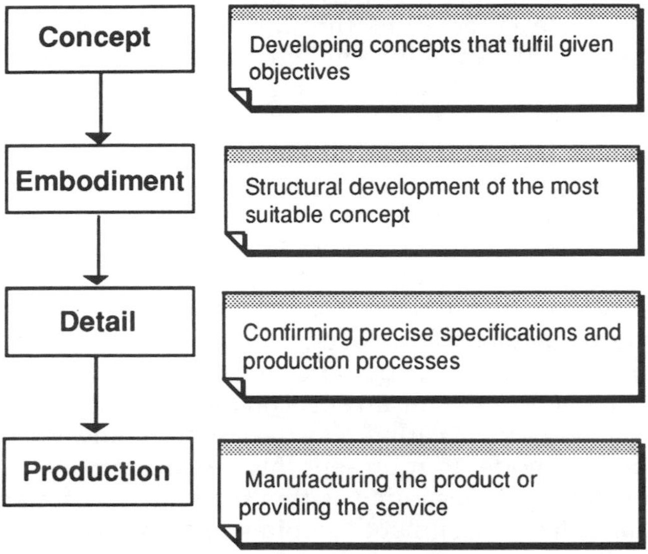

Concept	Developing concepts that fulfil given objectives
Embodiment	Structural development of the most suitable concept
Detail	Confirming precise specifications and production processes
Production	Manufacturing the product or providing the service

Hollins and Hollins are among those who have developed the concept of "Total Design" as a broader, more integrated definition of the design process.[56] Definitions of the design process, they argue, should include an indication of market pull or technical push, emphasise its multidisciplinary and iterative nature, explain that its purpose is to produce a product or service, and goes beyond the start of production, including issues such as product disposal. Total Design integrates market research, marketing strategy, engineering, product design, production planning, distribution and environmental monitoring within one cyclical model.

Total Design is consistent with Walker's model. Both see design as internally applying new technologies and developing product concepts and externally meeting the needs of the market and the wider environment. Both see design as cyclical and iterative, guided by a planning process. Both see design as a process involving more than just design skills. The only real difference is that Walker's "total process", in which "the design process is contained on one side by planning and on the other by production",[57] is described by Hollins as "total design". Both also make a differentiation between design and innovation.

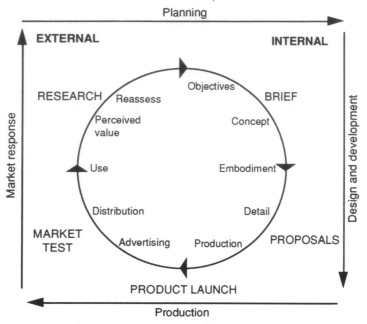

Figure 2.7 – The total process of design within management
Source: Walker, D. 1989

Many of the popular accounts of design in particular tend to use the terms *design and innovation* almost interchangeably. They must, however, be distinguished. Roy considers that the confusion arises because they are both creative activities.[58] Innovation and invention, he argues, are about making advances in technological state-of-the-art, while design is about making variations and applying that new technology. Design's role in the innovative process is defined by the shaded box in Figure 2.8. The design process thus interfaces with engineering, market research and basic research to develop a product which exploits new technology in meeting the needs of the market. It has a role in the very heart of the innovation process.

Gorb takes a similar, although more controversial, view. Because innovation, he argues, is the creative process in industry, "it follows that design is not a creative process", although it involves creative people.[59] Design is better regarded as a "thermostat for innovation", a process that "modulates, controls and encourages the innovative and creative inputs into the business". The design process may indeed reduce the application of innovation.

Figure 2.8 – The process of technological innovation, from *Product Design and Technological Innovation* edited by Roy and Wield, Open University Press, 1986 (with permission)

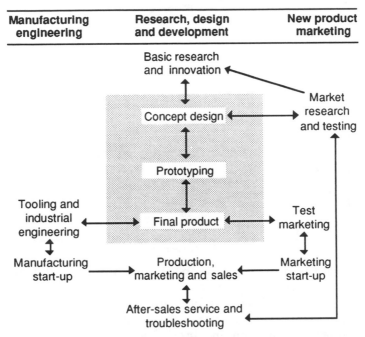

This is consistent with the concept of design published by the National Economic Development Office (NEDO) in a survey of international best practice. The Fairhead Report describes the design process as the strategic planning of products.[60] It is a process which collects information on markets, technological innovation and competitor activity, develops strategic planning on new product development and specifies product performance characteristics, product image, production processes and allied activities. This, argues Fairhead, characterises the view of design in many of the top performing Japanese companies. Indeed, it transcends the notion of process and becomes something far more fundamental: a culture which infuses the organisation; a culture of commitment to and passion for what the firm makes and how it makes it. Figure 2.9 represents this concept graphically.

Figure 2.9 – Design as a planning process.
After Fairhead (1987)

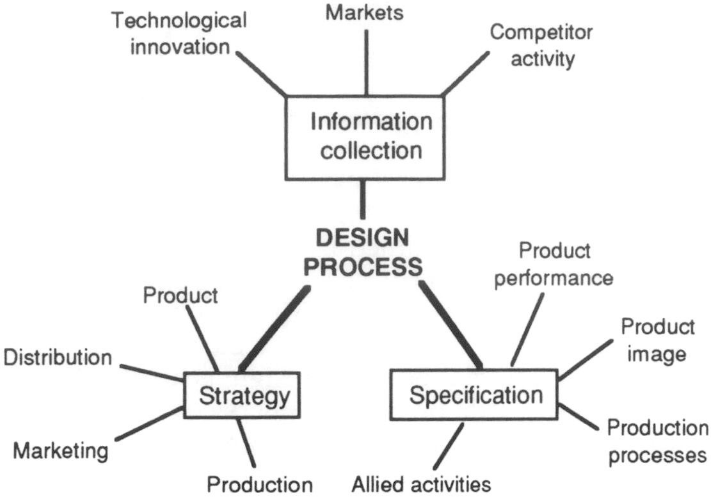

The discussion has revealed four broad approaches to viewing design as a process:

- Design as an internal creative process

- Design as an external productive process

- The total process of design within management

- Design as a planning process

These approaches could be related to Walker's notion of design maturity, in which he argues that the more mature an organisation becomes, the greater use it makes of more varied design specialisms and thus the broader its concept of design and its management becomes.[61] The designer–maker producing one-off furniture thus sees design essentially in terms of an internal creative process, while a medium sized furniture business launching a new design every year or so will see it more as an external productive process that can be bought in and used when required. A large manufacturer of household goods may see design as a more integrated part of its total management process, while an internationally competitive firm in a rapidly changing sector such as consumer electronics may regard design as the planning process which expresses its cultural commitment to its product and keeps it ahead in the market.

Perspectives of the design process are therefore determined by the size of the enterprise, the complexity of its production system and the nature of the corporate culture, issues which will be elaborated in following chapters. They are also to some extent determined by national culture. In the summer of 1992, this country's engineering designers were hailed as the creative force behind Britain's Olympic cycling and Nigel Mansell's Formula One victories. The act of designing, the creative process of design, is justifiably held to be a British strength. British designers conceive bicycles and cars which win gold medals. Regrettably they have long since fallen below bronze position in the race for customers. Design certainly is a creative process, but in increasingly competitive global markets design must also be seen as a planning process. The challenge for management is to appreciate that in the new physics of industry, design is both a particle and a wave.

Conclusion

How are we to make sense of the different views of design, some apparently contradictory, that have been presented in this chapter?

Design can be conceived from being an individual activity, such as designing a chair, through to a corporate planning process that regulates innovation to meet market demands. Its disciplinary boundaries, seemingly ever-shifting, range from engineering on one side to fine art on the other. Some claim that it has a duty to function, while others commit design to expressing emotion. Design can be lauded as a model of Thatcherite entrepreneurialism and willing servant of industry, or as a means of expressing the oppositional values of the punk sub-culture.

These differing perspectives have been presented to demonstrate design's diverse and changing role as an activity or process that links the realm of technology, production and economy with that of consumption, culture and ideology: the base and superstructure of society. A fuller understanding of the dynamic processes involved between design, culture and economy will develop in the following chapter, but at this stage some broad points can be made and some of the dilemmas raised so far addressed.

The methods and concerns of design have evolved in relation to the developing system of production. The largely functional and integrated nature of craft in pre-industrial society, where designing and making were performed by the same person, was replaced by an industrial division of labour that separated design from the tasks involved in manufacture. Increasing technological complexity demanded increasing specialisation on the part of designers and more marked professional boundaries between them. The pattern of educational specialisation has, in Britain at least, tended to create three largely separate cultures of management, engineering and "art-based" design. The tribal territorialism this has engendered has restricted the integration of these three functions within industry, manifested in both "silent design" and design's "distancing" as a consultancy service. The failure to address this problem seriously is a major factor behind Britain's lack of competitiveness, as we will see in more detail in the next chapter. The more competitive, knowledge-based industries of Japan recognise in design its potential as an integrating corporate process that can promote a culture of creativity and innovation and act as a synthesiser of technological potential and market needs sensitive to a changing cultural context.

Design's relationship to cultural and ideological change became most evident in the 1980s. In giving form to the material culture of consumption, design has had to meet the emotive and playful requirements of a postmodern consumerism. The "aestheticisation of everyday life" has challenged the relevance of functionalism as a central principle in design and eroded many former distinctions between art, craft, design and architecture. The ideological shift that championed consumption – Thatcherism – promoted a view of design that made it subservient to the needs of industry and commerce, concerned with stimulating ever more consumption and encouraged to develop as a model free enterprise service industry. Design was about buying – and directed to the service economy. In the context of the de-industrialisation of the British economy, it was less about making. The very concept of "design management" that has developed over the last decade or so reflects the idea that design must be more effectively defined and controlled by the processes of management.

Design has therefore been redefined and has taken on more diverse forms as a consequence of its changing industrial and cultural context. Some of the perspectives on the nature of these changes examined in this chapter are critical of this change: design pandering to the *nouveaux riches*, led by marketing to place novelty above usability, turned into a commodity or a debased form of quasi-art. Such perspectives are often grounded in an opposition to the dominant ideology of consumption. To what extent are these views valid?

The previous decade's consumer culture had provided design with more work and opportunities than ever before. In the headlong rush to set up new consultancies, design yet another shopping mall and create a new identity for the latest privatised utility, the profession could pull a discreet veil over the principles and philosophies about design having something to do with the quality of life or truth to materials that now seemed as relevant to modern life as steam engines and trade unions. Anything seemingly was possible, and was often backed with a government grant. This period enabled much bold, new and effective design to be undertaken that both improved the quality of life and accrued profit. It also enabled much derivative, unnecessary and poorly executed design to be done, which also accrued profit. Confronted with the latter, those such as Dieter Rams and Peter Dormer responded by defending design's "eternal values". Such reactions against a shift of emphasis from design as "the art of problem solving" to design as "stylistic diversity to raise sales" raised valid questions about both the quality of much design work and the interests that it served. However, in focusing upon the negative developments in consumer culture, critics such as

Dormer and Rams neglected the positive aspects of change through their imposition of their own value judgements on mass culture.

Why should the act of consumption not be more pleasurable? Why should consumers not manifest lifestyle through a more creative assemblage of consumer goods and services? Why should all CD players be black? The notion that marketing, and hence design, is about manipulating consumers to raise sales does not fit with the experience in many markets where firms have faced problems in responding to rapidly changing and diverse consumer demand. The new consumer culture, and the design that serves it, can be manipulative, superficial and exclusive to particular social classes, but it can also be creative, playful and supportive of social and cultural diversity.

Within the field of contemporary crafts, Dormer is right in pointing to an increasing output of poorly executed work pretending to be art. However, he neglects to recognise the cultural assertiveness of women and ethnic minorities, who, for historical reasons, have been excluded from the world of fine art and have used the crafts as a legitimate vehicle that places artistic expression above the exercise of craft skills. Their work has extended the possibilities and vocabulary of crafts such as textiles, jewellery and ceramics.

The scope, methods and objectives of design are not fixed. They change over time and vary according to economic and cultural context. But this is not to say that design is passively determined by economy and culture. It is a social activity, the practitioners and users of which play a part in determining its direction. The experience of recession, the tempering of Thatcherism and the changing public values on issues such as the environment have redefined some aspects of consumer culture and thus the role of design within it. Designers have indeed started to reassess the values that their professions uphold. By analysing the value of design in commercial, economic, symbolic and social terms we can gain a better understanding of its current and likely future role in economy and culture. This is the task of the following chapter.

Summary

• Design as art

Design has acquired a status similar to that of art in contemporary culture. This is manifested in stylistic diversity, artists designing prestige goods and experimental craft and design. One critical interpretation of this is as a marketing strategy that seeks to elevate everyday objects into art and feeds the needs of the *nouveaux riches*. An alternative interpretation sees such developments in terms of the "aestheticisation of everyday life" as a consequence of postmodern consumer culture. Consumers, it is argued, look increasingly to goods and services to symbolise meaning relevant to their lifestyles. While design shares some methods and cultural roles with art, it differs in terms of its concern with problem solving and meeting user needs.

• Design as problem solving

Design as a problem-solving activity involves balancing a range of factors: technology, production and use. While many designs work well, some consumer products fall short in terms of ease of use. One explanation argues that designers put aesthetic criteria first, design predominantly for themselves and are subverted by the pressures of marketing to place novelty above function. Blaming the designers should be tempered by evidence that shows that many design decisions are taken by non-designers. Design involves a synthesis of aesthetics and function.

• Design as creativity

The act of designing requires a combination of logical and intuitive thought which is encouraged in design education. As a solution-led creative activity, design does not always fit easily into the traditional culture of management. One goal of design management is to provide an environment that stimulates and supports creative design thinking.

• Design as a family of professions

Design encompasses a broad range of activities – a family of professions – that share common craft traditions. On one side it borders with art, while on the other it borders with engineering. The tribal hostilities between industrial design and engineering design derive from different educations and cultures and are reinforced by managerial separation. The four broad areas of industrial design most used within business are product, environmental, information and corporate identity design.

• Design as an industry

Britain's educational system, popular culture and design-orientated retail sector are three factors that account for a strong design consultancy industry in this country. The industry grew significantly in the 1980s, but has since undergone major decline. The dominance of design as a consultancy-provided service has tended to prevent its full integration as a core activity of British companies – the distancing of design.

• Design as a planning process

Design can usefully be viewed as a strategic planning process that applies the innovative potential of the enterprise with the changing requirements of the market. The extent to which design is viewed as an individual creative activity or as a corporate planning process depends upon company size and technology, the nature of the corporate culture and national culture.

Design's nature evolves in relation to changes in the mode of production and in the context of cultural and social development. It has become more complex and specialised over time. Consumer culture and the ideology that championed it in the 1980s made design a more market-orientated and managed process. This had negative consequences in terms of design's commitment to quality and the social interests that it served. However, some critiques of design's role in this period have neglected the positive potential of consumption as a cultural activity. A fuller view of design's role is gained by analysing its value in commercial, symbolic and social terms.

References

1 Tawney, R.H. (1961) *The Acquisitive Society,* Fontana, London, p.9.
2 Futrell, J. (1991) 'Emotional cars are go!' *Arena*, autumn.
3 *Business Week* (1990) 'Rebel with a cause', 3 December.
4 Cited in Holt, S. (1990) 'The art of design', *Art News*, April 1990.
5 Bayley, S. (1991) *Taste: The Secret Meaning of Things*, Faber and Faber, London.
6 Cited in Hancock, M. (1990) 'Moderate anarchy', *Design*, September 1990.
7 Morrison, J. (1987) *The sweet smell of design*, in Crafts Council (1987) *The New Spirit in Craft and Design*, exhibition catalogue.
8 Lucie-Smith, E. (1990) 'Comment', *Design*, December 1990, p.9.
9 Thackara, J. (ed.) (1986) *New British Design*, Thames and Hudson, London, p.12.
10 Dormer, P. (1990) *The Meanings of Modern Design*, Thames and Hudson, London, p.141.
11 Dormer, P. (1988) *The ideal world of Vermeer's little lacemaker*, in Thackara, J (ed.) (1988) *Design After Modernism*, Thames and Hudson, London, p.142.
12 Dornberg, J. (1992) 'Dieter Rams: The passionate purist', *Art News*, April 1992.
13 Featherstone, M. (1991) *Consumer Culture and Postmodernism*, Sage, New York.
14 Bayley, S. (ed.) (1989) *Commerce and Culture*, Design Museum, London, p.12.
15 Forty, A. (1986) *Objects of Desire: Design and Society* 1750–1980, Thames and Hudson, London.
16 Potter, N. (1989) *What is a Designer: Things. Places. Messages*, Hyphen Press, p.23.
17 Cited in Jones, J.C. (1980) *Design Methods*, John Wiley, Chichester, p.3.
18 Norman, Donald N. (1988) *The Psychology of Everyday Things*, Basic Books, New York.
19 Pye, D. (1978) *The Nature and Aesthetics of Design*, The Herbert Press, p.150.
20 Norman, Donald, N. (1988) *The Psychology of Everyday Things*, Basic Books, New York, p.156.
21 Gorb, P. and Dumas, A. (1987) Silent design, *Design Studies*, **8**(3), pp150-6.
22 Pye, D. (1978) *The Nature and Aesthetics of Design*, The Herbert Press, p.13.
23 Evans, P. and Deehan, G. (1988) *The Keys to Creativity*, Grafton Books, London.
24 Koestler, A. (1964) *The Act of Creation*, Hutchinson, London.
25 Lawson, B. (1990) *How Designers Think*, Butterworth Architecture, London.
26 Lawson., *op. cit.*, p.105.

27 Glegg, G.L. (1986) *The design of the designer*, in Roy, R. and Wield, D. (eds) *Product Design and Technological Innovation: A Reader*, Open University Press, Milton Keynes, p.86.

28 Papanek, V. (1984) *Design for the Real World*, Thames and Hudson, London.

29 Evans, P. and Deehan, G. (1988) *The Keys to Creativity*, Grafton Books, London.

30 Walker, D. et al. (1989) *Managing Design: Overview: Issues, P791*, Open University Press, Milton Keynes, p.22.

31 Heap, J. (1989) *The Management of Innovation and Design*, Cassell, London, p.22.

32 Bayley, S. (1989) Design in a mature economy, *Journal of Art and Design Education*, **8**(2), 1989, p.197.

33 Toffler, A. (1991) *Powershift: Knowledge, Wealth and Violence at the Edge of the 21st Century*, Bantam Press, London, p.213.

34 Pilditch, J. (1989) *Winning Ways*, Mercury Business Books, p.158.

35 Gorb, P. (1990) The future of design and its management, in Oakley, M. (ed.) *Design Management: A Handbook of Issues and Methods*, Basil Blackwell, Oxford, p.16.

36 Barlow, W. (1988) The importance of design, in Gorb, P. (ed.) *Design Talks!* Design Council, London.

37 Walker, D. et al. (1989) *Managing Design: Overview: Issues, P791*, Open University Press, Milton Keynes.

38 Owen, I. (1990) Industry and design, in Gorb, P. (ed.) *Design Management*, Architecture Design and Technology Press, p.41.

39 Gorb, P. (1990) *Design Management*, Architecture Design and Technology Press.

40 Olins, W. (1990) *The Wolff Olins guide to corporate identity*, Design Council, London, p.12.

41 Cited in Aldersey-Williams, H. (1992) *World Design: Nationalism and Globalism in Design*, Rizzoli International, p.56.

42 Myerson, J. (1992) History, structure and growth, in Lydiate, L. (ed.) *Professional Practice in Design*, Design Council, London, p.10.

43 Huygen, F. (1989) *British Design: Image and Identity*, Thames and Hudson, London, p.69.

44 Fitch, R. (1988) Impact of design on the retail landscape, in Gorb P. (ed.) *Design Talks!* Design Council, London, p.154.

45 Lewis, J. (1988) *The Distancing of Design*, Open University/UMIST Design Innovation Group, working paper WP-11.

46 Pilditch, J. (1989) *Winning Ways*, Mercury Business Books, p.144.

47 Jones, M. (1991) Going public, going bust, *Design*, January 1991, p.13.

48 *Design Week* (1992) 1992 consultancy survey, 27 March 1992.

49 Ibid., p.31.

50 Rawsthorn, A. (1990) Design directions, *Marxism Today*, December, p.35.

51 McDermott, C. (1987) *Street style: British design in the 80s*, Design Council, London, p.122.
52 Lewis, J. (1988) The Distancing of Design, Open University/UMIST Design Innovation Group, working paper WP-11.
53 Cited in Pilditch, J. (1989) *Winning Ways*, Mercury Business Books, p.136.
54 British Standards Institute (1989) *Guide to Managing Product Design*, BS7000.
55 Walker, D. et al. (1989) *Managing Design: Overview: Issues, P791*, Open University Press, Milton Keynes, p.34.
56 Hollins, G. and Hollins, B. (1991) *Total Design: Managing the Design Process in the Service Sector*, Pitman, London.
57 Walker, D. et al. (1989) *Managing Design: Overview: Issues, P791*, Open University Press, Milton Keynes, p.38.
58 Roy, R. (1986) Introduction: Meanings of design and innovation, in Roy, R. and Wield, D. (eds) *Product Design and Technological Innovation: A Reader*, Open University Press, Milton Keynes.
59 Gorb, P. (1990) *Design Management*, Architecture Design and Technology Press, p.19.
60 Fairhead, J. (1987) *Design for a Corporate Culture*, National Economic Development Office, London.
61 Walker, D. (1990) Design maturity: the ladder and the wall, in Oakley, M. (ed.) *Design Management: A Handbook of Issues and Methods*, Basil Blackwell, Oxford.

The Value
3 of Design

"Latest figures on the UK's invisible exports – which exceeded £117 billion in 1991 – reveal that they are larger than any other country's except the US. Designers' services make up a large part of that 'invisible' figure. The types of consultancy that have found new markets abroad are many and varied, but vehicle design remains a particularly popular export service. MGA Developments, for example, has recently completed the design and prototype build of a 1.5 tonne truck for the Chinese market that is expected to be built at the rate of 60 000 a year."

Design, February 1993

"The latest twist in the Leyland DAF saga came as the first casualties of the uncertainty about the manufacturer's future were told they were being made redundant. At least 250 skilled engineers and designers employed by Leyland DAF on plans for a new van were told they would be laid off and were unlikely to be paid for January."

The Guardian, 6 February 1993

Within 24 hours during early February 1993, two news stories demonstrated the double-edged value of design to the British economy. This country's designers are in demand worldwide, their services gaining valuable invisible export earnings for Britain. The products they design for international clients often compete well in world markets. Unfortunately, they compete against British made products. The irony of the cases above is that while this country congratulates itself on designing a truck to be made in China, the British truck industry is undergoing the latest episode in its rapid decline, with its first victims being British truck and van designers.

In the British economy, the creative process of designing successful products would appear to be strangely dislocated from the process of accruing profits from the manufacture of goods. British automotive designer Martin Smith adds value, not to the products of the UK car industry, but to those of his German employer for whom he conceived the Audi Quattro. Denmark's Bang and Olufsen competes against strong Japanese competition with its high quality consumer electronics designs, many of which come from the drawing board of Englishman David Lewis.

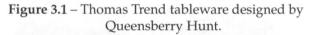

Figure 3.1 – Thomas Trend tableware designed by Queensberry Hunt.

Thomas Trend tableware designed by Queensberry Hunt. Europe's top selling tableware range is produced by the German Rosenthal group, but designed by London-based Queensberry Hunt. This consultancy has few major British clients. The concept for Trend emerged after considerable research into changing eating habits and ergonomic requirements. It meets a growing demand for modern unpatterned ware that British ceramic manufacturers have yet to take seriously

The Thomas Trend range of ceramic tableware, produced by Germany's Rosenthal group, competes successfully in those European markets where British tableware firms have yet to gain a major presence. The company's advertising copy reads, "What makes Thomas Trend one of Europe's best selling modern tableware ranges? The answer is Style, Choice and Value." These qualities were designed into the product by the London-based Queensberry Hunt consultancy (Figure 3.1). This design company has virtually no clients among British ceramics manufacturers.

Chapter Map

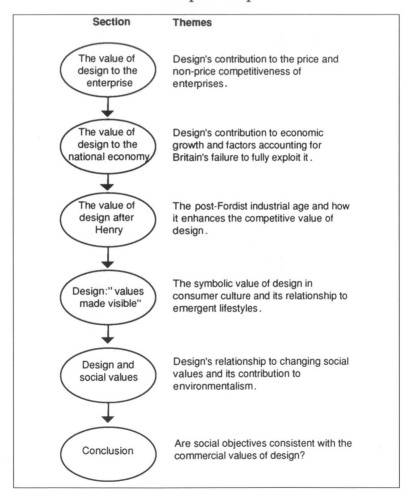

Section	Themes
The value of design to the enterprise	Design's contribution to the price and non-price competitiveness of enterprises.
The value of design to the national economy	Design's contribution to economic growth and factors accounting for Britain's failure to fully exploit it.
The value of design after Henry	The post-Fordist industrial age and how it enhances the competitive value of design.
Design:" values made visible"	The symbolic value of design in consumer culture and its relationship to emergent lifestyles.
Design and social values	Design's relationship to changing social values and its contribution to environmentalism.
Conclusion	Are social objectives consistent with the commercial values of design?

The previous chapter identified design as a multidisciplinary creative problem solving and planning process, linking the needs of the market to the potentials of production, producing goods and services that consumers desire. The task now is to explore in detail how design adds and expresses value. In doing so it is necessary to transcend the economistic, managerial view of design which dominates much design management literature. Design is certainly a tool of business and must be analysed in terms of its ability to add commercial value to the products of industry. However, as the previous chapter suggested, it is also a cultural phenomenon that evolves historically. The following discussion on the value of design will thus draw upon cultural theory, design history, economic theory and design management sources to provide a multidisciplinary view of the subject which will suggest its likely future orientation.

The Value of Design to the Enterprise

"The trick of discovering which set of attributes prospective purchasers would value, and of discovering a product configuration capable of embodying them at the right price is the exercise known as designing. Design, in the commercial context, is identifying the conditions which will create value."

Professor Bruce Archer, CBE[1]

Britain's post-war decline in manufacturing has led to many of this country's domestic markets becoming dominated by imported goods. Half of all cars, over one-third of footwear and clothing and three-quarters of electronic consumer goods bought each year in Britain are manufactured overseas.[2] Why, then, do British consumers prefer imported goods and why are foreign markets less attracted to a *Made in Britain* label?

Successive governments have put the problem down to price competitiveness. Cheap imports were perceived as the external threat, and high wages were British industry's enemy within. This *Skoda and Scargill* theory of industrial malaise made good copy in the popular press, but research suggests a more complex interplay of factors, with design playing a significant role.

Consumers take a number of factors into account when they make purchasing decisions. According to conventional wisdom, if there are two competing goods roughly the same in quality and design but differing in price then the rational economic person will go for the cheaper one. If there is no price difference, then the consumer will choose the product having an edge in terms of quality and design.

Clearly it is not quite as simple as this. The increasing symbolic value of many goods and services, brand loyalty and the strategies of advertising complicate the supposedly rational nature of the purchasing decision. There is also a common assumption that a higher price must imply a higher quality. But broadly we can differentiate between the price factor and non-price factors in purchasing decisions. The non-price factors include product uniqueness, quality, reliability, ergonomics, packaging and after-sales service, among others.

Various studies have tried to examine the relative importance of these. One study of British trade performance concluded that non-price factors accounted for 45% of British export performance and 80% of import penetration.[3] Domestic manufacturers, on the other hand, would appear to be less convinced. A comparative study of British and overseas companies showed that more UK firms attributed competitiveness to price factors than their foreign rivals.[4]

Design is an important element in all of this. It constitutes a non-price factor in its own right and, as Table 3.1 shows, determines other non-price factors as well. Significantly, design can also determine price.

Much of the literature on design fails to differentiate between engineering and industrial design, especially in terms of how they contribute to cost savings. Furthermore, the 'design evangelists', with an interest in furthering their own consultancy interests, have made bold

Table 3.1 – The role of design in competitiveness
Source: Walsh, V. *et al.* 1992

Factor	Influence of design
Price	Can reduce manufacturing costs
	Can determine cost of use and maintenance
Non-price	Product performance
Quality	Uniqueness
	Reliability
	Ease of use
	Durability
Company image	Product presentation
	Display
	Packaging
	Promotion
Delivery time	Design for ease of development
After-sales service	Design for ease of service and repair

and often unfounded claims for the commercial value of design. Below we will attempt to disentangle the two, and focus upon empirical research rather than evangelising assertion.

While design can be a minor factor in the total costs of any product, it has been claimed to be the process that can determine up to 85% of all costs.[5] The designer, it is argued, specifies the materials to be used, the component configurations and the manufacturing processes involved. Over the years design methods have been developed to help designers to investigate the cost implications. Value analysis, a design strategy which reduces cost by identifying the cheapest means of performing each essential function in a product, can lead to total cost savings of up to 20%.[6]

A more recent approach that has dramatic cost saving claims made for it is called *design for manufacturability and assembly* (DFMA). Developed by two British academics, the system attracted little interest from industry in this country. Now settled in the United States, the partners work for American corporate clients. It has been reported that the DFMA process, which calculates the economic implications of design decisions, has cut the assembly time of IBM printers by 90% and reduced Ford's manufacturing costs by $1.2 billion.[7] According to Ford, design decisions are ten times more effective than production planning decisions and one hundred times more effective than production changes in reducing costs and improving quality.[8]

Recent research in the United States has differentiated the cost implications of decisions taken at different stages of the new product development process. This suggests that industrial design decisions account for around 40% of costs, the rest being established by engineering decisions on manufacture and materials, together with broader managerial decisions on labour, plant and distribution.

Clearly as a factor acting in its own right and in determining others, it is difficult to isolate design as one determinant of competitiveness and measure its influence. However, considerable work has been undertaken by the Open University's Design Innovation Group examining the contribution made by design in industry.[9]

The group's most recent research project for the first time provides evidence on a most crucial question: what are the benefits and costs of investment in design? The research team surveyed 221 small and medium sized companies that had made use of DTI grants for design. Their three-year study examined firms that had used design in a variety of ways. About half of the companies had made use of product designers, one-third were concerned with engineering design issues, and the rest had taken on designers to do packaging and other product-related graphic design. The survey sample was broadly representative of the structure of British industry and the conclusions pointed to a very positive contribution by design:

- At an average cost of £60 000, 90% of design projects made a profit with an average payback period of 15 months.

- Compared with previous products, sales increased on average by 41%, new home markets were opened up in 25% of cases, with 13% of projects securing new or increased export markets.

- In total, the projects examined earned £500 m in export earnings over 6 years.

The researchers concluded that "investment in design improves financial performance, retains and regains market share, enhances exports and affects the competitiveness of British industry".[10] However, the researchers still saw a problem. One objective of the DTI support programme was to promote long-term investment in design together with more effective and deep-rooted design management in industry. The research discovered little evidence that this had occurred.

The relationship between design management and competitiveness has been the subject of a number of studies. These have focused in many cases on management attitudes to design as a useful measure of design orientation. Shortcomings here have received much attention in the literature. According to Wally Olins, a leading design consultant, the failure to recognise design as a coherent resource which can be managed like any other resource has led many companies to regard it as a somewhat arcane jobbing activity that transcends the need for managerial or strategic perspectives.[11] Other studies support this general view, including Borja de Mozota's case study analysis of eleven design projects, which concluded, "managers have a poor understanding and perception of how design works on a company's results".[12]

The Design Innovation Group's research on firms in the plastics industry concluded that "design conscious" companies performed better in terms of turnover growth and return on capital.[13] These findings are consistent with a Staffordshire University study of design management in the ceramic tableware industry. Manufacturers with generally positive views on design, who displayed evidence of design management, had higher sales, profits and especially export growth than companies with less positive views and an absence of design management.[14]

Researchers at the University of Strathclyde carried out a large survey of 369 companies, which examined management attitudes to design and design management practices, correlating them against sales performance and comparison with major competitors. Their study concluded that firms which wedded technical expertise to marketing skills, were committed to new product design, had the skills to carry it out, had design represented at board level and ensured that it was properly managed had the greatest success in the market.[15]

Much of the research cited above has been concerned with identifying the value of product design and its management to enterprises. However, there are a number of industries in which the product or service produced may be immune to the enhancing powers of design. In such cases it is the image of the company that is a more competitive factor. In meeting the needs of such industries has evolved the sophisticated business of corporate identity design, which is today a multi-million pound industry. Design is used to project a coherent and distinctive identity for an organisation, using a visual language to communicate its values and function. As the leading corporate identity designer, Wally Olins explains that this is to overcome the lack of any perceivable difference in the values of their products and services:

"It is virtually impossible to detect quality differences between the products of major financial service companies, or petrol retailers or the various chemical companies for instance. This means that companies and their brands have increasingly to compete with each other on emotional rather than rational grounds. The company with the strongest, most consistent, most attractive, best implemented and manifested identity will emerge on top in this race".[16]

BP, for example, recently spent £171 million on a new identity. Their corporate redesign, involving a subtly reshaped logo, aims to associate BP with the colour green in the public's eye. The design group Addison set out to make BP executives "fall in love with green", associating it with freshness, quality and vitality.[17] The new identity also made a timely link with consumers' increasing environmental concerns. As we will see in more detail in the following chapter, corporate identity can lead to long-term cost savings, greater employee motivation and higher consumer awareness. However, quantifying the value of investment in corporate identity is no easy task. Many of the claims made for it are largely anecdotal and often provided by the design industry itself. One independent case study of Fuji showed how the Japanese film manufacturer carefully researched its image in western markets before embarking on a new identity programme aimed at increasing its market share. The study concluded that the corporate identity programme helped to double its US market share to over 6%.[18]

The contribution made by environmental design to competitiveness is also difficult to quantify, although there are some cases which indicate that it can enhance efficiencies in the service sector. In advanced economies now more reliant on services than manufacturing for employment and wealth creation, desk bound employees have yet to make the same gains in productivity as those on the factory floor. While industrial efficiency has increased fourteen-fold in the postwar period, office efficiency has only doubled. As trade unions and researchers have argued, the introduction of new technology into offices has been more associated with sick building syndrome, repetitive strain injury, increasing job stress and higher absenteeism.

At its Stockholm sales office, the Digital computer company has used radically new office design to cut power bills by half, raise sales to 60% above target, cut paper consumption by 70% and reduce absenteeism to zero. The new office environment is designed to high ergonomic standards. Through careful analysis of its employees' work activities, Digital introduced a novel degree of flexibility into the office design. Space savings have been made by having desks appear only when they are needed. A report in *The Guardian* explains how:

"In the centre of the office is a large artificial tree on which appear to grow peaches and mangoes. The fruit house the buttons to lower computer terminals from their storage places in the ceiling to the individual's preferred work height (which could be standing up). ... Staff do not have allocated desks but wheel their mobile work station next to a fully-networked terminal and take their pick from a choice of ergonomically designed chairs".[19]

Thirty other employers in Sweden are working with Digital and Swedish government departments to explore how this new experiment in the design of office environments, equipment and the jobs that use them can be applied elsewhere. The value of design to enterprises in the service sector increasingly includes efficiencies in the delivery of those services.

From the studies and examples described above, it can be concluded that design and the way in which it is managed contribute to both price and non-price competitiveness, helping to determine the consumer's perception of value-for-money, which is itself a crucial purchasing factor. But clearly design does not guarantee success; it is far from being a panacea for all the ills of uncompetitiveness. As we will explore in the next chapter, it is the appropriateness of the overall corporate strategy to prevailing market conditions and the way in which this integrates effective design with other activities that determines success.

Prevalent attitudes to design are also determined by national culture. Having explored the value of design to the enterprise, we shift our attention now to the macro-level to examine how design contributes to national economic development.

The Value of Design to the National Economy

"The worse an object is designed the better it sells in the export market. China dogs apparently are really popular abroad."

Senior British Government Treasury official, 1951[20]

According to the Treasury, Britain's post-war industrial recovery would owe nothing to design and thus the Design Council's predecessor should be abolished. The export markets that British manufacturers had to gain would be won with traditional, even poor, designs.

In 1950 Britain accounted for 25% of world manufacturing exports. In 1984 the import of manufactured goods into Britain exceeded the level of exports for the first time ever, while the country's share of world manufacturing exports had slumped to 8%. Could the Treasury have been mistaken?

As the extent of Britain's industrial decline became evident, a number of reports from the late 1970s onwards began to identify design as a neglected resource in the British economy. The 1979 Corfield Report drew on the evidence of National Economic Development Office (NEDO) working party reports and case study material to argue that "better product design would make a significant contribution to improving UK economic performance".[21] Although Corfield has been criticised for presenting more of an article of faith in design than an analysis fully grounded in empirical research, subsequent studies have supported this commitment.[22] A Committee of Enquiry investigating the standards of design in a number of consumer goods markets drew the following conclusion in its 1983 report:

"While British industry has both design and manufacturing capability in plenty, the necessary synthesis of the two remains elusive, to the detriment of our industrial survival. In the current context of world trade, it is not feasible for the UK to compete on price alone. Only by outperforming our competitors in terms of product design and quality are we likely to keep our place in world markets."[23]

Despite the government-supported design initiatives described in the previous chapter, British industry still remains reluctant to embrace design fully. A survey of British design professionals highlighted shortcomings in the corporate view of design and considered that *"British industry continues to lack the capacity to make full use of a vig-*

orous indigenous design profession".[24] More recently, a survey of attitudes to design among senior managers from 200 British, French and German companies showed that UK manufacturers place design low on the corporate agenda. By their own admission, a majority of UK managers agreed that British companies place a lower value on design than do their French or German competitors.[25]

Some industrialists may be cautious that *design* has become a postmodern soundbite; yet another stick to beat ourselves with. Regrettably, the stick has been wielded for a great many years. It was in 1832 that Sir Robert Peel argued in Parliament that Britain's declining exports resulted from poor design, initiating a movement to raise the overall standards of taste in British culture and improve standards of design. The Victorian Design Reform Movement led to the establishment of the National Gallery and a number of design schools. The Great Exhibition of 1851 sought to

Table 3.2 – Cultural and economic factors accounting for Britain's poor integration of design

Factor	Effect
Conservative Protestant culture	Provides Britain with a strong sense of pragmatism and utilitarianism, eschewing the outward display of decoration and taste
Rural-based ruling class	Legacy of anti-industrial, anti-urban values, in which business was "ungentlemanly" and the status of engineers was low
Dominant concern with heritage	British values are held to be better signified through traditional crafted prestige products such as fine china and luxury motor cars
Reliance upon sterling markets	Post-war export focus on low growth, low innovation markets with little competition
High defence expenditure	R&D expenditure drawn from private indus try to defence, with a high reliance of the UK electronics sector on defence rather than consumer markets
Emphasis on basic R&D	Concern with prestige projects leads to insufficient importance or investment placed upon incremental innovation or product design

demonstrate Britain's technological and manufacturing superiority. In this it succeeded, but according to one account, "the first industrial nation had, inevitably, achieved another first, namely the embodiment of poor taste and dubious quality in cheap consumer goods".[26]

Design is formed at the nexus of culture and economy. Consequently, accounting for British industry's relatively poor integration of design requires an examination of relevant cultural and economic factors. Table 3.2 summarises six key factors, which are elaborated further in the text below.

Frederique Huygen's wide ranging study of British design makes some useful cultural observations.[27] In her view, Britain's conservative Protestant culture has "no love of outward display".[28] Its strong sense of pragmatism was better suited to utilitarian, technological innovation rather than the less definable domain of decoration and taste. Its rurally-based ruling classes provided the legacy of an anti-industrial, anti-urban culture which continues to permeate British society. Business became regarded as an "ungentlemanly occupation", and, unlike other countries, the status of engineers remained low. Although this cultural critique of Britain's decline has been subject to recent empirical challenge,[29] the tenacious hold of traditional values is clearly an important factor.

The attempts at design promotion since Peel's initiative have fought against this conservative culture. There is a dominantly held view that it is precisely this heritage that accounts for Britain's success and is increasingly projected as Britain's *corporate identity*. British values are signified through the products of Laura Ashley, Rolls-Royce, Burberry and Wedgwood. Modern design is encouraged, but almost like a childhood pursuit that the establishment hopes manufacturers will eventually grow out of. As Peter York has observed, "It's typically English and paradoxical that the Duke of Edinburgh presents his yearly prize for elegant design for the Design Council talking in precisely *that* kind of English voice and wearing *that* kind of English suit that hasn't changed since the 1930s. The Duke of

Edinburgh does not wear 'designer' clothes – he wears *tailored* clothes. His style is the antithesis of design as the design professional knows it; so are his houses".[30]

From these cultural foundations, other economic and political factors must be considered. Britain's former imperial superiority, of which its monarchy is a symbol, provided two post-war legacies which further divorced design and innovation from the needs of creating a competitive industrial base: reliance upon imperial markets and high military expenditure. The sterling area that Britain concentrated its export drive on after the war offered less competition than either North America or Europe and a fondness for things traditionally British. As a major study has concluded, "British exports concentrated in low growth markets [and] British design was concentrated in low growth and low technical innovation sectors – or in high technology, frequently defence related sectors".[31]

Drawing out the implications of this latter point, Martin Walker has argued compellingly that the British defence sector acts as a giant magnet attracting R&D funds and expertise away from private industry. Britain and the United States, with the lowest industrial growth rates, spend over 30% of their total R&D funds on defence. In contrast, the post-war economic successes, Japan and West Germany, spend less than 7% on defence.[32] A recent NEDO report argued that the UK electronics industry's reliance upon defence contracts has reduced the abilities of companies to compete in the consumer electronics and information technology sectors.[33]

In considering R&D expenditure, we highlight a further problem besetting the use of design in Britain. A number of studies have suggested that this country places too much emphasis on basic R&D and technological innovation, thus underestimating the role played by incremental product design in contributing to national economic performance. As a former IBM vice president has observed, "product leadership can be built without scientific leadership if companies excel at design and the management of production".[34]

This view is echoed by the chairman of a company whose global rise has mirrored Big Blue's global eclipse. In a lecture delivered to British industrialists in 1992, Sony's Akio Morita made the following point: "The key to competitiveness in a borderless, 'high tech' world does not lie beneath the microscope lens of the laboratory scientist, but on the drawing boards and computer screens of electrical engineers, software developers and design experts".[35]

To understand the value of design to national economies we need to explore further the relationship between design and innovation first raised in the previous chapter. It was argued that while innovation is concerned with advances in state-of-the-art technology, design is concerned with applying that technology and making product variations. In Table 3.3 the Open University's model of four stages in the spectrum of innovation and design is applied to advances in consumer electronics.

Table 3.3 – The spectrum of innovation and design

Basic product and component innovations	Major product and component innovations	Incremental product and component innovations	Design variations and new models
Transistor	Transistor radio	Sony pocket radio	
Magnetic tape	Philips compact cassette	Sony Walkman	Sony Sports Walkman
Microprocessor	Personal computer	Apple Macintosh	Apple Mac Performa
Laser	Compact disc	Kodak Photo CD	

The basic technological innovations, such as the transistor and the microprocessor, emerged from extensive R&D programmes, in both cases funded largely by the US Defense Department for military purposes. But such innovations do not necessarily result in products that have a commercial value. It is the job of engineering and industrial design to apply basic innovation to the demands of the market. According to Walsh *et al.*, designing is involved in all four stages, although probably 90% of it is concentrated in the latter two.[36]

The job of design is often to incorporate new technologies into existing products, thereby creating a new concept, such as the use of transistors in radio sets leading to portable radios. Design can also be directed towards refining an existing technology to create a new product, as Philips did by miniaturising magnetic tape technology into the form of the compact cassette. Such new consumer technologies can be refined further through industrial design. The Sony Walkman has been described as a piece of innovative technology by seemingly everyone except its conceiver, Akio Morita, who queried, "Where is the technology? Frankly, it did not contain any breakthrough technology. Its success was built on product planning and marketing".[37] The hundreds of different Walkman models produced since its original development, and the application of new recording technologies to the original concept, has given the product a broadening and durable market presence.

One factor accounting for Japan's success has been the concentration of its R&D efforts on new product and applied research rather than basic research. Only 15% of the country's total R&D expenditure is allocated for basic research.[38] This is perhaps the most appropriate strategy given the types of industries that form the backbone of the Japanese economy and their levels of technological and economic maturity. Japan's strategic identification of future growth industries and the targeting of appropriate R&D support on them has been in contrast to Britain's industrial economic strategy. As Japan shows increasing evidence of increasing its basic research investment, the country's policy makers would appear to be in step with economic models that suggest a strong relationship between economic cycles and patterns of innovation.

In the 1920s a Russian economist, N.D. Kondratieff, identified half-century cycles in economic activity. The Kondratieff cycles predicted an economic downturn from the early 1970s, bottoming out in 1989, and thus for obvious reasons Kondratieff has attracted new-found interest. Perhaps more so than the cycles themselves, attention has focused on a theory to account for them. A former Austrian finance minister and later Harvard academic, Joseph Schumpeter, linked the cycles to innovation.[39]

Schumpeter's theory, summarised very broadly, was that the upturn of each Kondratieff long wave was largely due to a corresponding wave of technological and industrial innovation. These two waves are plotted against each other in Figure 3.2. Innovations in the cotton and iron industries – the original industrial revolution – triggered the build up to the first economic boom. As economic decline set in, the development of railways and the steel industry helped to initiate the second period of growth, and so on.

Figure 3.2 – Innovation and economic activity

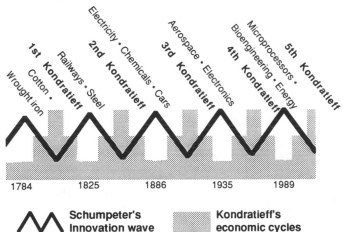

While there is considerable debate over the causal relationship between innovation and economic activity, and the validity of the specific innovations cited by Schumpeter, long-wave theories do have important implications and provide insights to the development of economies. As Freeman argues, the role of innovation was neglected in Keynes' economic theory, which made no allowance for the impact of new technologies on economic development.[40]

Freeman develops Schumpeter's approach to propose a three-fold taxonomy of innovation. The first are major *technological revolutions*, which lie at the heart of the long wave, such as electrification or information technology. These bring with them a whole new technoeconomic paradigm which restructures economies, ushers in new industries and destroys redundant ones, initiating social and cultural changes. The second group are *radical innovations*, which are spread throughout the cycle, and may lead to major adjustments for firms in particular industries. An example would be a new material in the textile industry. Third are *incremental innovations*: "a relatively smooth continuous process leading to steady improvement in the array of existing products and services and the ways in which they are produced".[41]

Design clearly plays a vital role throughout these cycles, but its role changes as the cycle develops. When a new industry emerges, design is concerned with radical product innovation. As dominant products emerge, design's focus moves more towards efficiency of their manufacture and design refinement. In a mature industry, product differentiation and incremental innovation is design's main domain. Walsh *et al.* conclude from this that "radical innovations, and incremental and design innovations, are thus equally important in economic terms, but in different ways".[42]

Freeman considers that Japan's ability to ride the current wave owes much to its ability to redesign products and production processes and to develop the national educational and strategic mechanisms which allow this to occur. Britain's obsession with counting its Nobel prizes and neglecting commercially exploitable innovation suggests, in the view of Professor Peter Hall, the need for a Japanese future-orientated industrial strategy: "That, however, will need a new kind of civil servant: the kind who can spot future commercial winners, rather than backing Concorde".[43] It also requires that Britain consider the implications of evidence suggesting that we are entering a new technoeconomic paradigm.

The Value of Design after Henry

"The revolution in retailing reflects new principles of production, a new pluralism of products, and a new importance for innovation. As such it marks a shift to a post-Fordist age."

Robin Murray, University of Sussex[44]

Kondratieff's Fifth Wave, Toffler's Third Wave,[45] Halal's Post-Industrial Paradigm,[46] Lash and Urry's Disorganized Capitalism,[47] Harvey's Flexible Accumulation,[48] Murray's Post-Fordist Age – different labels and different theoretical frameworks, but a shared view that the form of capitalist production characterised by Henry Ford's organisational and technological innovations is undergoing a radical transformation, as is the system of consumption that it serves. One result of the new industrial age is to enhance the value of design greatly.

The so-called *Fordist* system of mass production combined various elements together in the production of a complex commodity – the motor vehicle. These elements comprised a standardised product, a factory structured around an assembly line where the product flowed past workers undertaking specific tasks and the use of machines which were each dedicated to producing or assembling one component of the final product. The economies of scale created by the Fordist system accrued profit as long as the factory could be operated around the clock, and as long as there were consumers who desired a standardised product. This system of production transformed all the major consumer goods industries, including food, furniture, clothing and textiles, and domestic appliances, creating affordable goods for increasingly affluent populations in industrialised countries.[49]

From the 1960s problems in this system became evident, and, with the onset of recession in the early 1970s, came to a head. Mass producers had always faced the problem of forecasting demand: if too little is produced market share is lost, and if too much is produced then it is necessary to hold expensive stock. The rise of an individualistic consumer society was creating a market where people no longer desired a standardised product, but the organisation of labour and machinery on assembly lines was geared around the standard product. Simply increasing capital and labour input to increase diversity was no solution since it would increase costs at a time of uncertain demand and increasing price competition from newly industrialising economies. According to Murray, the groundwork for a new system was laid in the shopping aisles of stores such as Sainsbury.[50]

The problems faced by producers in forecasting demand for a few products pales in comparison to those of Sainsbury, which holds over 12 000 product lines. Since the 1950s, leading retailers had been using computer systems to monitor sales and co-ordinate distribution to their outlets, thereby matching supply to the shifting patterns of demand. They were among the first to realise that the mass consumer was being replaced by diverse market segments which could be identified by various measures such as social class, household type and lifestyle group. Stores could then segment themselves into a range of new outlets, each attracting a different type of consumer. Burton, for example, splintered into Top Man, Top Shop, Principles and Dorothy Perkins: "In all these shops the emphasis has shifted from the manufacturer's economies of scale to the retailer's economies of scope. The economies come from offering an integrated range from which customers choose their own basket of products".[51]

Retailers were using information technology to generate knowledge about the nature of their changing markets and act appropriately and flexibly in response. It was this same strategy that began to transform manufacturing industry, enabled by a new wave of largely computer-based innovations.

Figure 3.3 – Flexible manufacturing system

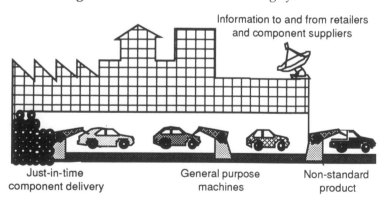

Information to and from retailers and component suppliers

| Just-in-time component delivery | General purpose machines | Non-standard product |

Flexible manufacturing systems (Figure 3.3) enable one production line to produce a number of different models and variants geared to different niche markets. The factory is geared to respond to changing consumer demand as quickly as possible. Information systems enable the manufacturer to communicate with retailers and component suppliers and co-ordinate all aspects of production. Replacing single-purpose machines are general-purpose multi-task robots. Sharp's robotised electronic calculator line can produce up to six different models simultaneously. Even in industries where more heavyweight production equipment is needed, new technologies have been used to increase flexibility. Whereas car panel presses in the United States recently took 9 hours to change their dyes, Toyota's modern presses have reduced this to 2 minutes.

However, Japan's competitors have not been slow in learning their lessons. When an American customer orders a General Motors Saturn, as soon as the salesperson keys the order into the showroom terminal specifying colour, accessories and other specifications, the computer at the Tennessee plant sets up the robots on the shopfloor to make a car to these specific requirements. As the factory sees its orders developing, it orders the components it requires from nearby suppliers using a supply system called *just-in-time*. Instead of holding stocks of components, the manufacturer ensures that their suppliers are all based within a short travelling distance from the plant and are geared up to deliver components as they are needed – just in time for final assembly – thus reducing costs and storage space. This system of component supply was pioneered by Toyota after the company's founder visited an American supermarket chain and observed how its stock was ordered.

At Panasonic it is claimed that over 11 million variations of bicycle design according to individual customers' ergonomic and feature requirements can be produced from their flexible factory.[52] Such production systems also make it viable to produce short runs of particular product variations geared for niche markets. Some Japanese firms claim to be manufacturing complex products such as photocopiers in batches as small as 500. Flexible technologies also offer opportunities for decentralised production, thereby opening up new opportunities to small and medium sized firms.

Evidence from northern Italy, where competitive industries such as clothing and furniture are built upon small enterprises using advanced technologies, supports this claim.[53]

Some have argued that Italy has been particularly successful in rising to the challenge of post-Fordism. As the textile and clothing industries of Britain and the United States continue their decline, those of Italy remain largely buoyant. With the Italian textile industry retaining a strong small firm character, it has been suggested that perhaps sweat shop wage rates account for Italy's competitiveness.

In fact, textile and clothing labour costs in Italy are higher than those in Britain and America.[54] Italy's performance in these sectors can be accounted for by an appropriate mix of innovation in production and distribution technologies, together with effective design strategies.

From the early 1970s the large textile firms such as Gruppo GFT and Marzotto offered manufacturing and marketing support to designers in the then embryonic Milan fashion houses. The intention was to use Armani and Versace to create a prestigious image for Italian design which would rival that of France. Promoting distinctive Italian design accompanied heavy investment in new automated plant. This has enabled Italy to create a price-competitive mass market in fashion.

Combining an eye for controversial advertising with new technology, flexible production and high design content, Benetton has secured a place on virtually every high street in Europe and North America. The company's 200 strong design team produces 5000 different garment designs each year. Benetton's trick has been to supply each of its franchises with precisely the clothes demanded by each store's customers. Undyed garments are made to Benetton's design by a network of small businesses which send them to the company's automated dying plant. Computerised checkouts in each store monitor consumer's colour tastes, sending data to the dyeing plant where appropriate batches of coloured garments are produced and shipped to the stores within 8 days. Applying many of the principles of post-Fordism, these examples demonstrate how design can unite with more radical production innovation to provide export earnings, employment and a marketable national cultural identity.

The post-Fordist thesis comprises five main elements:

- The identification of Fordism as a formerly dominant technological paradigm.
- A shift away from Fordist mass production.
- A shift away from mass consumer markets.
- The development of new production technologies, creating opportunities for small firms.
- The increasing skill requirements of workers using flexible technology.

While there has been considerable and continuing debate over these claims, David Harvey, Professor of Geography at Oxford University, considers that the evidence for increasing flexibility is overwhelming.[55] Although not employing the "post-Fordist" label as such, his notion of flexible accumulation shares many common elements, but in a balanced view which acknowledges the period of transition that industrial economies are currently undergoing.

Flexible manufacturing plants are an important element of post-Fordism but, as Harvey suggests, it would be a mistake to characterise the new industrial age solely in terms of hi-tech factories and a shoppers' paradise. Flexibility in production has also been gained by exporting Fordist mass-production systems to low-wage economies, increasing sub-contracting to small businesses and promoting home-working. Many of these developments have brought with them greater insecurity and exploitation in employment. The multi-tier labour markets that some economists are identifying indicate that many millions of consumers, even in the west, buy goods simply for need rather than to express lifestyle. For every Sainsbury with its 12 000 lines is an Aldi or Kwik-Save with a far more modest selection of cheap, basic goods. Despite the attractions of a GM Saturn, the market for second-hand Ladas remains buoyant.

However, for those with spending power post-Fordism enables bewildering choice and the means of expressing identity through consumption. An accompanying aesthetic shift has been the decline of modernist functional styling, very much a product of Fordist production, and the rise of a postmodern eclecticism. As the previous chapter explained, "postmodernism" has been used as a term to describe the overall cultural transformation that the new technoeconomic paradigm has enabled, elevating the act of consumption to a new cultural activity. The new postmodern consumers and the values they ascribe to design are considered more fully below, but at this stage it is relevant to reflect on how the new "economy of innovation", as Murray describes it, increases the value of design.[56] The culture of consumption increasingly drives the engine of production in many markets, rather than the other way around, generating employment both in retail itself and in other cultural industries. The retail boom of the 1980s created a massive market for design, with 86% of UK retailers investing in design.[57] Designers shaped the emergent lifestyles, designed the segmented shops, promoted their images and conceived the goods that they sold. Design was not only essential to the processes of consumption, but also in exploiting the flexible manufacturing potential that the new production systems offered by increasing the choice to consumers.

The post-Fordist paradigm raises the value of design as a bridge between new production opportunities and more diverse consumer needs. It is how to understand those needs and how they relate to developments in contemporary consumer culture that we now turn.

Design: "Values Made Visible"

"The word 'values' implies both aesthetic and commercial values, and the phrase hints at interpretation, at communication."

David Bernstein, advertising executive[58]

Compared with other definitions of design, "values made visible" has the apparently paradoxical advantages of both brevity and scope. It is a useful window through which to view design's historical development and changing cultural role.

The postmodern consumer culture, introduced above, has enhanced the act of consumption and as such it has fundamentally altered the relationship between consumer and commodity. According to Tomlinson, "the commodity has acquired, in late consumer capitalism, an aura beyond just its function. The commodity now acts *on* the consumer, endows him/her with perceived qualities which can be displayed in widening public contexts. ... It is the difference between buying an object mainly for its function, and acquiring an item for its style".[59] It is therefore crucial to appreciate how design is becoming more a communicator of values and meaning required by consumers than just a functional problem solving activity.

The design of any artefact involves arranging materials into a configuration whereby they fulfil a particular function and meet a human need. The resulting product therefore has a use-value which reflects its utility. In pre-capitalist societies this use-value is the only value that products are required to embody and express. According to Marx, as soon as products are bought and sold they acquire a new value – their exchange-value.[60] In so doing they cease to be utilitarian objects valued solely in terms of their use, and instead become commodities valued in terms of their exchange.

Within consumer culture this exchange-value dominates over a design's use-value and necessarily changes the design process itself. Products are bought not just for their utility, but perhaps more importantly for what they symbolise in terms of meaning and value. Cars are bought increasingly as a means of communicating a consumer's lifestyle, values and social status. Henry Ford's realisation of this in 1926 led him to abandon production of the "any colour you like as long as it's black" Model T, spend $18 million on styling a new car and, in what has been described as "the most expensive art lesson in history", demonstrate in his new Model A that it is form rather than function that sells a product.[61] In the United States this helped to refocus the activity of industrial design away from European functionalism to product styling.

Many of the American product stylists emerged from the advertising industry. This helped in cementing the relationship between the design of a product and the imagery used in advertising to sell it. Some cultural theorists argue that products are consumed purely as symbols for the imagery offered by the advertisement. According to the French sociologist Jean Baudrillard, the rise of consumer society has heralded "the passage from use value to sign value".[62] He has gone so far as to argue that our media-orientated culture has created an "aesthetic hallucination of reality" in which the real and the imaginary become indistinguishable in an overwhelming proliferation of signs. Semiotics, the science of signs, has proved a useful means of understanding the relationship between designed products and contemporary culture.[63] Products, to use a semiotic term, become "signifiers" of meanings and values, and are consumed as such. Consequently, their design becomes a complex process which weaves together various messages of meaning into desirable products.

The sign-value of a product is clearly most important when its use-value is indistinguishable from that of its competitors in the market. Instant coffees taste much the same, but it is the tantalising romantic mythology of the Gold Blend couple that has made the brand a market leader. Design therefore focuses on the creation of a myth, of which the jar of coffee is a signifier. Similarly, no one but a few cola connoisseurs can tell the difference between Pepsi and Coke. Coca Cola's disastrous attempt to differentiate their product with a new recipe has been followed by the safer option of a massive investment in a new advertising image which, through the signifier of a distinctive logo, sells a can of coloured water.

Selling a product using an image totally disconnected with its function is not restricted to coffee and cola. Benetton invests considerably in the distinctive design of its clothing. This is sold using powerful, often controversial, images of human suffering rarely featuring the actual product. The company claims to be communicating its social values to consumers, inviting them to share concerns over AIDS and famine through the act of buying a jumper (Figure 3.4).

Figure 3.4 – BenettonAdvertising

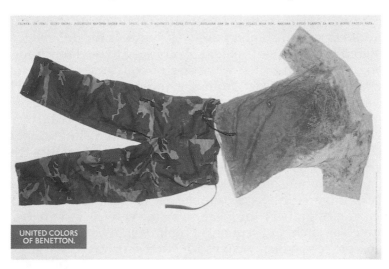

The bloodstained clothes of Marinko Gagro, a victim of the Bosnian war, feature in Benetton's 1994 billboard advertising campaign. Claiming to be "an expression of our age", Benetton uses powerful, often controversial, imagery which focuses on world issues such as racism, poverty, pollution, AIDS and war. Benetton combines effective advertising with bold depiction of current social values

Motor vehicles, as functionally more complex and differentiated products, use design in a variety of ways to express symbolic value. The creation of images to "take your breath away" are an integral part of the mythology that the car signifies. It is also signified through a greater investment in product and engineering design: the features and performance offered, the materials used and the vehicle styling. The distinctive identity of the manufacturer is also asserted in the product using a logo as a metaphor. According to the French semiologist Roland Barthes, "the Citroën emblem, with its arrows, has in fact become a winged emblem, as if one was proceeding from the category of propulsion to that of spontaneous motion, from that of the engine to that of the organism".[64]

Sign-value therefore begins to erode price as a factor considered important by consumers. Japanese automotive designer Naoki Sakai argues that this is leading towards what he describes as the *conceptual economy*: "In this economy value is imaginary. There need be no relation between sales price and production cost. Instead, in this system of artificial value, the psychological nature of the product is what determines its desirability and hence its cost. It's the sort of mechanism in operation in the world of fashion".[65]

Table 3.4 – Nine American Lifestyles
Source: Arnold Mitchell (1983)

Values	Lifestyle	Percentage of total US population
Needs-driven		11
	Survivor	4
	Sustainer	7
Outer-directed		67
	Belonger	35
	Emulator	10
	Achiever	22
Inner-directed		20
	I-am-me	5
	Experimental	7
	Societally conscious	8
Combined outer and inner		2
	Integrated	2

An important concept in consumer culture is lifestyle: self-expression and the assertion of individuality through the consumption of distinctive styles of goods and services.[66] From the fields of sociology and market research have arisen various attempts at lifestyle typologies. Mitchell's classification, shown in Table 3.4, identifies four value groups and nine lifestyles deriving from them.

It is lifestyle that determines why two consumers sharing the same occupation, status, education and social class background will be attracted to different products. Outer-directed consumers with a more socialised lifestyle buy products to assert their belonging to social groups or to express their status and achievement to others. Inner-directed people consume fewer products. Less materialistic, they may choose goods on environmental or ethical grounds.

The Japanese Ministry of International Trade and Industry has not been slow to draw out the implications of lifestyle for design. According to a report that the Ministry published in 1988, "People no longer base their decisions for purchase only on fundamental criteria such as function, economy and safety. Now there is a growing tendency to select on the basis of secondary criteria such as comfort, warmth, elegance, humour and personal statements conveyed by individual life and taste. ... The future of design would seem to indicate greater individualism and design diversification, possibly leading to an inordinate variety of products".[67]

It is one thing to identify the lifestyle that a consumer may be wishing to express, and quite another to predict or control the goods and services they will purchase from the inordinate variety on offer to express it. Lifestyle-orientated retailers, such as Next and Habitat, sought to package lifestyle. Perhaps their demise is evidence of consumers' growing sophistication in assembling their own stylistic codes of consumption. Certainly consumers are far better advised on lifestyle choices by the media which, through the *Clothes Show, Elle Decoration* and serious documentaries on taste, provides semiotic guidance. The market research industry is responding with sophisticated research methods that map individual purchase decisions to specific lifestyles.

Marx's notion of commodity fetishism has clearly reached new heights of ecstatic pleasure. And pleasure is indeed a useful guide to the contribution made by design to the act of postmodern consumption. We consume in order to gain pleasure. As John Walker argues, given the central importance of pleasure in design, fashion, shopping and consumption, the lack of analytical attention it has been given is surprising.[68] He identifies five sources of pleasure in the act of consumption. Table 3.5 shows these, together with the contribution that design makes to each of them.

Table 3.5 – Design's pleasure principles
Adapted from J.A. Walker (1990)

Source of pleasure	Design contribution
Desire	Conceiving and expressing the myth or fantasy
	Advertising
Purchase	Packaging
	Display
	Retail environment
The object	Qualities of newness
	Tactile qualities
	Aesthetic appeal
Use	Performance
	Ergonomics
	Ease of use
Perception by others	Symbolic value

The pleasure derived from owning and using an object is bound up with the pleasure of its desire, the act of its purchase and the perception that others have of the consumer by virtue of that ownership. Design should therefore aim to enhance the pleasure derived from each of these sources: a seductive mythology, a celebratory environment for purchase, a tactile and appealing object, a comfortable and reliable mode of operation, and a symbolic code that suggests status, identity, wealth or even sexual desirability.

As we indicated in the previous chapter, interpretations of lifestyle and consumer culture polarise between viewing it as manipulations of the mass market to seeing it as extensions of individual autonomy beyond direct control. Mike Featherstone argues for a perspective that transcends the limitations of these opposing views and relates to a class analysis of contemporary society. While much of his analysis is beyond the scope of this discussion, one key argument is essential in appreciating that the designer is not just a cog in the larger wheel of capitalist growth, but plays a partly autonomous role in determining the nature of consumer culture.

Featherstone argues that consumerism has given rise to a new petite bourgeoisie, an expanding class fraction responsible for the "production and dissemination of consumer culture imagery and information ... concerned to expand and legitimate its own particular dispositions and lifestyle".[69] This group includes designers, artists, educators and caring professions, sharing with intellectuals a progressive world view:

"The new petite bourgeoisie, therefore, identifies with the intellectuals" lifestyle and acts as intermediaries in transmitting the intellectuals' ideas to a wider audience. They also act as cultural entrepreneurs in their own right in seeking to legitimate the intellectualization of new areas of expertise such as popular music, fashion, design, holidays, sport, popular culture, etc. which increasingly are subjected to serious analysis. ... They have abandoned the narrow asceticism of the petite bourgeoisie in favour of promoting more hedonistic and expressive consumption norms."[70]

This perspective suggests a more autonomous cultural and social role for designers than that suggested by much design management literature. It is to the relationship between design and changing social values that we now turn.

Design and Social Values

"The goal of design is neither to fill the purse of management nor inflate the glory of the designer, but rather to strive for civilised design that will better serve the needs and aspirations of humans".

Arthur J. Pulos, Emeritus Professor of Design, Syracuse University[71]

Design both reflects and often seeks to promote the changing values of society. As an activity often concerned with aesthetics, visual order and beauty, its practitioners have often been driven by a missionary zeal to bring "good taste" to the masses, embrace radical political movements and when appropriate celebrate the optimism of the time.

The social and cultural changes already evident in the 1990s will be reflected in new concerns and priorities on the part of designers and those who employ them. Some in design are developing proactive strategies around issues such as environmentalism, global culture and demographic change which are already influencing industry. Before these are examined in detail, it is necessary to explore the historical relationship between design and social values.

The 1980s was perhaps the low-point in terms of design's recognition of its social responsibilities. Design had come of age as a fully fledged industry in its own right. When Moselli Design, creators of the Maserati and the Gaggia coffee machine, designed decoy replicas of Phantom fighter bombers for the Iraqi Government during the Gulf War, the consultancy was expressing an overriding responsibility to its bottom line.

A century earlier, William Morris helped to found a design movement asserting the designer's moral responsibility to the common good. The Arts and Crafts movement embraced socialist ideology and a naturalistic aesthetic as a reaction to the inequities and ugliness of industrialisation. The craft aesthetic and working method posed an alternative to the questionable design quality of manufactured goods and the alienated labour involved in their production. The aesthetic and the political were inextricably bound together in the Arts and Crafts movement, although ironically not in its patrons. Morris himself lamented that he was ministering "to the swinish luxury of the rich".[72]

Morris's ideas were influential to the pioneers of the Modern movement earlier this century, although they were expressed through a very different aesthetic. The Modernists shared the Arts and Crafts notion of design's moral responsibilities and the use of design to express and further political ideals, but achieving social objectives was to be attained through the use of new technologies and mass production rather than through their rejection. The machine age, it was hoped, could provide prosperity and good design for all. Modernist design, encapsulated by principles such as "form follows function", developed an aesthetic characterised increasingly by geometric form, new materials and bright colours. The Modern movement eventually succumbed to the same commercial realities as Morris in an industrial system which bought the aesthetic, but left the politics on the shelf.

The post-war ideals of social democracy in the context of rising consumer affluence were manifested in the Contemporary design style. Unlike Arts and Crafts or the Modern movement, designers of the 1950s Contemporary period were not challenging capitalism, but sought to express and exploit its potential for reform. Like its two predecessors, the Contemporary style was concerned with establishing a dominant aesthetic based on functionality. In the realms of both design and political economy, the greatest progress was made in northern Europe. Scandinavian designers and manufacturers reunited craft and industry, as the early Modernists had done, using natural materials to manufacture affordable products with simple organic forms. In Norway a market for these products was created through social reforms that included furniture grants to newly married couples. Classless consumerism fed by well-made modern design aiming to improve the general aesthetic quality of life was a concept shared by Terence Conran's Habitat.

During the 1960s designers celebrated the new pop culture and optimism with a style that stressed fashion and disposability. Form no longer followed function in throwaway paper chairs or gaudily decorated bean bags. The social and cultural optimism of pop evolved into the more clearly articulated critique of the dominant Modern aesthetic: postmodernism. Stressing cultural pluralism, greater stylistic diversity and a more critical view of technology, postmodernism severed design from functionality and married it to semiotics. The Memphis Group's plastic laminated furniture and Alessi kettles became the icons of the new ideology.

Reflecting the need for stylistic novelty in an age obsessed with consumerism, postmodernism is undergoing both intellectual and aesthetic challenges. Its frivolity is less appropriate to the post-recessionary insecure 1990s. Although its semiotic observations and assertion of pluralism will no doubt endure, there are indications that postmodern design will more thoroughly embrace new social and cultural concerns. While all work and no play may have made Modern design a rather dull boy (the gender label is used deliberately), the postmodern partying made design more of a wayward adolescent who often disturbed the neighbours.

Design in the 1990s is already evolving to respond to new social values. Concern for the environment, the changing role of women in society, the needs of the disabled and elderly, together with cultural and national identity are among the issues that are equipping design with new responsibilities.

"There are professions more harmful than industrial design, but only a very few of them".[73] The opening sentence to Victor Papanek's Design for the Real World, published in 1973, began a powerful critique of the environmental and social problems that design contributed to. The call for design to address real problems – those of the disabled, the elderly and the Third World – drew upon the Schumacher "Small is Beautiful" ethos and posed a new agenda for design. Eclipsed by the designer eighties, Papanek's ideas are being rediscovered and are contributing to the concept of Green Design today.

With increasing popular concern over environmental issues, often expressed through legislation, design methods which value the environment are filtering into the mainstream. The cradle-to-grave approach considers a product's design in environmental terms from raw materials, through manufacture to use and disposal. Using methods such as lifecycle analysis, the designer seeks to reduce material, energy use and waste at each stage in the product chain. One objective is to increase the recyclability of materials or components. Both Philips and BMW design products that can be easily disassembled, enabling parts to be reused. Designers at AEG addressed the environmental impact of their company's products in use, redesigning washing machines to use less energy and water.

As a major source of waste, packaging has been subject to environmental design attention. Concentrated detergents sold in flexible pouches use 80% less plastic than conventional bottles. There has also been an increase in the use of recycled plastic for packaging. The fashion industry, itself seemingly a promoter of disposability, is promoting eco-friendly styling. Many designers and textile manufacturers are experimenting with recycled materials, natural fibres and less polluting dyeing and finishing processes. Even typographers have demonstrated that they can help to save the planet through the redesign of British Telecom phonebooks. A new typeface combined with four column layout has reduced paper requirements, retained clarity and in the process saved 8000 trees annually.

There is evidence that the marketing led "green consumerism" of the late 1980s is maturing into a more deep-rooted and considered approach to the design of all products. As Dorothy Mackenzie explains in her wide ranging review of green design, "the designer's task will become more difficult and more important than ever, demanding changes in attitude, education, approach and sophistication".[74] Research into the environmental impact of materials, processes and use becomes more critical to the design process, requiring new information systems and methodological tools. Figure 3.5 shows some of the principles and guidelines that promote more environmentally conscious industrial design.[75]

Figure 3.5 – Green design

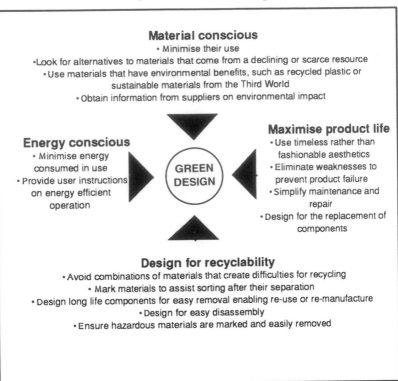

Excluding the needs of the environment from the design process is a deficiency that is gradually being overcome. Excluding the needs of most consumers is taking longer to rectify, although changes are evident. Most products are designed by relatively young white men, with women making up less than 1% of the industrial designers profession.[76] The past two decades have witnessed the rise of feminism, which has changed women's aspirations and roles in society, a greater awareness of the requirements of those with special needs, and a recognition of the multicultural nature of our society. The design of those products, services and environments that we all use is necessarily evolving to enhance accessibility and use by all sections of society.

Decorative fields of design, within which women have traditionally worked, such as textiles, are becoming recognised as equally crucial to our economic well-being and quality of life as the "male" domain of industrial and engineering design. Furthermore, women are being positively encouraged into areas which formerly excluded them, bringing new perceptions to design problems and processes.

Demographic change will create a whole new set of needs to be catered for through design as those aged over 50 will increase in number by 20% during the next 20 years.[77] New strategies are being developed to meet them such as Transgenerational Design (Figures 3.6 and 3.7). Pirkl argues that we should "design products at the outset for use by a transgenerational population, including the aged as well as the young and able bodied. I see no reason a fire extinguisher or a faucet control should not be as useable by a septuagenarian as by a teenager".[78]

Figure 3.6 – Third age fashion shirts by Julie Nock

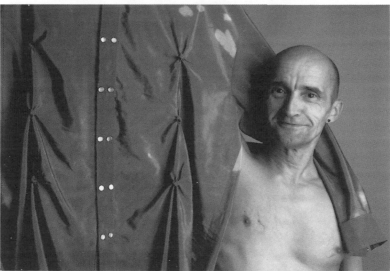

Textile designer Julie Nock used cultural, market and sociological research to develop clothing ideas for the new generation of "fiftysomething" men. The specific ergonomic requirements of a mature market requiring greater warmth and easier fastenings were combined with an understanding of the values this age group is seeking to externalise through clothing. Her lifestyle research led to designs that use classic styles as vehicles for the playfulness required by men who were among the first generation to express individuality through clothes

Figure 3.7 – Design Age jar by Gavin Pryke

The Design Age project at the Royal College of Art aims to promote design which better integrates older people into society. Glass designer Gavin Pryke worked with the project to design jars for the Safeway supermarket chain. The conical form is more stable and comfortable for a range of hand sizes. Easier to grasp on the supermarket shelf, the jar also has finger indents and a form less likely to slip with improved leverage

Cultural pluralism is gradually being acknowledged through the design of the public environment. In Smethwick, for example, recent local authority funded public art has asserted the Asian culture of this West Midlands town.[79] While industrial design has yet to rise to the challenge of cultural diversity within Britain, the differing nature of national cultures is being addressed. The aspiration of globalism, in which the same product can be sold worldwide, has foundered upon the realities of national culture. While there has been a growing uniformity in some product areas, there remain significant differences in taste and requirements between countries. Flexible manufacturing offers opportunities to globalise a core technology, but to adapt its styling to specific national or regional requirements. Design is also used to assert national cultural identity. This may increase further as the new nations of Eastern Europe and elsewhere compete in international markets. According to Aldersey-Williams, design nationalisms "could encourage product diversity, stimulate market demand and perhaps even do a little to improve mutual understanding among the peoples of different nations and cultures".[80]

Furtherance of progressive social and cultural values does not contradict design's value as a commercial and economic resource. Political change in the world's largest economy would appear to be rejecting the blinkered "design as marketing" notion that was dominant in the 1980s. America's President Clinton called together a team of 23 design professionals and industrialists to meet in conference at Little Rock, Arkansas, to propose a national strategy for design that would contribute to the country's economic and cultural renewal. In the context of an economy suffering a decline in manufacturing, environmental problems and the increasing social fragmentation and alienation that resulted in the LA riots, the team set its sights on directing design "to build an America that is economically preeminent, sustainable, proud of its diversity and accessible to all".[81] Table 3.6 summarises the main elements of the Little Rock design strategy.

The Little Rock strategy views design in broad multidisciplinary terms that embrace product and information design, together with architecture, planning and strategic development. It furthers and reflects those values that won the presidency for Clinton: the need to create employment by improving America's competitiveness, the importance of harnessing the potential of new technologies, tackling the environmental problems faced by industrial society, improving the quality of life for those living in urban areas, enabling and celebrating America's cultural diversity and richness, and developing new mechanisms appropriate for new times in furthering democracy. How much of the Little Rock programme is adopted by Clinton's administration remains to be seen, but it represents a visionary restatement of design's potential as a progressive element in social change.

Table 3.6 – Little Rock design strategy presented to President Clinton

Initiative	Aim	Policies
Strategic Design Initiative	Foster collaboration between designers, manufacturers and investors in key areas of innovation	Establish US Design Council
		National Design Consortium bringing together teams of designers, engineers and planners to accelerate growth of tomorrow's key industries
		Making Government a model client by setting high design standards
		Presidential Design Leadership Award to endorse design excellence
		Government support for design research projects
		Tax incentives for design investment
		Appointment of design 'tsar' at highest level of government
		Declare 1994 the 'Year of Design in America'
Urban Design Initiative	Restore cities and towns and create new and sustainable communities for the 21st century	Encourage sustainability through urban planning and transport systems
		Creation of an urban research laboratory to develop visionary plans for community development
		Target innercities including commitment to the homeless
		Design as a medium for education through training programmes in building trades

References

1 Archer, B. (1976) *A new approach to Britain's industrial future: Design*, text of a lecture given at the Royal Society of Arts, 15 March.

2 Roy, R. and Potter, S. (1990) *Design and the Economy*, The Design Council, London, p.13.

3 Cited in Roy, R. and Potter, S. (1990) *Design and the Economy*, The Design Council, London.

4 Roy, R. (1990) Product design and company performance, in Oakley, M. (ed.) *Design Management: A Handbook of Issues and Methods*, Basil Blackwell, Oxford.

5 The Design Council (1992) *Design and Business Performance: A Chief Executive's Handbook*, Department of Trade and Industry, London.

6 Jones, J.C. (1980) *Design Methods*, John Wiley, Chichester, p.113.

7 *Business Week* (1989) Pssst! Want a secret for making superproducts? 2 October.

8 Roy, R. and Potter, S. (1990) *Design and the Economy*, The Design Council, London.

9 Much of their research is discussed in detail in Walsh, V. et al. (1992) *Winning by Design*, Basil Blackwell, Oxford.

10 Potter, S., Roy, R., Capon, C.H., Bruce, M., Walsh, V. and Lewis, J. (1991) *The Benefits and Costs of Investment in Design: Using Professional Design Expertise in Product, Engineering and Graphics Projects*, Open University/UMIST Design Innovation Group, Report DIG-O3, July.

11 Olins, Wally (1985) The mysteries of design management revealed, *Journal of the Royal Society of Arts*, January, 103–114.

12 Borja de Mozota, Brigitte (1990) Design as a strategic management tool, in Oakley, M. (ed.) *Design Management: A Handbook of Issues and Methods*, Basil Blackwell, Oxford.

13 Walsh, V., Roy, R. and Bruce, M. (1988) Competitive by design, *Journal of Marketing Management*, **4**(2), pp 201–217.

14 Press, M. (1991) *Design management in the ceramics industry*, Staffordshire University Design Research Centre, research paper, July.

15 Service, L.M., Hart, S.J. and Baker, M.J. (1989) *Profit by Design*, The Design Council, Scotland.

16 Olins, W. (1990) *The Wolff Olins Guide to Corporate Identity*, The Design Council, London, p.70.

17 *Business* (1989) Green shield stamp, December, 111.

18 *International Management* (1985) How western-style corporate identity programmes aid Japanese firms, **40**(3), pp 66–74.

19 Weston, C. (1993) Uprooting the traditional office with Digital's tree of knowledge, *The Guardian*, 4 August, 13.

20 Maguire, P. (1991) Designs on reconstruction: British business, market structures and the role of design in post-war recovery, *Journal of Design History*, **4**(1), p.26.

21 Corfield, K.G. (1979) *Product Design*, National Economic Development Office, London.

22 Oakley, M. (1985) The influence of design on industrial and economic achievement, *Management Decision*, **23**(4), pp 3–13.

23 The Design Council (1983) *Report to The Design Council on the design of British consumer goods by a committee under the chairmanship of David Mellor OBE, RDI, p.14.*

24 Davies, H. (1989) *The designer's perspective: Managing design in Britain, Journal of General Management*, **14**(4), pp 77–88.

25 *Design Week* (1991) UK industry undervalues design, 22 March.

26 Stewart, R. (1987) *Design and British Industry*, John Murray, Edinburgh, p.9.

27 Huygen, F. (1989) *British Design: Image and Identity*, Thames and Hudson, London.

28 Huygen, F. (1989) *British Design: Image and Identity*, Thames and Hudson, London.

29 Rubinstein, W.D. (1993) *Capitalism, Culture and Decline in Britain 1750–1990*, Routledge, London.

30 York, P. (1988) *Culture as commodity: Style wars, punk and pageant*, in Thakara, J. (ed.) *Design after Modernism*, Thames and Hudson, London, p.162.

31 Maguire, P. (1991) Designs on reconstruction: British business, market structures and the role of design in post-war recovery, *Journal of Design History*, **4**(1), p.26.

32 Walker, M. (1986) Defence spending: Britain's self-inflicted wound, in Roy, R. and Wield, D. (eds) *Product Design and Technological Innovation*, Open University Press, Milton Keynes.

33 NEDO (1988) *Performance and Competitive Success in the UK Electronics Industry*, National Economic Development Office, London.

34 Cited in Roy, R. and Potter, S. (1990) *Design and the Economy*, The Design Council, London, p.24.

35 Department of Trade and Industry (1992) *The First United Kingdom Innovation Lecture by Akio Morita*, Department of Trade and Industry, London, p.4.

36 Walsh, V. et al. (1992) *Winning by Design*, Basil Blackwell, Oxford, p.26.

37 Department of Trade and Industry (1992) The First United Kingdom Innovation Lecture by Akio Morita, Department of Trade and Industry, London, p.4.

38 *High Technology* (1985) Japan's technological agenda, **5**(8), August 1985.

39 The following sources provide fuller discussions on innovation cycles: Freeman, C. (1985) *The economics of innovation*, IEE Proceedings, **132**(4), July 1985; Roy, R. and Wield, D. (eds) (1986) Product Design and Technological Innovation, Open University Press, Milton Keynes, Section 6.
40 Freeman, C. (1985) The economics of innovation, IEE Proceedings.
41 Freeman, C. (1985) The economics of innovation, IEE Proceedings, p.217.
42 Walsh, V. et al. (1992) *Winning by Design*, Basil Blackwell, Oxford, p.31.
43 Hall, P. (1986) *The geography of the fifth Kondratieff cycle*, in Roy, R. and Wield, D. (eds) (1986) Product Design and Technological Innovation, Open University Press, Milton Keynes.
44 Murray, R. (1988) *Life after Henry (Ford)*, *Marxism Today*, October, 8–13.
45 Toffler, A. (1981) *The Third Wave*, Bantam Books, London.
46 Halal, W. (1986) *The New Capitalism*.
47 Lash, S. and Urry, J. (1987) *The End of Organised Capitalism*, Basil Blackwell, Oxford.
48 Harvey, D. (1990) *The Condition of Postmodernity*, Basil Blackwell, Oxford.
49 This discussion of Fordism and its transformation is necessarily superficial. The reader is referred to Harvey (*The Condition of Postmodernity*, Basil Blackwell, Oxford, 1990), who elaborates a richer argument and examines varying interpretations.
50 Murray, R. (1988) Life after Henry (Ford), *Marxism Today*, October, 11.
51 Murray, R. (1988) Life after Henry (Ford), *Marxism Today*, October, 11.
52 Goldhar, J.D. and Lei, D. (1991) The shape of twenty-first century global manufacturing, *Journal of Business Strategy*, **12**(2), March/April 1991, pp 37–41.
53 Piore, M.J. and Sabel, C.F. (1984) *The Second Industrial Divide: Possibilities for Prosperity*, Basic Books, New York.
54 Toyne, B., Arpan, J.S., Barnett, A.H., Ricks, D.A. and Shimp, T.A. (1984) *The Global Textile Industry*, George Allen and Unwin, London.
55 For debate on this issue, see especially Pollert, A. (1988) *Dismantling flexibility, Capital and Class*, (34), spring; Clarke, S. (1990) *New utopias for old: Fordist dreams and Post-Fordist fantasies, Capital and Class*, (42), winter, 133; Harvey, D. (1990) *The Condition of Postmodernity*, Basil Blackwell, Oxford.
56 Murray, R. (1988) Life after Henry (Ford), *Marxism Today*, October, 8–13.
57 Walsh, V. et al. (1992) *Winning by Design*, Basil Blackwell, Oxford, p.14.

58 Bernstein, D. (1988) The design mind, in Gorb, P. (ed.) *Design Talks!* The Design Council, London, p.203.

59 Tomlinson, A. (1990) *Consumption, Identity and Style: Marketing, Meanings and the Packaging of Pleasure*, Routledge, London, p.9.

60 Marx, K. (1954) *Capital: A Critique of Political Economy, Vol. 1*, Lawrence and Wishart, London, Chapter 1.

61 Sparke, P. (1986) *An Introduction to Design and Culture in the Twentieth Century*, Unwin Hyman, London, p.34.

62 Cited in Tomlinson, A. (1990) *Consumption, Identity and Style: Marketing, Meanings and the Packaging of Pleasure*, Routledge, London, p.20.

63 An introduction to semiotics is beyond the scope of this text. The reader is therefore referred to the following concise reading, which details further sources: Walker, J.A. (1989) *Design History and the History of Design*, Pluto Press, London, pp.141–149.

64 Barthes, R. (1972) *Mythologies*, Jonathan Cape, London, p.89.

65 Platt, E. (1991) Form follows fashion, *Design*, July, 12–18.

66 For further discussions on lifestyle, see Featherstone, M. (1987) *Lifestyle and consumer culture, Theory, Culture and Society*, 55–70; Walker, J.A. (1989) *Design History and the History of Design*, Pluto Press, London, pp.166–170.

67 Cited in Pilditch, J.(1989) *Winning Ways*, Mercury Books, London, p.65.

68 Walker, J.A. (1989) *Design History and the History of Design*, Pluto Press, London, pp.185–187.

69 Featherstone, M. (1991) *Consumer Culture and Postmodernism*, Sage, New York, p.84.

70 Featherstone, M. (1991) *Consumer Culture and Postmodernism*, Sage, New York, p.91.

71 Pulos, A.J. (1991) Is there such a thing as design management? *Design Review*, spring, 64–70.

72 Cited in Lambourne, L. (1982) *Utopian Craftsmen: The Arts and Crafts Movement from the Cotswolds to Chicago*, Van Nostrand Reinhold, London, p.25.

73 Papanek, V. (1984) *Design for the Real World*, Thames and Hudson, London, p.ix.

74 Mackenzie, D. (1991) *Green Design: Design for the Environment*, Laurence King, p.154.

75 Burall, P. (1992) How to be green, *Design*, August.

76 Bruce, M. and Lewis, J. (1990) Women designers – is there a gender gap?, *Design Studies*.

77 Bound, J. and Coleman, R. (1992) *Activities and products for the Third Age: A survey of expectations and attitudes*, Design Age Conference, Royal College of Art, London.

78 Pirkl, J.J. (1991) Transgenerational design: A design strategy whose time has arrived, *Design Management Journal*, fall.

79 Jennings, R. (1992) A brighter prospect, *Crafts*, July/August.

80 Aldersey-Williams, H. (1992) *World Design: Nationalism and Globalism in Design*, Rizzoli, p.13.

81 Pearlman, C. et al. (1993) Designing America, *Industrial Design*, March/April, 55.

82 Walker, D. (1991) Comment: David Walker on the marginalisation of design, *Design*, August, 5.

Corporate Design
4 Strategies

"In strategy it is important to see distant things as if they were close and to take a distanced view of close things."

Miyamoto Musashi, 1645[1]

"Strategy is understood as the analysis of the objectives to be achieved in the light of the total military situation and the overall ways of reaching these objectives."

Che Guevara, 1959[2]

"Design management is the implementation of design as a formal program of activity within a corporation by communicating the relevance of design to long-term corporate goals and coordinating design resources at all levels of corporate activity to achieve the objectives of the corporation."

Robert Blaich, 1993[3]

While military analogies may be less appropriate in today's management literature, with its talk of "flatter organisations" and "employee empowerment", business at its heart is a commercial game of war. There is market territory to be won or lost, price wars to be fought and campaigns to be launched. Perhaps the most durable and critical military concept in management is strategy.

The publishers of a 300 year old guide to *samurai* strategy exploited this in the dust jacket copy, which read "Japan's

---

executives have long applied its teachings to their business methods – with startling success". This no doubt helped to make the volume an international best-seller. Che Guevara's manual on guerrilla warfare has yet to find its niche in the business section of airport book shops, but as a concisely written account of how a guerrilla band can take on and defeat a well-resourced regular army, it offers useful advice for the small business. Should Cuba become the world economic miracle in 300 years' time, then Che will find his place alongside Tom Peters and John Harvey Jones.

Che Guevara's definition above captures the essential components of strategy: having clear objectives and plans for achieving them which follow from analysis of the situation. To this, Miyamoto Musashi adds the insight that any analysis must embrace a predictive long-term view and a careful critical examination of immediate conditions. If corporate strategy is about defining business objectives and how they are to be achieved, then design clearly has a strategic role to play. As former Design Director of Philips, Robert Blaich is well qualified to define this strategic role of design management.

The previous chapter outlined the value of design in various terms, which included improving the competitiveness of enterprises, contributing to national economic growth and expressing the values of consumers and their culture. This chapter now considers how companies can accrue this potential value by harnessing design as a strategic resource. The emphasis is on describing specific examples of best practice within the field of design management to demonstrate design's strategic role for companies large and small. Many of these examples draw from published research undertaken during the 1980s. Given the changes of recent years, this chapter seeks to temper some of the buoyant design evangelism that underlies such examples with a more critical view of design's future strategic role in the concluding section.

Chapter Map

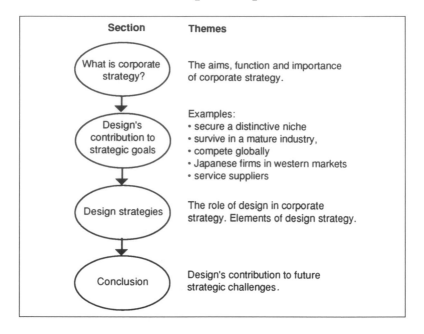

Section	Themes
What is corporate strategy?	The aims, function and importance of corporate strategy.
Design's contribution to strategic goals	Examples: • secure a distinctive niche • survive in a mature industry, • compete globally • Japanese firms in western markets • service suppliers
Design strategies	The role of design in corporate strategy. Elements of design strategy.
Conclusion	Design's contribution to future strategic challenges.

What is Corporate Strategy?

"Strategy is to do with long term prosperity. It is to ensure that the business is still around in ten or twenty years time. It is concerned with long term asset growth, not short term profit."

Gordon Pearson, Strategic and General Management Consultancy Group, Staffordshire University[4]

Strategy is easily confused with planning. The latter is administratively tidy, can be closely monitored and is an ideal function of traditional hierarchical management structures. Planning is rational and sufficient for companies operating in predictable and secure market environments. Regrettably, the reality of business in the 1990s is that no market can be considered either predictable or secure. In such circumstances the detailed map of planning must be complemented by the guiding compass of strategy. Much like design, strategy is a creative and visionary, yet critically functional, element of business. Both require similar conditions within which to flourish, both reinforce each other and both are concerned with "making values visible", not to mention profitable.

The overall aim of strategy is to identify and secure a long-term competitive advantage for the enterprise. This is based upon a clear vision or mission from which a sense of direction can be derived. Plans can be developed to move the business in the right direction, but these must be flexible enough to respond to the shifting contours of the market and reconsidered as necessary. The strategic firm shifts from being a classical orchestra playing to those who always demand the "Jupiter" symphony as Mozart wrote it, to jazz players expected to provide surprise through improvisation appropriate to the changing mood of the audience.

Pearson identifies four essential purposes of strategy: setting direction, concentrating effort, providing consistency and ensuring flexibility. These will be discussed briefly in turn.

Setting direction

"Any new company, once it has sorted out its financial needs, must be driven by a vision, a dream, by something that energises and motivates the company from top to bottom". Steve Shirley, director of the FI Group, expresses a view common to virtually all successful companies, which represents the heart of corporate strategy.[5]

When in 1976 Steve Jobs sold his VW Microbus to make computers in his parents' garage, he was driven by a clear vision for his then embryonic Apple Computers. Seventeen years later Apple, with a turnover of $7 billion, has the highest rate of return on equity and net assets of any manufacturing company in the world. While Jobs has long since left Apple, his vision remains. The very different technologies and markets of the 1990s has meant that Apple is evolving more towards being a software and systems designer. According to former chief executive John Sculley, "It's highly likely that by the time I eventually retire from Apple, it will be a completely different kind of company. But not in terms of its vision and core competency, which is to change the world by making sophisticated technology approachable to normal people".[6] In Apple's 1976 business plan this was linked to the ambition of being the first recognised leader in the PC market with a market share double that of its nearest competitor. Much the same ambition drove the founder of a company which has been locked in a legal battle with Apple Computers over the use of the Apple name. According to John Lennon, "We always wanted to be bigger than Elvis because Elvis was the thing".[7] Substitute IBM for Elvis Presley and sophisticated technology for rock and roll and you have a similar business vision.

Other notable entrepreneurs rose to success on clear, achievable visions. Despite his recent setbacks, Sir Terence Conran built a retail empire by "Constantly striving to offer customers better designed, better quality products at good prices. We must not allow ourselves to be deviated from this goal. The search for new ideas and new retailing formulas, the investment in technology, and the need to attract and motivate staff gathers pace as this new retail philosophy gains strength and conviction".[8] Anita Roddick attributes the appeal of her 300 outlet Body Shop to the guiding principle pinned above her desk: "We *will* be the most honest cosmetic company".

Such visions are based upon an accurate understanding of future trends and a realistic view of how future opportunities can be exploited. This vision can act as a spark to inspire and motivate employees in addition to attracting consumers. Vision, translated into action, sets the enterprise on course.

Concentrating effort

Vision should encapsulate the firm's competitive advantage, whether it is producing understandable technology, affordable good design or ethically sound cosmetics. Strategy should then ensure that all investment decisions and activities concentrate effort to attain this goal.

Peters and Waterman describe this in terms of "sticking to the knitting". Their study concluded that a lean staff and simple structure focused on a core business is a key to success.[9] Winning companies, in their view, are the ones which play to their competitive strengths rather than get diverted by other objectives. However, according to Pearson, "no other principle of effectiveness is violated as constantly as the basic principle of concentration".[10] As businesses grow and diversify, and particularly when they acquire new subsidiaries or are absorbed by larger conglomerates, such concentration can be lost.

From the mid-1980s a number of commentators were suggesting that Habitat's mission of providing good design at affordable prices was being lost as Sir Terence Conran's energies were diverted towards stitching together his large Storehouse retail business. As a consequence, Habitat started losing its distinctive identity and market share. Pearson cites the example of Jaguar, which in the days of British Leyland was in danger of losing its reputation as a producer of high quality up-market cars as the short-term financial objectives of the parent company dominated. Now under Ford's ownership, Jaguar has a clear, focused mission. The former parent company itself, following its "Roverisation" programme, claimed in 1993 to have replaced 90% of its model line-up over the previous 40 months and is repositioning itself as a premium marque.[11] From being an unsuccessful low-export high volume producer, a leaner Rover now has aspirations to be an export-orientated manufacturer now of course, under the control of its German parent BMW. Jaguar and Rover's knitting is high quality cars, and they seem to be sticking to it.

Providing consistency

Consistency, according to Pearson, is simply concentration over time. Strategy ensures that the enterprise builds upon its expertise and market experience rather than shifting aimlessly from one activity or product to another. Consistent concentration of effort does not imply becoming permanently rooted to one market; rather, there is a rational progression in a firm's attainment of its goals.

Apple identified its competitive advantage in the user interface of the Macintosh. It concentrated its efforts in developing this one product, first for niches in design and education, and more recently for business and general consumer markets. Its success in moving from being a low volume, high margin computer firm to being a high volume, low margin producer provides Apple with new opportunities to exploit its user-friendly software strengths. Collaborations with Sony and IBM enabled Apple to apply its concepts progressively to new consumer product and business markets.

The Sony Walkman is in many respects a microcosm accounting for the success of Japanese consumer electronics companies in western markets. Building upon imported product and component innovations, design and marketing are used to generate product concepts of high quality that appeal to western markets. Such an approach is applied within a long-term strategic view of increasing market share across a range of product segments: a good example of consistency. Particelli describes this in terms of Japan's *cascade* through western markets.[12]

Starting in a large protected home market, economies of scale are developed which can then be directed at a well-focused usually low-end foreign market. Success in that segment will be followed by targeting another, thereby developing a brand presence. Market share is then progressively built across related product segments. For example, Sony's initial beach-head in America and Europe based on transistor radios has been followed by a cascade through the television, VCR and audio equipment markets. The Walkman continues to be marketed in hundreds of different design variations as a high profile relatively cheap product aiming to secure brand allegiance from western consumers. Its success can be gauged by a recent international survey showing Sony to be second only to Coca Cola in brand recognition. The cascade is continuing from entertainment hardware to software. Recent acquisitions by Japan's electronics firms mean that Mickey Mouse is Japanese from the knees down and through Sony's purchase of CBS Records, Michael Jackson is Japanese in his entirety. Japan's competitive strategy is clearly a thriller in more ways than one.

Ensuring flexibility

But what happens when you are "bigger than Elvis" or try to sell "better design" to customers with less appeal for it? Simply break up the band or the holding company? In a fast changing world, strategy ensures not only that organisations are flexible enough to respond to and predict change, but also that the strategy itself recognises its own built-in obsolescence and can adapt appropriately.

There is a temptation, perhaps promoted by the journalistic style of much management literature, to see strategy as solely the product of creative entrepreneurs such as Steve Jobs and Sir Terence Conran. Individual visionaries are often critical factors in the initial success of enterprises, but as both Apple and Storehouse have discovered, companies can survive – at times can *only* survive – without their charismatic founders. Developing and adapting strategy is in most cases a corporate activity.

In his most recent book *'Power Shift'*, Alvin Toffler describes the rise of what he describes as the *flex-firm*, in which managers loosen the reins of bureaucracy to allow their companies to adapt to changing conditions.[13] He describes how in such firms there are faster, freer flows of information, more use of information from outside the firm and more a feeling that the enterprise is "a living creature" than "a well oiled machine". Flexibility is often achieved by decentralising large companies into smaller profit centres with greater autonomy. The case of Xerox demonstrates how such flexibility is essential in enabling corporate renewal and survival.

The company fortunate enough to own the patents for what Fortune magazine described as "the most successful product ever marketed in America" was able to prosper for over 20 years with little notion of its future direction. It was only when Japanese firms started producing superior photocopiers that Xerox was forced to grasp the nettle of strategy. As the only American corporation to regain market share from Japanese competitors, Xerox's corporate approach to strategic renewal is instructive.[14]

Between 1976 and 1982, Xerox's share of the world photocopier market was halved. In response, Roger Levien was brought in as a new vice president to head the corporate strategy office, and he soon set in train the Xerox '95 programme. The aim was to involve all senior management in an exercise identifying the likely market environment 10 years ahead. A series of off-site meetings enabled a range of future scenarios to be generated which were distilled into 24 assumptions about the external environment. From this, together with an analysis of the company's strengths, evolved a strategic direction based on document processing. Xerox is now focused on delivering "products and systems to the market that bridge the present chasms between paper and electronic filing and retrieval".[15]

This strategy of market leadership in information processing and integration systems is further enabled by strategic planning based on five-year, three-year and one-year time horizons, in addition to a significant cultural shift in how Xerox views its markets and technologies. The intention is also to reconsider the company's ten-year time horizon every five years. Xerox's renewal is also related to organisational changes in which the company was broken down into twenty "strategic business units" to improve flexibility and enhance innovation. The case of Xerox demonstrates why strategy is essential for corporate survival in providing direction and thus focusing effort on specific products and market segments. The company has also built into its strategy a system of review to enable a flexible approach in the context of fast changing market conditions.

Design's Contribution to Strategic Goals

"Only one company can be the cheapest – all the others must use design."

Rodney Fitch, Chairman, Fitch RS PLC[16]

Whether a firm supplies computers, clothing or cosmetics, it needs strategy. Strategy provides direction and focus in an increasingly competitive environment. Markets are becoming more global and increasingly segmented; consumers are becoming more sophisticated and demanding more product differentiation; technologies are changing rapidly, giving rise to new production systems and product concepts. As a process which bridges the desires of the market with the potential of production, design clearly has a strategic dimension. In this section we draw upon specific examples to demonstrate how design and the way it is managed plays a part in contributing to strategic goals (Table 4.1).

Table 4.1 – Strategic role of design

Challenge	Strategic goal	Role of Design	Examples
Small firm in consumer electronics market	Secure distinctive international niche	Provide niche through unique styling, identity and product innovation	Consumer electronics B&Q Linn Psion
Survival in a mature industry with keen price competition	Concentrate on added value markets or processes	Add value through fashion orientation	Textiles Leeds Group Issey Miyake
Transnational manufacturer with diverse world markets	Coherent identity and appropriate exploitation of scale economies	Corporate identity and co-ordination of design resources to target global markets	Electronics Philips
Japanese companies in competitive western markets	Quickly develop products appropriate to diverse lifestyles	Integrate innovation process and humanisation of product	Electronics/ motor vehicles Canon Ricoh Sony Toyota
Service supplier in newly competitive market	Develop distinctive identity	Corporate identity and environmental design	Services Prudential Scottish Power Royal Mail

Design to secure a distinctive niche

Small to medium sized companies competing in advanced technology markets have often managed to secure a market niche, and thus their survival, through the use of design. While the European consumer electronics industry has generally withered in the face of high volume, globally marketed Japanese products, two relatively small manufacturers have employed design-led strategies to gain a distinctive market presence.

A recent analysis of international design has argued that of all European countries, Denmark has the strongest national design identity.[17] With a small domestic market, and thus less opportunity to manufacture on a large scale, Denmark has tended to wed its craft traditions to modern technology, thereby winning high quality niche markets. One firm that typifies this strategy is Bang and Olufsen.

Employing little more than 3000 people, compared with Sony's staff of 80 000, Bang and Olufsen manufactures a range of hi-fi and television products noted for their distinctive styling and innovative features. The well-engineered, sleek designs of Bang and Olufsen, exploiting wood and metal finishes rather than plastic mouldings, became the design icons of the 1970s and earned sixteen places in the collection of New York's Museum of Modern Art. Having launched the first record deck with an electronic tangential tracking arm, Bang and Olufsen has kept innovation to the fore and is currently developing advanced home information network products with support from the Danish government.

Bang and Olufsen's innovation is clearly based on design rather than technological R&D. According to Jørgen Palshøj the company's director of public relations, "As a small company we cannot carry through basic research in the electronic area. But we can implement the newest technology with creativity and inventiveness".[18] Promoting a distinctive culture of creativity has been essential to Bang and Olufsen's success. Rather than maintaining an in-house design team, Bang and Olufsen has worked only with freelances as a means of introducing fresh ideas. Reinforcing this outward orientation, the company established the Design Reference Group, comprised of individuals from outside Bang and Olufsen, which assisted in evaluating the application of Bang and Olufsen's almost evangelical design policy. The seven principles at its core assert the primacy of simplicity in operation, faithful reproduction of sound or picture, and design as a language that expresses "the time in which we live rather than passing fashions".[19]

Unfortunately, in the early 1990s, the Bang and Olufsen style itself looked like becoming a passing fashion. Faced with trading losses, some in the company began to question aspects of design strategy in the light of new market conditions. Bang and Olufsen's product development manager has been quoted as arguing that "We need more products, and we need to get them into the market faster. The way B&O designs and develops products at the moment, we wouldn't know how to do that".[20] A design-led strategy secured a global niche for a family run Danish firm. Whether Bang and Olufsen has the flexibility to adapt that strategy, perhaps requiring a shift down-market, remains to be seen.

One company in the same market has seen its recent fortunes shift in the opposite direction to those of Bang and Olufsen. With sales of £3 million in 1991, Linn Products' total turnover represented less than half the development costs for Bang and Olufsen's latest audio system. As a Scottish manufacturer of top range record turntables, the CD age had dictated that Linn either perished or adapted. The company chose the latter option, involving new investment in design and manufacturing totalling £2.75 million. As a consequence, Linn has grown rapidly and accrued profits of £11 million in 1993.[21]

Linn's success derives from using its high quality market profile in turntables as a springboard to launch complete hi-fi systems. A new marketing and distribution policy is used to exploit fully innovative product design. The new investment enabled a larger team of designers to be recruited, which has been responsible for developing and launching 24 new products. With its top end systems retailing for £22 000, Linn has to satisfy the buyer that the product is a lifetime investment. Given the rapidly evolving audio technology, Linn achieves this through the modular design of its products, whereby design enhancements can be bought and added easily to a user's existing equipment.

Another British company has used design to gain a global niche in computers. Although it was the country that gave birth to the principles of computing, Britain now has only two firms designing and making computers. With its new Series 3 pocket computer, Psion is pitched against strong Japanese competition, but the firm has used design to give its product a distinctive presence in the market.

The first company to open up the hand-held computer market with its rugged Organiser, Psion was soon overwhelmed by the electronic organisers that flooded the market from the Far East. The Series 3 meets this challenge with a new product concept: a pocket computer with a QWERTY keyboard, PC compatibility, a word processor and a distinctive alternative to the matt black aesthetic of most organisers – all for under £200. Dr David Potter, Psion's managing director, sees design as an essential part of the Series 3 product development process: "Design is not something added on to make it look attractive, it's absolutely intrinsic".[22] The Frazer Designers consultancy were involved at all stages: identifying market needs, solving complex technical problems, getting manufacturing costs down and creating an appearance right for the market.

The product was launched to critical acclaim and considerable market interest both in Britain and abroad, demonstrating how design contributes to gaining market share. But as Japanese competitors exploit the market that Psion has opened up, the modest sized UK firm will clearly require more than well-managed, innovative design to survive.

Carefully focused design and marketing strategies are winning Linn Products and Psion growing international market niches that avoid head-on competition with Japan's mass manufacturers. These companies demonstrate the need for flexibility and an eye for opportunity in fast changing consumer electronics markets. Such characteristics are no less necessary in those industries that built the industrial revolution.

Design to survive in a mature industry

Few industries are more mature than textiles, and in Britain few industries have declined quite as spectacularly. The lesson from various studies, both in this country and overseas, is that survival in textiles depends on continual innovation in production technology and design.

Of the 200 000 jobs in the UK cotton industry in 1960, barely 10% remain today. During the 1970s textile production in this country was halved. The popular theory of cheap Third World imports to account for this decline does not fully fit the facts, because more significant imports to Britain come from higher wage economies in the EC and North America. The chief executive of the former Tootal textile group points the finger of blame elsewhere: "The real culprit was obviously management and the absence of any real understanding of what the customer wanted and any commitment to marketing. The approach had been entirely production based. Fortunately out of the ashes, marketing emerged and gained status. And from the 80s design was recognised, with designers being taken on across the industry".[23]

Textile manufacture in Britain had remained doggedly Fordist; it was a mass production industry that assumed a standard market and produced a standardised product. While rising consumer affluence in the post-war period was creating a more fashion conscious buyer-led market, the design diversity this demanded could not be met without investment in new production technologies. Roller printing in the cotton industry meant that repeat sizes were limited by the circumference of the roller and variation limited by the high cost of engraving it.[24] Britain was slow in both developing the more flexible technology of mechanised screen printing and exploiting new techniques to texture synthetics.

Allied to these technological constraints is evidence of a lack of commitment towards market orientated design. A Committee of Enquiry on British design standards made the following observation on the design of household textiles: "Although there are distinguished exceptions, British manufacturers are not generally looked to for fashion-setting merchandise. In volume markets there is obviously a bias towards caution and conservatism".[25] Another study of design management in textiles underlined Britain's comparative disadvantage together with arguing the case for design: "There is some large measure of truth in saying that the design function is more cohesively managed and marketed on the continent. ... Good design is of key importance; conceivably, it can to some extent even redress unfavourable factors like a strong currency or low cost imports".[26] With the production of commodity textiles shifting seemingly relentlessly to newly industrialising countries, the survival of the industry in older economies would appear to rest on exploiting indigenous design talent and more flexible technology to meet the needs of fashion conscious markets.

Such is the strategy of the Leeds Group, an old established Yorkshire textile printer. Over the past decade, while the industry as a whole has continued its steady decline, the Leeds Group has grown in both sales and profitability, with its stock increasing in value by 2000%. Seemingly immune to the recession, the Group recently expanded by acquiring two Dutch textile companies. Company chairman Robert Wade explains how success is based on "sticking to the knitting", which in Leeds' case involves no knitting at all: "We own no looms, no knitting machines, no spindles and no clothing manufacturing interests. Our fundamental principle is that we operate only with colour and design. We dye and we print".[27]

Leeds has risen to the challenge of a domestic market that demands more design variety, delivered more quickly and in smaller batches. Leaving the actual manufacture of cloth to others, the company's flexible printing technology, investment in design and just-in-time delivery have secured major orders from companies such as Liberty and manufacturers of boxer shorts, for whom great design variation is essential.

In other industrialised countries more committed to retaining textile manufacture, closer links have been formed between the industry, clothing manufacturers and fashion designers. The example of Benetton, described in the previous chapter, illustrates the flexible design-orientated strategy that has gained a future for Italy's clothing and textile sectors. In Japan, various forms of collaboration with fashion designers have benefited a textile industry that has certain structural disadvantages. Organised almost like a cottage industry, textile manufacture in Japan is fragmented by regional specialisation. New wave Japanese fashion designers from the early 1980s onwards built international appeal for their garments on the aesthetic of the natural materials produced by this traditional industry. These designers married together the craft of Japanese fabric with advanced technology.

Leading designer Issey Miyake developed laser printing techniques and introduced computer driven looms to craft weavers. Investment in Miyake's design studio by the Toray chemicals company has accompanied continued innovation by Miyake in new methods of texturing synthetic materials.[28] Comme des Garçons is another Japanese fashion house that has built a presence for itself on the international market. All of their fabrics are produced by Hiroshi Matsushita's Textile Research Centre, which co-ordinates a network of producers nationwide.[29] Miyake and Comme des Garçons have in a short time secured positions as leading international fashion houses, exploiting western interest in Japanese style. As a consequence, they have also secured new markets for Japanese textiles.

Both in Britain and Japan, textile producers are finding a niche through greater integration of design as a means of meeting the needs of fashion-based markets. This is either through buying in fabric and applying design appropriate to national consumer needs, or developing long-term relationships with fashion designers, who provide the main market for fully manufactured and finished material.

Competing globally

The examples discussed so far have concentrated on small companies that have used design strategically to develop a sustainable niche or overcome cost competitive disadvantages. In such cases design is often used flexibly, either as a bought in consultancy-based resource or through ongoing collaboration with a prominent design group. For globe-straddling transnational corporations, the strategic role of design can take on new dimensions by offering a means of integrating and providing a coherent focus for diverse corporate activities.

Thanks largely to the prodigious publicity and analysis generated by Robert Blaich, its former managing director of design, Philips is held as a model for the strategic use and management of design.[30] On his appointment to Philips in 1980, Blaich was confronted by a company that produced "just about anything that could be plugged into an electrical outlet" – from light bulbs and shavers to computers and telephone exchanges.[31] The company employed 17 000 people in product development, with 270 designers distributed over 25 countries.

The Dutch conglomerate's problems were considerable. In the face of Japanese competition, the consumer electronics division was operating at a loss, with overpriced products often brought late to the market. Product quality often left much to be desired, as an internal company report observed when it described Japanese portable radios as having a "better technical finish and production quality" in comparison to Philips' models.

Design and manufacturing were being duplicated in different countries, leading, for example, to Philips' subsidiaries in twelve European countries having their own separate development projects for colour televisions, generating a total of 90 basic models. Throughout such projects design was regarded as a styling operation, with designers given little more than a fortnight in the product development process. The marketing emphasis of the company centred on its strengths in technological innovation rather than connecting with the actual needs and desires of consumers. Although Philips developed the Compact Cassette, it virtually gave the innovation away, thereby enabling others – particularly Sony – to profit through its application to lifestyle products such as the Walkman. With a plethora of different brand names, product styles and advertising campaigns, Philips had a fragmented identity worldwide. In short, the company was inefficient, production-centred and poorly perceived.

Blaich's design revolution succeeded in cutting development times, reducing duplication and exploiting the benefits of the firm's global reach, winning new markets for new high quality lifestyle products and helping to create a modern identity for Philips. The problems that new design management sought to solve and the methods by which solutions were developed are summarised in Table 4.2.

Table 4.2 – Design Strategy at Philips

Problem	Policy	Solution	Results
Improve product quality	Design policy	• Better evaluation of design quality • Better integration of design into product development • Improve design standards	• Design as managed process • New criteria for evaluating design quality • Professional development programmes for design staff
Fragmented design resources	Renewal program: new design management structure	• Implementation design policy • Co-ordination of design activities • Design linked to product divisions	• Design is planned strategically • Increased productivity of design teams
Lack of visual unity in Philips' products	Harmonisation programme	• Reduce duplication • Project clear identity • Global marketing	• Quality improvements • New markets • Corporate identity

Underlying Blaich's philosophy was the belief that industrial design is central to the public perception and thus success of any manufacturing company: "The product is the most important statement a company can make about its image. It is the image".[32] His design policy set the overall agenda for improving product quality through design. It defined a new design management structure, identified the criteria for assessing design quality, set in train staff development programmes to enhance the skills and standards of design staff and integrated design into the mainstream of new product development.

Critical to this strategy was Blaich's "Renewal Programme", which reshaped the management structure of design. Corporate Industrial Design (CID) based in Eindhoven had unclear relationships with the company's various product divisions. Blaich introduced a new structure, which balanced centralised co-ordination with devolved design responsibilities for product divisions, including CID groups based in various countries. A further element in the strategy was a harmonisation programme to reduce duplication of effort and provide a clearer visual identity for the company expressed through its products.

Blaich's design strategy has achieved many of its objectives. Increases in the efficiency of Philips' large design group are evident from the three-fold rise in completed projects over the 1980s with no major change in staffing levels. Many of these projects were driven by a keener sense of identifying global product markets in which Philips had competitive advantage and placing design at the centre of product development. The "Moving Sound" audio equipment range brought Philips success in the fashionable youth market through exciting designs linked to aggressive marketing. Opening up the youth market for electric shavers exploited CID's global reach. The design group in Japan had been developing a shaver for their local market. The design criteria of compactness, portability and light shaving head matched those for the western youth market where it was successfully marketed as "Tracer" (Figure 4.1).

Figure 4.1 – Philishave Rota 93

Since Robert Blaich's retirement from Philips in 1991, design in the company has been under the direction of Stefano Marzano. This former professor of design has championed a design philosophy in tune with changing times. Greater concern for environmental issues and more cultural intelligence is informing the design process. The Rota 93 range of electric shavers best expresses this new concept of "high design". Anthropologists played a part in conceiving the product range, along with ergonomists and designers. Software is used to create an "intelligent" product needing fewer controls on a carefully sculpted form containing a less polluting power source.

Overall, the new approach to design has enabled Philips to bring more, higher quality products to the market more quickly and efficiently than before and more carefully designed to meet specific market requirements. Philips uses its international design resources to produce for globally stratified markets in addition to specific national markets.

In so doing it has had to deal with the issue of globalism in design.

Ever since The Beatles recorded "I Wanna Hold Your Hand" in German, international marketers have sought to test the limits of how far goods and services can be sold globally without adaptation. While The Beatles need not have worried, firms such as Philips and Ford do, and they have found design to be a critical process in tailoring their products to particular national or regional requirements.

Some market analysts have identified a new group of global consumers known as *universal users*. Based predominantly in the industrialised nations, these consumers share similar education, access to technology and popular culture. This global young generation, numbering around 600 million, consume similar goods whether they come from Japan, a rich Brazilian suburb or a European city. Wearing Levis and Walkmans and eating Big Macs, they probably all settled down in 1985 to watch Live Aid. As this generation gets older, so their global consumption fills out into new products and services.

The question is, how far do their global tastes reach? Smart branded goods, branded luxuries and fast cars all have global appeal, but volume cars, most clothes, food and financial services have national or, at best, regional markets. Domestic appliances is one market where national preferences have remained immune to the global challenge. With washing machines, the French prefer top loaders, the British prefer access from the front, Italians prefer machines with a slow spin, while Germans go for high performance.

Ford sought to exploit its global economies of scale through the world car concept. Components for the Ford Escort were sourced from plants worldwide, and assembled close to their markets. However, the model for North America had to be so heavily adapted to meet the needs of the local market that it became a totally different car. The global market thesis, at best limited to certain products, is now having to cope with the resurgence of nationalism and more assertive cultural identity, especially in Europe.

According to Ford's former vice president of design, "Some regional characteristics will become stronger again. The variety of products needed to meet the aspirations of smaller groups of customers will create the need to find ways to combine or retain a high level of economy of scale but create a level of flexibility to respond to different segments".[33]

Philips and the Japanese companies described below all use design to tailor product concepts to different national needs, while continuing to exploit those truly global markets that do exist. In selling their world products they have tended not to repeat those mistakes from the early days of global marketing. In marketing the Vauxhall Nova as a world car, General Motors had neglected to note that in Spanish "nova" means "it doesn't go".

Japanese firms in western markets

Philips would not have been fighting for its survival had it not been for the Sony Walkmans, Hitachi videos, Sharp televisions and other Japanese goods that flooded western markets from the 1960s onwards. While there are many industrial, economic and social factors that account for Japan's success, the strategic status of design and the evolving mechanisms of its management play a crucial role.

Product innovation is recognised more in Japan than in other countries as vital for competitiveness. In a survey of business executives, 80% of those in Japan considered that a great deal of product innovation was needed in their enterprises, compared with 56% of those in Europe and 49% of North Americans.[34] As explained earlier, Japanese companies regard design as a key process within innovation, often lying at the very heart of product innovation and thus at the heart of the company itself. The predominant western view of innovation is often that of a fragmented, compartmentalised process comprising engineers, marketers, designers and sales staff, all tightly guarding their disciplinary boundaries. In many Japanese companies innovation is seen as a multidisciplinary process, with design providing the vision and communication to bind the process together and provide direction.

There is no one single model of how design is managed in Japanese firms. It varies between companies – and it changes over time. Just as the west was beginning to understand how Sony managed the design process, the company completely restructured its famous PP Centre. Japan, then, is a culture of change and experimentation. This is expressed not only in the design of products, but also in the way that design itself is managed. There are some broad principles in the management of design that appear characteristic, summarised in Table 4.3 and elaborated further below. It must be emphasised that not all firms apply every principle, and there are considerable organisational variations. There are no magic formulas in the strategic use of design by Japanese manufacturers, but some elements of best practice that deserve scrutiny.

Table 4.3 – Design management in Japan

Design management principle	Strategic role	Example
Product planning section	Co-ordination and promotion of innovation	Sony PP Centre
Design represented at and reviewed by board	Higher status and monitoring of design	Sony • Canon
'The Rugby Approach' to product development	Reduce product development times Better links between engineering, design and marketing	FujiXerox • Honda
Humanware design philosophy	Adapt technology to cultural specific user needs	Ricoh • Sharp
Lifestyle research Antennae showrooms Satellite design studios	Ensure design meets user requirements and increase cultural influences into design	Mazda • Honda • Toyota

As Bill Evans explains in his survey of Japanese design management, many companies have a product planning section or similar body that directs and harnesses the innovation process.[35] Design may be a department within product planning or it may be structurally separate. To confuse western analysts further, Sony's design division was renamed the PP Centre, although it was separate from the firm's existing product planning function. However design is related to product planning, it usually finds itself represented at board level. At Sony there is a design director who sits on the board and is accountable directly to the chairman. In addition, there are monthly meetings between members of the board and the design staff, with a similar arrangement existing at Canon. Such mechanisms reflect the high status accorded to design and provide top level monitoring of its performance.

However design is structured organisationally, there is invariably a very close link between design and marketing. Marketers are wedded into the design process to ensure that market factors inform design decisions. In some companies, designers are briefed with the specific job of coming up with creative ideas, which are then given to engineers to develop technologically. But most firms try to build an environment that can exploit ideas that originate from anywhere. One way this works is through a design management technique known as *the rugby approach*. To understand how it works it must be compared with the traditional product design and development process.

Figure 4.2 – Linear product development vs
"The Rugby Approach"

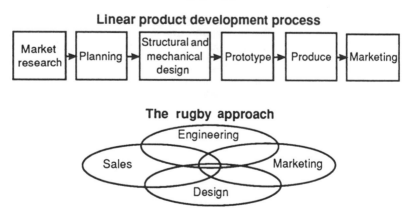

Linear product development process

Market research → Planning → Structural and mechanical design → Prototype → Produce → Marketing

The rugby approach

Engineering

Sales

Marketing

Design

In the conventional linear approach to product development, shown graphically in Figure 4.2, market research identifies a need, the concept is planned, and the is product designed, prototyped, produced and finally marketed. The process been likened to a relay race, where the baton of product development is passed from department to department. In the rugby approach problems are worked on simultaneously and ideas passed around between team members. Senior management hand-picks a multidisciplinary team that is given broad goals and hands-off support.[36] At FujiXerox this method is called the *sashimi* approach – named after the Japanese presentation of slices of raw fish which overlap each other.

The result of such methods is that product development times are greatly reduced. This means that more products can be brought to the market more quickly, which is the key to Japan's competitive strength. In motor vehicles, an average product lead time of 3.5 years in Japan compares with 5 years in Europe and North America.[37] In other industries the rate of product development can be startling. In 1981 Yamaha took on Honda in a bid to dominate the motorcycle market. Honda's response was to launch 113 new models in less than 18 months, representing one new model every four days. That is a somewhat lethargic performance compared with Seiko, the watch manufacturer, which introduces one new model every working day.

According to Evans, new ways of managing and speeding up product development are being accompanied by new philosophies of design appropriate to flexible manufacturing and the diverse lifestyles of global consumers. Just as new access to information allows manufacturers to understand consumer demand and adjust production accordingly, so too it is allowing designers to create a wider range of products with specific market appeal. Products are becoming pieces of applied knowledge manifesting need, lifestyle, values and aspirations. New methods and processes in design make products more tailored, adaptable and desirable to the consumer. Some Japanese companies are describing this shift as the humanware age of design.

Typical of the future-orientated view of many Japanese firms, Ricoh analyses design's evolution in terms of three phases, shown graphically in Figure 4.3.[38] The first two phases – hardware and software – were concerned with technology: producing and integrating it efficiently, styling it attractively and making it easy to use. Now "we have the technology", as Ricoh claims, the emphasis is on exploiting the opportunities of flexible manufacturing systems to inject consumer lifestyle into products, to make the technology more intelligent and more appropriate to the specific cultural context of its use – the humanware age.

Figure 4.3 – Evolution of design philosophy at Ricoh
Source: Evans, B. 1985

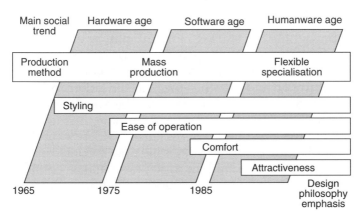

Other firms such as Sony, Canon and Sharp now ensure that design starts with an understanding of the social and cultural context of products. Kiyoshi Sakashita, corporate director of Sharp, says that "many companies have shifted their marketing strategies from a merchandising to a needs oriented basis. As a result, the role of the designer has changed. 'Humanware' is the consideration of the product in terms of the total environment in which it will be used".[39]

The humanware age is fundamentally changing the methods of design. As products move closer to becoming fashion items, so industrial designers are learning to become fashion designers. Success in the world of fashion requires an acute understanding of the fast changing markets and creative ways of translating this information into surprising, desirable products. Evidence from Japan shows how designers are gaining this lifestyle information.[40] In many firms, design departments have established units known as *Trends Research Centres or Lifestyle Centres*, where sociologists and psychologists work alongside industrial designers. At Mazda design research is not just reading technical reports on carbon fibres. Required reading for the teams include *Vogue* and *The Face*, and designers get sent on people-watching trips where they sit around in European bars and restaurants. All this means that design problems are defined in a very different way. At Honda the design team working on the Honda Accord was given a one-line design brief: *a rugby player in a business suit*. The idea is that the product must express perfectly the lifestyle – the aspiration – of the target consumer. All else follows from this.[41]

Another new development has been *Antennae Showrooms*. These are basically showrooms for products, but in fact are used by manufacturers to study scientifically the behaviour of consumers as they look at and use the products. CAD systems in these showrooms let consumers design their own dream cars – ideas from which will be studied by designers.

The need to design close to the target market has led firms to establish *satellite design studios*. All of the Japanese car makers now have such satellites within 60 miles of Los Angeles. Sony have also developed a network in Europe and North America. Toyota's California satellite has developed what it describes as a "fine arts" approach to automotive styling. Wet balloons filled with plaster were photographed, then projected at distorted angles to generate ideas for the forms of the new Lexus range. As the director of a prominent Japanese design consultancy whose clients include Nissan and Olympus has said, "We make fashion. We are not product designers".[42]

The examples above demonstrate how design is used strategically in many Japanese firms as a visionary tool to provide direction and often as an integrating element within the whole product development process. Design is the process by which the core technologies produced in Japan are tailored to culturally specific lifestyle needs, thus gaining relevance and demand worldwide.

Design in the service sector

Considerably more than just a logo, the whole business of corporate identity has today evolved into the complex science of Visual Management. For service companies and suppliers of relatively undifferentiated commodities such as petrol or detergent, corporate identity is crucial to competitiveness. While the discussion here will centre on the strategic role of Visual Management in the service sector, it is no less important to manufacturers. For firms such as Apple, Bang and Olufsen, Philips and Sony, whose identity derives from their physical products, corporate identity is vital to the public perception and demand for their branded product.

Financial services is a sector that has undergone a revolution in recent years. Deregulation, increased competition between suppliers, technological change and far more discerning, market-aware consumers have transformed the formerly austere user-unfriendly world of banking, insurance and mortgages. While competition has increased radically, there is relatively little differentiation in terms of the products on offer: loans cost much the same, insurance policies provide broadly similar cover and interest rates differ only fractionally. Although companies have developed lifestyle specific services, such as telephone banking and youth accounts, competition has centred mainly on corporate identity.

From the mid-1980s, financial services companies became some of the major clients of corporate identity designers. Sir Brian Corby, chairman of the Prudential Corporation, was quick to recognise the strategic contribution of design: "To me it seemed that the justification for the use of design skills at our strategic level must lie in the fact that they will make a clear contribution to improved economic performance of the business".[43]

As Britain's third largest financial institution, the Prudential had a solid, respected image in the market. However, as a survey commissioned by the company in 1985 showed, the public perception of the Prudential was also staid and old-fashioned, with little awareness of the company's activities other than insurance. Images such as the "Man from the Pru" obscured the company's position as the largest investor on the London Stock Exchange and the country's largest estate agent. This was not the identity required in the changing competitive environment of the 1980s.

The corporate identity consultancy Wolff Olins created a new image based on an up-to-date interpretation of Prudence, after whom the company was originally named. This new icon of modern, human and caring values became the focus for a corporate identity programme that has helped the corporation to maintain its market lead, as demonstrated in a second survey conducted in 1989. As Sir Brian Corby explains, "We are now seen as contemporary and going places. Most different socio-economic and age groups find us appealing and this is particularly so with the younger middle class, exhibiting an efficient, businesslike approach which they regard as desirable".[44]

While the new logo featuring Prudence is the symbolic focus for the company's profile, its new corporate identity involved a complex design and implementation programme covering all aspects of the corporation. Of equal importance to physical design was the process of communicating the company's values as expressed through this identity to all 25 000 employees, thereby gaining their commitment. The Prudential's design management team has been responsible for applying this identity to literature, office interiors, signage and advertising. Design standards were clearly defined and carefully monitored in their implementation. Implementing the identity has also brought unexpected new business to the Prudential. The 16 strong in-house design team recruited to apply the Wolff Olins plan now pitches for work outside the corporation and has succeeded in attracting a number of clients.[45]

According to Sir Brian Corby, the strategic role of design in the company is three-fold. Firstly, it enables more effective and clear presentation of financial products, thus enhancing customer satisfaction. Secondly, it has improved working environments for staff, leading to greater employee satisfaction and motivation. Thirdly, it has changed the overall public perception of the company, creating more interest in its services.

Changing public and employee perception is a key strategic objective of some of the world's largest and newest companies. The transformation of state-owned monopolies into privately owned competitive enterprises through privatisation involves a massive and challenging shift in corporate identity. Consumers need to be persuaded that a profit-orientated company will not exploit its monopoly position; financial institutions need assurance that the new enterprise will deliver a good return on their investment; and employees need to understand and support the new management regime.

Working in tandem with the organisational, financial and management changes that privatisation involves is a corporate identity programme to achieve these goals. As a public utility, the main job of the South of Scotland Electricity Board was to supply power to most of Scotland's industrial and domestic users. With privatisation, the management placed a greater focus on customer services and opportunities to sell power to England. The new values and priorities of the Board were expressed through a new name and logo, and effectively implemented identity programme. So successful was the highly profiled launch of Scottish Power that, according to a MORI poll, out of all the new electricity companies floated on the market, the company has the highest ratings of favourability among institutional investors.[46]

One public utility that has yet to undergo privatisation is that of postal services, but continued state ownership does not ensure immunity from competition or the strategic importance of corporate identity. The Royal Mail not only sorts and delivers 61 million letters every day, but pays pensions and unemployment benefit, and competes vigorously in the express delivery market.

Binding together its four business units and providing a focus for its 170 000 staff is a recently implemented visual identity programme that has enhanced its market competitiveness. A Royal Mail management team that includes members from the Sampson Tyrell consultancy has been responsible for co-ordinating and monitoring the implementation of this identity. While the popular press tends to focus on the high cost of corporate identity programmes, less attention is given to the cost savings that can result. In the case of Royal Mail, replacing varied signage and identity systems with a more coherent unified approach reduced printing costs and, through a consistent image, reduced marketing costs. New signage alone saved the organisation £750 000, according to the claims of its designers.[47]

Corporate identity plays a clear strategic role throughout the manufacturing and service sectors. In the case of the latter it helps to differentiate services and provides a focus for the organisational changes required by enhanced competition. For utilities, both private and public, identity expresses the cultural shift required to attract consumers and investors.

Design strategies

"Design is the only process through which the technological, ergonomic and stylistic specifications can be configured into viable products, services or environments. Thus it should be at the centre of all business activities."

Professor Colin Clipson, University of Michigan[48]

In the previous section we have considered the strategic role of design in helping organisations to meet successfully the challenges posed by their differing market environments and competitive positions. It is now possible to draw some general observations and conclusions that relate to the earlier discussion on corporate strategy and explain more specifically how design plays its strategic function at the centre of all business activities. Table 4.4 sets out the general goals of corporate strategy together with the objectives of design strategy that serve them and the tools of design management that follow from such objectives.

Table 4.4 – Corporate strategy, design strategy and design management

Corporate strategy goal	Design strategy objective	Design management tools
Set direction "vision"	Visualise and communicate corporate objectives	• Corporate identity programme • Design for quality
Concentrate effort "stick to the knitting"	Produce goods and services appropriate to the firm's competitive advantages	• Design policy focused on clear objectives • Integration of design
Provide consistency "concentration over time"	Ensure consistent development and application of design policy	• Design standards • Design monitoring • Effective design leadership
Ensure flexibility	Adapt the focus of design resources to changing external environment	• Culture of innovation • Outward directed design organisation

Setting direction through a clear vision that motivates employees and attracts consumers and investors is enabled through a design strategy that aims to visualise and communicate corporate objectives. From the examples of the Prudential and Philips, corporate identity was essential in confronting new competitive challenges and asserting the innovation and relevance of the companies. The process of corporate identity, based on methodical research of consumers' and employees' attitudes, focused through a potent symbol of the firm's values, and applied to environments, information and products, is particularly important in cases where a company's products or services are relatively undifferentiated from those of its competitors. However, in the case of manufacturing industry, Blaich is generally correct in asserting that "the product is the image". The strategic goal of design to communicate corporate objectives and values can therefore be realised by ensuring that quality is a key priority of design. This indeed accounted for the success of the Blaich strategy at Philips. At Bang and Olufsen the premium quality of its product, achieved through design, has given this small company a distinctive identity in the market.

Bang and Olufsen have also "stuck to the knitting". Design strategy is clearly essential in ensuring that companies concentrate their efforts on products and services that play to corporate strengths, rather than dissipate their resources and identity. A design policy can be developed with clear objectives which relate to a firm's internal and external environment: its market, the technology used, access to investment and so on. Bang and Olufsen's seven-point design policy provides a strategic focus for design by identifying the parameters of the firm's market and capabilities together with the design criteria for which the firm has become known. For such policies to have effect design must be appropriately integrated within the culture and organisation of the company. Japanese manufacturers are perhaps exemplars in this respect. However design fits into corporate structures, many firms have used it to provide vision and direction, integrating it with other functions to maximise creative interaction and focus in the new product development process. Philips especially demonstrates how this integration requires an appropriate design management structure that can balance centralised design resources with the geographical and product diversity of a large transnational. In smaller companies, such as Linn Products or the Leeds Group, this integration may just represent a greater investment in design and its recognition as the key competitive advantage for the firm.

Concentration over time, which as we saw earlier is also a characteristic of Japanese manufacturing, requires a forward looking design strategy to ensure consistent development and application of design policy. The definition of design standards and systems of monitoring is common to many of the examples discussed. Design direction at Bang and Olufsen was evaluated by the firm's Design Reference Group, while at Canon and Sony design is regularly reviewed at Board level. Such consistency is also achieved by clear and appropriate design leadership, which may include design managers represented at Board level.

Particularly in today's fast changing market environments, flexibility is an essential strategic goal. Design must therefore be adaptable, opportunistic and forward looking. Virtually all of the examples above show how, in different ways, a culture of innovation can be engendered within companies. As the creative engine room of many firms, the design department itself needs to be more outward directed and prepared to develop new ideas. At Bang and Olufsen this has been achieved through the use of external consultant designers rather than an in-house team. At Philips, with its large design staff, Blaich's employee development programme led to a much stronger market orientation and exciting new product concepts. In some Japanese companies in-house designers have become more "semi-detached" through the growth of satellite design studios. Other initiatives such as antennae showrooms and lifestyle research groups have broadened the research base of Japanese design.

Moving away from the specific examples cited above, is there any empirical evidence that explains the contribution of design strategy to competitiveness? In 1989 the Design Council published a University of Strathclyde survey which examined the relationship between product design strategy, design management and company performance in 369 British companies.[49] From their research the following characteristics were among those common to the top performing companies:

- Market-led orientation
- Use design as competitive tool
- Multidisciplinary approach to new product development
- Adaptive and willing to change
- Good company image
- Continuous product improvement
- Design on board
- Top management commitment to new product development
- Attention to technology and market trends

The Strathclyde research therefore supports the view drawn from our examples that well-managed strategic design is correlated with good company performance. The specific focus of design strategy and the mechanisms of its management vary according to companies' internal resources and culture, together with the relationship with the external market and technological environments. Figure 4.4 summarises the common elements of design strategy and the stages in its development.

Figure 4.4 – Design strategy: main elements and stages of development

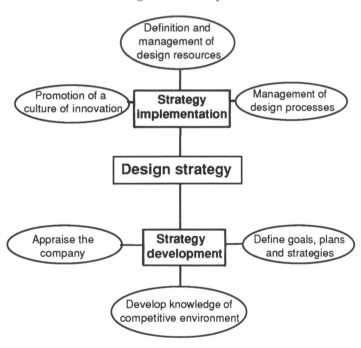

Conclusion

This chapter has necessarily focused on design's strategic role in gaining market share and competitive advantage in companies where it is a managed resource. Design management can therefore be seen as the process that directs design to fulfilling corporate objectives. But in the changing market and cultural environment of the 1990s, design can also contribute to broadening its responsibilities, through helping to define those objectives. The social concerns and responsibilities of design discussed in the previous chapter, while they may transcend the prosaic goals of management, are not necessarily inconsistent with them. If strategy is about meeting the challenges of the future, then design's visionary potential has much to offer companies that will be required to respond to the changing values of our age.

At a design conference held in Glasgow in 1993, one speaker made the following point: "Design is a political act. Every time we design a product we are making a statement about the direction the world will move in. The solutions we choose are political decisions. We must be aware of our power".[50] Far from being a fiery radical from the days of the Red Clyde, these words were spoken by Stefano Marzano of Philips Corporate Design. This statement is indicative of an increasing recognition by employers and designers that industry must respond to both the material and social aspirations of an ever smaller and integrated world.

Concerns over the environment, the need to humanise increasingly complex and powerful technology, the challenge of an ageing population and dissatisfaction with globally styled and marketed products – these are strategic issues for business to which design can contribute through its intermediary role bridging economy and culture. As such it has advantages over marketing as a discipline to help companies to respond effectively to these concerns, as the example of the "green market" shows.

From the late 1980s marketers identified the "green consumer" as a market segment worthy of targeting. Supermarket shelves rapidly filled with recycled toilet rolls and biodegradable detergent, while BMW and other motor manufacturers trumpeted their green credentials. After a short period of growth, sales of such products went into decline and many have since been discontinued. Some studies have indicated consumer disillusionment with misleading advertising claims, inconsistent labelling and high pricing. The environmental lobby was also critical of the notion that shopping would save the planet. Marketing may help in identifying consumer concerns, but perhaps not in responding to them. Design, while it has certainly helped to create many environmental problems, does have the potential to start tackling them. Methods described earlier, such as lifecycle analysis, can reduce energy and material use in manufacturing and increase the rate of recycling and reuse. Design is a discipline that can take a wider view of problems, with concerns ranging from designing a car through to concepts for urban transport systems.

In 1991 Japan's Ministry of International Trade and Industry (MITI) called on the country's manufacturers to stop designing so much. Model changes and variations, the Ministry argued, should be drastically slowed down. While this call for less design reflects the economic logic that design in recession reduces profitability, it is also indicative of other changes. MITI's Design Policy for the 1990s argues that design must shift its emphasis from increasing the quantity of goods to improving the quality of life. Ryuya Aoki is one of many Japanese designers who are looking beyond the varied styling of Walkmans to considering how their talents in designing consumer electronics can meet these broader concerns: "Reliance on sophisticated marketing analysis techniques has obscured the bigger picture. ... Computer technology offers the first opportunity to change Japanese society radically since our industrialisation".[51] Perhaps the concept of humanware described earlier to express design philosophy in Japan is already giving way to "cultureware", in which the design needs of individuals as consumers are being supplemented by the wider cultural aspirations of the society within which they live.

The challenge for both industry and the design professions is to develop a new relationship in which design can better exploit its abilities to consider "the bigger picture" and thus contribute to industry more effectively, reflecting the changing values of our age.

Summary

• Corporate strategy and design

Corporate strategy aims to identify and secure a long-term competitive advantage for the enterprise. The four essential purposes of strategy are setting direction, concentrating effort, providing consistency and ensuring flexibility.

Especially in fast changing technological and market environments, design has the potential to contribute to strategic goals.

• Design distinction

Small companies in consumers electronics have used design to provide unique styling, identity and product innovation, thereby securing a distinctive niche in world markets.

• Survival by design

Survival in a mature, cost competitive industry such as textiles can be secured by using design to provide fashion orientation, thus concentrating companies on added value markets or processes.

• Global design strategies

As a large transnational confronted with Japanese competition, Philips successfully developed a coherent corporate identity, targeted new global markets and raised product quality, fully exploiting its global reach in production and markets. This was enabled through a well-formulated design strategy and appropriate mechanisms of design management.

• Strategic use of design

Japanese manufacturers have maintained quality, reduced product lead times, introduced new product concepts and tailored core technologies to diverse western lifestyle groups through distinctive design organisation and methods. Design in Japan tends to be seen as a visionary force that can provide direction to new product development.

• Strategic values made visible

Financial service suppliers have differentiated themselves in the market through corporate identity and environmental design as competition in their market has increased. The successful transformation of public utilities into privatised companies uses corporate identity to raise employee commitment, reassure consumers and attract interest from investors.

- **Design strategy and company performance**

Coherent design strategy supported by mechanisms of design management clearly contribute strongly to corporate strategic goals. Empirical research has demonstrated the correlation between the elements of design strategy and good company performance. The central elements are defining and managing design resources, managing design processes and promoting a culture of innovation.

Design offers a means for companies to meet their social responsibilities during a period of changing cultural values. This suggests a re-thinking of the relationship between industry and designers.

References

1 Musashi, M. (1974) *A Book of Five Rings*, Allison and Busby, p.54.
2 Guevara, C. (1969) *Guerrilla Warfare*, Penguin, Harmondsworth, p.19.
3 Blaich, R. and Blaich, J. (1993) *Product Design and Corporate Strategy: Managing the Connection for Competitive Advantage*, McGraw-Hill, New York, p.13.
4 Pearson, G. (1990) *Strategic Thinking*, Prentice Hall, Englewood Cliffs, New Jersey, p.21.
5 Shirley, S. (1991) Corporate strategy and entrepreneurial vision, in Henry, J. and Walker, D. (eds) *Managing Innovation*, Sage, New York, p.211.
6 *The Independent on Sunday* (1993) Renaissance manager, 2 May.
7 Cited in Wenner, J. (1972) *Lennon Remembers*, Penguin, Harmondsworth, p.70.
8 Conran, T. (1988) Design and the building of Storehouse, in Gorb, P. (ed.) *Design Talks!* The Design Council, London.
9 Peters, T.J. and Waterman, R.H. (1982) *In Search of Excellence*, Harper and Row, New York.
10 Pearson, G. (1990) *Strategic Thinking*, Prentice Hall, Englewood Cliffs, New Jersey, p.23.
11 *Marketing* (1993) Can Rover overtake BMW? 8 April.
12 Summarised in detail in Lorenz, C. (1987) *The Design Dimension*, Basil Blackwell, Oxford, pp.152–155.

13 Toffler, A. (1990) *Power Shift*, Bantam Books, London, Chapter 16.

14 This discussion on Xerox is drawn from Kennedy, C. (1989) Xerox charts a new strategic direction, *Long Range Planning*, **22**(1), 1989, pp. 10–17; reprinted in Henry, J. and Walker, D. (eds) *Managing Innovation*, Sage, New York.

15 This discussion on Xerox is drawn from Kennedy, C. (1989) Xerox charts a new strategic direction, *Long Range Planning*, **22**(1), 1989, pp. 10–17; reprinted in Henry, J. and Walker, D. (eds) *Managing Innovation*, Sage, New York.

16 Cited in the Design Council's promotional brochure, *Are You Prepared to Take on the Challenge of the Nineties*? (1989).

17 Aldersey-Williams, H. (1992) World design: nationalism and globalism in *design*, Rizzoli, p.48.

18 Palshøj, J. (1990) Design management at Bang and Olufsen, in Oakley, M. (ed.) *Design Management: A Handbook of Issues and Methods*, Basil Blackwell, Oxford, p.41.

19 Palshøj, J. (1990) Design management at Bang and Olufsen, in Oakley, M. (ed.) *Design Management: A Handbook of Issues and Methods*, Basil Blackwell, Oxford, p.41.

20 Cited in Platt, E. (1991) The quality trap, *Design*, February, 40–42.

21 Southam, H. (1993) Turning the tables at Linn, *Marketing*, 20 May, 20–21.

22 Jones, M. (1991) A very British co., *Design*, October.

23 Maddrell, G. (1990) Design and strategic change, in Gorb, P. (ed.) *Design Management*, Architecture, Design and Technology Press, London, p.139.

24 A detailed account of post-war developments in the design and production of British textiles can be found in Schoeser, M. (1986) Good design and good business: A survey of the changes in the British textile industry, in Sparke, P. (ed.) *Did Britain Make It*? The Design Council, London, pp.146–186.

25 The Design Council (1983) *Report to The Design Council on the design of British consumer goods by a committee under the chairmanship of David Mellor OBE, RDI*, p.38.

26 Cotton and Allied Textiles EDC (1984) *Designing for Success: Approaches to Managing Textile Design*, National Economic Development Office, London, p.24.

27 Levi, J. (1993) Wade's winner, *Management Today*, June, 44–47.

28 For further discussion of these and other developments in textile design, see Colchester, C. (1991) *The New Textiles*, Thames and Hudson, London.

29 *Axis* (1991) Hiroshi Matsushita's reorganisation of textile industry, **38**, winter.

30 Discussion on design management at Philips can be found in the following sources: Aldersey-Williams, H. (1992) *World Design: Nationalism and Globalism in Design*, Rizzoli, pp.174–179; Blaich, R. (1988) Design as a corporate resource, in Gorb, P. (ed.) *Design Talks!* The Design Council, London, pp.9–26; Blaich, R. (1988) From experience: Global design, *Journal of Product Innovation and Management*, **5**, December, 296–303; Blaich, R. and Blaich, J. (1993) *Product Design and Corporate Strategy: Managing the Connection for Competitive Advantage*, McGraw-Hill, New York; Heskett, J. (1989) *Philips: A Study of the Corporate Management of Design*, Trefoil; Lorenz, C. (1987) *The Design Dimension*, Basil Blackwell, Oxford, Chapter 9.

31 Blaich, R. and Blaich, J. (1993) *Product Design and Corporate Strategy: Managing the Connection for Competitive Advantage*, McGraw-Hill, New York, p.93.

32 Heskett, J. (1989) *Philips: A Study of the Corporate Management of Design*, Trefoil, p.36.

33 Cited in Aldersey-Williams, H. (1992) *World Design: Nationalism and Globalism in Design*, Rizzoli, p.12.

34 Cited in Pilditch, J.(1989) *Winning Ways*, Mercury Books, London, p.21.

35 Evans, B. (1985) Japanese-style management, product design and corporate strategy, *Design Studies*, **6**(1), 25–33. A version of this article also appears in Oakley, M. (ed.) *Design Management: A Handbook of Issues and Methods*, Basil Blackwell, Oxford, pp.393–405.

36 For further discussion on this issue, see Takeuchi, H. and Nonaka, I. (1986) The new new product development game, *Harvard Business Review*, **64**(1), 137–146.

37 Clark, K. and Fujimoto, T. (1989) Reducing the time to market: The case of the world auto industry, *Design Management Journal*, **1**(1), pp 49–57.

38 Clark, K. and Fujimoto, T. (1989) Reducing the time to market: The case of the world auto industry, *Design Management Journal*, **1**(1), pp 49–57.

39 Cited in Pilditch, J.(1989) *Winning Ways*, Mercury Books, London, p.63.

40 For more detailed coverage on this issue, see Platt, E. (1991) Form follows fashion, *Design*, July, 12–18; Aoki, R. (1991) Electric dreams, *Design*, July, 22; Pearlman, C. (1991) Satellite studios, *Industrial Design*, December, 40–43.

41 The Honda example is described more fully in Clark, K.B. and Fujimoto, T. (1990) The power of product integrity, *Harvard Business Review*, **68**(6), Nov-Dec 1990, pp 107–118.

42 Aldersey-Williams, H. (1992) *World Design: Nationalism and Globalism in Design*, Rizzoli, p.144.

43 Corby, B. (1990) Implementing corporate strategy, in Gorb, P. (ed.) *Design Management*, Architecture, Design and Technology Press, London, p.164.

44 Corby, B. (1990) Implementing corporate strategy, in Gorb, P. (ed.) *Design Management*, Architecture, Design and Technology Press, London, p.164, p.172.

45 Hoggard, L. (1990) The team from the Pru, *Design*, October, 20–22.

46 Sampson Tyrell (1992) *Identity issues*, company promotional literature, p.12.

47 Bowman, Josie (1993) North West Design Talks seminar, 20 May.

48 Clipson, C. (1990) Design as a business strategy, in Oakley, M. (ed.) *Design Management: A Handbook of Issues and Methods*, Basil Blackwell, Oxford, p.104.

49 Service, L.M., Hart, S.J. and Baker, M.J. (1989) *Profit by Design*, The Design Council, Scotland.

50 Cited in *Design Week*, 24 September, 1993.

51 Aoki, R. (1991) Electric dreams, *Design*, July, 22.

Design and the
5 Organisation

"Innovative management demands that all phases of the operation be seen as links in a single chain of innovation. Each link allowed to pursue its own challenges – but also aware of how it should integrate with the others"

Akio Morita, Chairman, Sony Corporation[1]

No matter what business an organisation is concerned with, there is always a need to innovate in order to maintain competitiveness and continue in business. As Akio Morita[2] has suggested, to innovate successfully functions need to be linked: "Each link is vitally important – but equally so. It is important that the 'prestige level' of each link be similar in order to keep high achievers motivated in each group. And the creation and promotion of this approach is the responsibility of top management".

A chain suggests perhaps one rather linear method of linkage; it may be more appropriate to see the functional links

Figure 5.1 – Functional links as interlocking building blocks

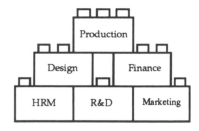 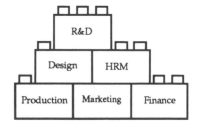

as interlocking building blocks (like that manufactured for children by Lego), which are all necessary for the end product, but combine in different ways to achieve the desired end (Figure 5.1). Most organisations now realise that the

Chapter Map

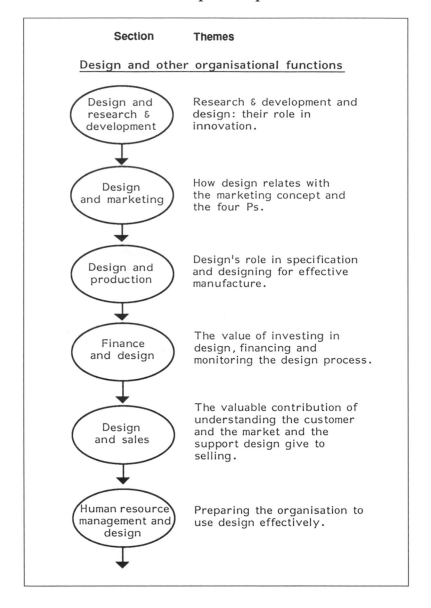

Section   **Themes**

Design and other organisational functions

Design and research & development — Research & development and design: their role in innovation.

Design and marketing — How design relates with the marketing concept and the four Ps.

Design and production — Design's role in specification and designing for effective manufacture.

Finance and design — The value of investing in design, financing and monitoring the design process.

Design and sales — The valuable contribution of understanding the customer and the market and the support design give to selling.

Human resource management and design — Preparing the organisation to use design effectively.

Design and other organisational issues

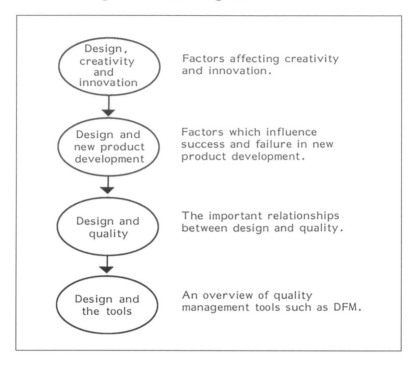

Design, creativity and innovation	Factors affecting creativity and innovation.
Design and new product development	Factors which influence success and failure in new product development.
Design and quality	The important relationships between design and quality.
Design and the tools	An overview of quality management tools such as DFM.

various functions are not independent – they are interdependent – and that interfunctional teams must work together in order to see a plan to a successful conclusion. However, the composition of these teams and the way in which they operate are always matters for considerable debate. The various organisational functions are addressed separately in this chapter, to identify how design and the design function impact on them, and to support the notion that designers or design managers should be involved in organisational teams.

In addition, there are many other issues that organisations are endeavouring to address – issues such as quality, innovation, creativity, new product development and tools that organisations use for process improvement, such as "quality function deployment", "failure mode and effects analysis" and "information technology". We consider each in terms of its impact on the design function and activity.

DESIGN AND OTHER ORGANISATIONAL FUNCTIONS

Design and Research and Development

Frequently in small and medium sized enterprises design and R&D activities are undertaken often by one group – in manufacturing industry it is the engineers. However, in larger organisations, R&D exists as a discrete function or is out-sourced from agencies or academia. R&D information is essential to designers working on product development: they need to know what is happening at the forefront of technology, in terms of materials, machines and manufacturing methods. Such knowledge feeds the creative process and enables designers to develop innovative and leading edge concepts. For example, Teflon was developed in the aerospace industry but later resulted in saucepans, skis and bearings. Because of the great diversity of R&D activity and operation, it is impossible to describe all of the potential design/R&D interaction. It is essential, however, to realise that communication of developments in R&D contribute to innovation and effective design, and therefore must be encouraged and supported through bringing the functions together. Indeed, not only does knowledge of advances in R&D increase the ability of design to produce innovative new products, but an understanding of design activities enables R&D to contribute more effectively to the design process.

Design and Marketing

Managers will find that very little has been written about design in marketing literature, and when it has been mentioned, assessment of its relative value and contribution to marketing has varied. Some writers have identified design as a strategic tool,[3] others define it as a significant part of the product development process,[4] and currently the debate includes whether design should be managed by, or integrated with, marketing.[5] It is worth while, therefore, to look at where design and marketing do interface with one another.

The marketing mix

Design has a connection with every one of the marketing mix tools.

In "Product" as a tangible artefact, design is a major factor. It influences the quality, function, service, usability and appearance, and it also contributes to product features and to the added value. Design has an impact on all the features that differentiate one product from another, as described by Kotler,[6] – features such as performance, conformance, durability, reliability, reparability, style: no more so than in the car market, where all of these terms are used by the manufacturers to describe their products and to differentiate them. These elements must therefore be designed into the product at the outset.

In "Product" as a service, the design factors are only marginally less central. For instance, in such industries as insurance or banking, advertising and communications design provides the information and evidence of the service, from the policy document and cheque books to sales literature. In hotels and catering and in the leisure industry, designers provide the environment for the service. Design also has a bearing on the service differentiation, delivery, installation, consultation, personnel differentiation and image differentiation. For example, in any airline the delivery of the service and the environment where that service takes place have an important impact on the consumer. The design of the departure lounges, aircraft interior, uniforms, meal packs, corporate literature – even the luggage labels – all contribute to the overall consumer perception of the company. The United States South West Airlines presents an efficient yet relaxed and informal image; one manifestation of this is through the uniforms, which consist of shorts, T-shirts and training shoes, a very different look from that of Virgin Airlines, which uses red lipstick and red shoes to express its corporate image through its air hostesses. It should be noted, however, that while such design cannot overcome poor quality personal service, it can only enhance the effectiveness of a good service.

In "Price", effective design can save money for an organisation by designing products that are economical in terms of materials, energy and manufacture. Design can also enhance a product, and therefore its perceived value, enabling it to sell at a higher price. KP Foods, for instance, in promoting its "Brannigans" brand, used the pack design (brown wrapping paper quality with Victorian style typography and salesman image) to present a more sophisticated image for the snack.

Design has an impact on "Place" or distribution, in that designers, when they are designing a product, take into account the means of distribution and will consider the nature of the packaging and storage. In addition, when the product relies on its location, design can make a major contribution to its success or otherwise. In 1993 flat pack furniture manufacturer MFI began a major refurbishment programme in its outlets to boost store traffic and sales. The redesign was created by the British design consultancy Fitch, whose brief from marketing was to increase consumer circulation around the stores, encouraging customers to shop in all areas rather than concentrate on one particular sector. Reporting on the design, a Fitch director said, "the design is quite radical, intended to increase profits for MFI while being cost effective work itself".[7]

Design has a key role in "Promotion". Packaging, promotional and sales literature, all forms of media advertising and point of sale displays are physically designed and specified by professional designers. For instance, when the clothing company Jaeger decided to shed its conservative image in favour of a more youthful, modern look, the marketers turned to design to implement a major part of their marketing strategy. Jaeger decided to launch its biggest ever advertising push. These ads were designed to appeal to women aged between 35 and 45, and tended to be sophisticated and understated, some having a slightly humorous tone.

Market Research and Design

The "marketing concept" concerns the corporate orientation towards the customer or consumer, addressing the basic premise that the company should endeavour to identify and serve the customer's needs and enable a successful transaction to take place between them. Market research is therefore an important element of marketing activities. It is frequently collected as quantitative data – for example, the size of the market, the market segment defined – and also includes forecasting in terms of trends in the market or identification of current gaps in the market in terms of the product need. Designers turn those needs into tangible products. In consumer durables, for instance, this might be a washing machine prototype offering innovative functions; in services it might be the literature to support a new financial service, or interior designing of a new leisure facility.

In order to do this, the designer needs not only quantitative information but also qualitative information. This type of information is extremely important to the designer in terms of putting his or her own knowledge into context. During the design process, designers rely on intuition based on information stored in their subconscious minds. This subconscious information is related to all five senses – visual, oral, tactile and so on – and is collected by designers making a conscious effort to observe the world around them. The type of market intelligence that designers need is that which will help them to understand the context in which their subconscious and sensory knowledge can be used to solve the design problem and their visualisation skills can be used to realise the concept. (Figure 5.1)

For example, when a textile designer is asked to design a new range of bedding, he or she would want to know as much as possible about the consumer. In marketing terms that may be quantitative information such as demographic, socioeconomic and geographical data. But in order that the resulting design is attractive to the market segment it is aimed at, more visual and lifestyle information is needed. The designer needs to understand the consumer, their taste and environment, and also their functional needs. This enables the designer to use his or her own innate knowledge and creativity to develop a design for that context. Frequently the designers themselves try to get their own information. However, communication between design and marketing is often enhanced when both undertake such research; this enables them to achieve a common understanding as to the required product orientation.

Figure 5.1 – The design process and market research

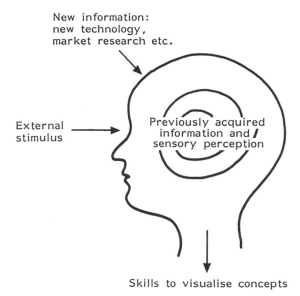

Understanding the consumer – getting into the head of the consumer – is important for designers, in order that they can develop a conscious and subconscious understanding of consumer needs, and translate that understanding into design features. Therefore "consumer behaviour" intelligence, in terms of what influences the consumers, is important – economic, cultural and occupational factors, peer group pressure, lifestyle and psychological factors are all relevant. These need to be collected and communicated in sensory terms to the designer.

There are a number of methods of communicating this type of qualitative information. Transmitting market intelligence through a mood board is a means of achieving common understanding between designers and marketing, and can often overcome misunderstanding at the onset of a project in relation to aesthetic and functional attributes. A mood or lifestyle board is a presentation of images that represent aspects of consumers, their lifestyles and environments, including textures, colours, shapes and so on. Mood boards are frequently used where design is a central feature of the product, for instance in fashion, textiles and small domestic appliances. However, their use can be valuable in a much wider range of situations, and development of such a board by both design and marketing frequently aids the definition of the product brief.

Another effective means of determining the product concept and conveying market intelligence is the use of metaphor as a definition. Clarke[8] gives an example used by Honda to describe the characteristics of the 1990 Honda Accord: "A rugby player in a business suit". This metaphor was used to capture the personality of the project. The metaphor was translated into key attributes, such as rugged but fair, socially recognisable, polite, sportsmanlike, strong and secure, orderly, likeable, bright and elegant, which in turn translated into features, such as friendly : soft touch interior, tough : larger engine and improved reliability in extreme conditions. Metaphors can be used to capture the feeling of the product throughout the development process and to develop detailed specifications, which everyone in the development team can relate to, and which the designer can translate into aesthetic and functional design forms.

Setting the scene for the product or developing scenarios is another method of providing usable market intelligence to the designer. This method actually tells a story; for examples, it chooses a fictitious couple and describes their daily life, and possibly more specifically their use of a product or a situation, such as how they shop for groceries, the process they go through and what guides their decisions. Again, this type of information helps the designer to focus on the sensory or functional problems, and aids in the development of appropriate design solutions to the problem.

Designers also often look for analogies to help in communicating the desired attributes. For instance, when designing a stereo or a video system, a designer might ask, "If this were a car, what would it be? A Rolls-Royce or a Mini?". This question focuses the team's thoughts on the product attributes consumers need, and gives the designer a tangible form with which to relate. It is, in effect, translating the knowledge the marketing professional has into a form from which the designer can use his or her own understanding to solve the design problems.

It is well understood that conventional market research frequently reveals only what the consumer already likes, wants or needs and indicates little about the future. For example, when the Sony Walkman was initially tested, consumer response indicated market failure. It is therefore essential that designers are provided with information from which they can generate future perspectives. Understanding consumer behaviour, in terms of how they operate from day to day, how much they spend, what make of car they drive, who makes dinner, who chooses the wallpaper, what that person's tastes are and how they perceive the various design features, are important to designers. Woodhuysen[9] points out that it is the cognitive and emotional issues and their likely evolution that are of interest to designers. Designers can use these in conjunction with the data they already have in their subconscious to generate designs for the future.

Marketing and the design brief

Where a market need has been identified, a product concept or a promotional campaign has been sort, and a marketing strategy formulated, the design brief is then constructed by management, frequently by marketing. The brief is often communicated to the designers by a project manager from marketing. In this situation designers often question the brief in detail, to establish that they and their client or project manager have the same understanding of the problem. If, however, the designer is part of a new product development process, it is often wiser to bring the designers in at the idea generation stage; they should in this case be working with the marketing and production team on the whole process. Specific design briefs can be written when alternative products or concepts need developing. This type of brief will arise from joint discussion among the team and will probably be drafted by the designers themselves. Whichever way the brief arises, market information and a clear understanding of the customer is important to the designer.

Marketing and product testing

Once a concept has been developed, it needs to be tested with the customer or a customer sample. The market research function often organises this aspect of product development. Frequently, it is the market research function or agency that is the contact with the customer. The results of such testing are extremely important to the designer; it is often the details of a design that can make a product successful or otherwise. Best practice suggests that even if the designer is not directly involved in this testing he or she should be involved, briefing the researchers and receiving feedback or, indeed, talking to the customers themselves.

Marketing and design and the organisation

Marketing and design interlink in many more aspects of an organisation's business. In understanding the market, in translating that understanding into innovative products, in testing and refining those products, launching, promoting and distributing them, the skills of the marketeers and the designer are needed. In order to work effectively, these two functions need to understand and respect each other's role and skills, communicate frequently and develop a common understanding of corporate goals and the customer.

Design and Production

The Design Council[10] suggests that "not only must designers have the best knowledge of what the market wants, but the better they are informed on the materials and manufacturing capabilities of their business, on what is available to their business and what is available for the future of their business then the better will be their designs". In every design discipline, the design concept must be transferred from the "drawing board" into reality. This involves a production process. The interface between designers and production will of course vary, depending on the design discipline, the product and the production process. For example, designer–makers of ceramics, jewellery and furniture frequently design and make as one process and, therefore, conflict and misunderstanding is not likely to occur. Where the product and manufacturing process are more complex and contributions to design come from a number of specialists (for example, in the telecommunications industry), transferring the design into production and manufacturing requires a high level of understanding and co-operation among all design and production functions.

Production and the design brief

In most design disciplines, when developing a design concept the designers must take into account production methods. Designers need to know how the design concept will be produced, where and by whom. For example, let us consider three different design disciplines.

Graphics

The outcome of the graphic design process is usually some form of print or packaging, which means that the designers must know how all aspects of production will occur. The designers must know how the type will be set, how the graphic items (photography, illustrations) will be originated, what type of printing method will be used (silk screen, offset litho, foil blocking etc.) and by whom this will be done. Without knowing the processes available, the graphic designer is completely limited in his or her creative ability; for example, using silk screen gives a thickness and opacity of ink, which enables the designer to create a design incorporating white or a very pale colour on a dark base. In addition, the quality and efficiency of production will vary from printer to printer. Designers must be aware of the services available and able to make judgements on the ability of the printer to achieve the quality desired. This will enable the designer, if necessary, to design to the tolerances available. For example, if, because of cost limitations, the corporate graphic designer must use an in-house reprographics unit with limited colour reproduction systems, there would be little point in designing a brochure using full colour photography.

Interior Design

Once again, an interior designer also has to understand how his or her design can be produced. The contributory elements are more complex than for graphic design; indeed, a complete specification for an interior project might include building modification, specifications for floor, ceiling and wall finishes, fixtures, lighting and services. The interior designer, therefore, must be able to select such details and be aware of the skills, facilities and standards of the suppliers and contractors who will implement the design proposals. In briefing interior designers, production/implementation of the project must be discussed. Indeed, the contractors should be brought in as early as possible. If the designers are working with contractors with whom they are familiar, this enables much better understanding and should result in much smoother and trouble free implementation.

Product Design

Mistakes frequently occur in the product introduction to manufacturing, because the production function is not represented when the design brief is initially developed. A UK plastic manufacturer found that such a problem occurred when their designers were provided with information on general manufacturing capabilities but not on specific machine capabilities. The resulting design for a plastic component, when brought to production, was limited to manufacture on one particular machine. Subsequently it was revealed by production personnel that, had it been designed differently, it could have been produced using an alternative machine, which would have resulted in substantial cost savings.

It is the responsibility of both the design and production personnel to collaborate with each other at the briefing stage, to ensure that the designers have as much information as possible on the manufacturing facilities available. They must also be given information on *when* and *where* test production is available in the development process, to enable them to schedule the design and development programme accordingly.

The basic premise is that at the briefing stage, in all design disciplines, production factors must be considered, to enable creative, effective and appropriate design to take pace. This means that – whether the designers are company employees or external consultants – they must discuss the project brief and its implications with production. Designers often fear that such discussions will inhibit their creativity; however, research shows that, given all the technical constraints and production capabilities, designers are more creative with than without them.[11]

Production and the design and development process

Once design development takes place, designers will at various stages consider implementation and manufacturability. They should be able, therefore, to refer to the production personnel, whether they are printers, contractors or production engineers. In all design projects, reviews occur at stages throughout the design development, and consultation on manufacturability is essential. Frequently, production may be able to contribute to the design development in terms of new technology or production techniques to overcome a design problem.

When the design has been approved and signed off for production, designers have the responsibility for providing clear, precise and detailed instructions to whoever is responsible for producing the end product. In graphic design, this means producing artwork, supplying the graphic material, giving details on the inks, the papers or board, etc. In interiors, there are detailed specifications of wall, floor and ceiling treatments, space plans and detailed drawings for fixtures and fittings. In product design, the transfer from product design to manufactured product is also complex, through tooling production and trials to test production. In each instance, there must be constant communication between designers, engineers and production personnel. Frequently, designers complain that design compromises occur because of production failings; production staff tend to complain that the design is not appropriate, or that they have not been given enough time for testing, and there are problems, therefore, in the manufacturing process.

In all instances of transfer from detailed design to manufacture or production, it is essential that the designers and the people responsible for production have direct contact with each other, throughout the design and development process. The discourse can not only prevent problems occurring later in the manufacturing process, but will also contribute to innovation and creativity in the design process, and result in time and cost savings on well planned and implemented projects. CAD has been identified as a significant contributor to this communication process, and companies are increasingly investing in CAD/CAM and MIS systems to improve communications and shorten product development time.

Design for effective manufacture

Designers frequently use models or mock-ups to test ideas in terms of performance, safety, functionality and other design details. The use of models helps everyone to get a "feel" for the product. Production can certainly contribute to the evaluation of the models. Many companies provide evidence of the need to involve production as early as possible in the design process. Rolls-Royce estimates that design decisions determine 80% of the final production cost of many of the components it makes.[12] Designing to take account of manufacture can result in substantial savings; in product design, for instance, the number of components can be reduced or changed, to enable easier assembly or automatic manufacture. There are a considerable number of issues, described in Table 5.1, which must be taken into account, at the interface between design and manufacture or production.

To enhance all production/design interfaces the organisation must ensure regular contact between production and design staff via team meetings or product development committees to discuss such issues.

Finance and Design

As discussed in earlier chapters, many British companies have been reluctant to invest in "design", there being little understanding among senior management about the value of design. British industry has traditionally concentrated on low added value products, making it susceptible to both low cost, low technological foreign imports and high added value, high cost products from competitors in Germany and Japan. In order to increase the added value element of their product or service, companies need to invest in the design and development process, and managers, particularly financial managers, need to understand the value of design to the company, whether it be related directly to the development of a product or service or to the promotional, PR and advertising supports to a core activity.

Table 5.1 – Checklist of issues that impact design and design disciplines in their decision making

- Materials; Advances, recyclability, safety, quality, storage, cost, waste
- Suppliers; quality, availability, time
- Machines/methods of production; quality, energy costs, reliability, flexibility
- Components; standard or special
- Stocks and inventories; standardisation on materials, just-in-time procedures
- Timescales; parallel working, (simultaneous engineering, etc.)
- Assembly; ease of assembly, automated assembly, reduction in components and machining
- Operations; finishing operations, etc.
- Distribution; such as packaging and transport costs
- Storage; space and facilities

In addition to the use of design for the core products or services and supporting communication material, managers must consider the financial benefits that accrue from a contented, comfortable workforce. Designing and providing a superior working environment has benefits in achieving a good corporate culture and increased productivity. It conveys an atmosphere of efficiency and quality that enhances the company and its products in the eyes of potential customers. For instance, the benefits a grocery store can offer in terms of parking, location and store layout not only provide the customer with benefits but also the employee. This is undoubtedly the same for a major manufacturing company such as the UK-based JCB, whose plant is located in the Staffordshire countryside, in a landscaped environment, with facilities for both their employees and prospective customers.

Good design, as we have seen earlier, helps in effective manufacture by considering manufacturability, sometimes reducing the number of components needed or shortening the assembly time, for example. In a study by the Design Innovation Group[13] on the costs and benefits of investment in design among 250 UK companies, it was found that 90% of implemented projects were profitable, with payback periods averaging under 15 months, and almost all recovering the total project investment. Also, where projects involved redesigns or updates of existing products, this generated an increase in sales, on average, of over 40%.

Having established, as has been done, that investing in design helps corporate competitiveness in all aspects of its business, it is important to understand how the finance function interfaces with design activity and function. Finance contributes in six major ways to:

1   Planning in terms of project or product and marketing plans

2   Forecasting sales and profit growth

3   Resource planning and allocation

4   Project cost monitoring

5   Project authorisation and expenditure

6   Project evaluation

Whether the project be a new product, a major advertising campaign or an exhibition or showroom – indeed, anything involving design expertise – financial managers should be part of the project team throughout the design and development process.

At the brief stage, the designers need to understand the budget for design and development, the limits to manufacturing costs, and their own contribution to the overall budget in terms of design development time. Managers responsible for finance should develop an understanding of the design process and design requirements, to enable them to plan more thoroughly and accurately, optimising the resources they have available.

Finance is often a contributing factor in the decision to employ design expertise or to buy in design consultants. Many companies decide to out-source design expertise, for a number of reasons, often because they feel they get a fresher creative approach to the problem or because they estimate that this practice is cheaper than retaining a design function. The advantages and disadvantages will be discussed in other chapters. It is important for finance managers to recognise these issues and make an informed judgement. Frequently, design is eliminated from within the organisation, particularly when the company is undergoing financial difficulties, because it is considered as a luxury, rather than its importance being recognised in product development or in corporate communications.

Time and resources must be allowed at the onset of a design project, for creativity at both the concept development and the detail development stage. These are the two crucial phases, the designers must have the time to develop their ideas, test them and transfer them into accurate details for production. Investing in the "up front" planning and design has been found to reduce the number of problems that occur later in the project development and implementation stages. In response to the question, "How do you get products to market so quickly?" Japanese producers often reply that they start earlier; that is, more time and funds are allocated to the concept stages of projects.

The DTI[14] recommend the following financial targets for cost effective management of the product creation process:

- Specify target product costs and design requirements.
- Set budgets for design and development expenditure.
- Forecast the expected benefits, such as increased market share and profit.
- Regularly review targets, budgets and forecast benefits,

against what has been achieved and what is achievable, and modify or abandon if necessary.

Monitoring and maintaining records not only aids good financial control, it also provides a basis from which to estimate the risk in future projects. Designers should record the time spent at all stages of a design development, plus overheads in terms of space, materials and bought in services. However, this should be seen as an investment rather than an expense.

Once a project comes up for final approval, the financial managers must undertake some assessment of risk. They should evaluate with the project team:

a) whether the proposal will meet all the performance and production specifications required of it;

b) consider the loss in profit potential if the project failed;

c) check that marketing have made an accurate assessment of the market potential; and

d) consider what impact delays in time to market will have on profits.

This process of financial control, although developed for product creation, can of course be modified for use with any design project. Once the checks have been made, the designers, with financial management and the chief executive (if necessary), must assess the design and formally authorise and sign off the job for production, or ask for further feasibility and financial planning to be undertaken. Communication here will increase awareness between all functions of the design and marketing objectives and the financial implications of implementation and manufacture.

Product evaluation takes place once the product has been brought to market. This evaluation should operate against the objectives set out in the brief or product plan, in terms of customer acceptability, cost of production and likely return on investment. Financial managers need to remember that return on investment may be other than monetary. It may take the form of increased awareness of the company, increased customer perception of the company's products or services, early entry into the market or a new market opportunity, better working conditions or improved productivity. There are a number of success/failure criteria and it is important that the project is assessed against those that are most appropriate, as identified at the start of the project. An appreciation by financial managers of the value of design in terms other than monetary is essential to effective use of design by an organisation.

Design and Sales

Sales personnel are frequently closest to the customer; they are also aware of the competition and the market situation. The knowledge they have is therefore very useful to designers; often a comment made by a customer can stimulate a new product innovation or an idea for a product modification. Sales staff are also aware of the support needs they require, for example a higher corporate identity profile, or more supporting promotional literature for the organisation, or, indeed, new order forms or a display stand – even a signage system for visiting customers. The existence of small well-designed material can positively affect customer perception of the organisation. The sales knowledge and support needs must be communicated both formally and informally within the organisation or company, either in terms of electronic mail or via such devices as an organisation "product book", in which comments are made and directed to the senior manager or director responsible for design.

During the design process, sales personnel have a valuable contribution to make in terms of their understanding of the customers' or consumers' current attitudes. They may also be able to provide information on trends, for example, in retailing on the shelf space or the display of products. However, caution should always be taken when presenting very innovative concepts to sales personnel. If the concept had not previously been available, whether it is a service or a product, sales personnel, depending on their own outlook and corporate culture, may err on the side of caution; that is, on what they – and what they believe their customers –

are familiar with, and may therefore reject what may be a profitable new idea as unacceptable to the market.

If designers are to develop successful design concepts, it is important that they understand the customer and the consumer. Therefore, where possible, it is useful for the designer to spend some time with the sales functions, visiting customers and consumers. This helps designers to develop first-hand knowledge of who they are designing for. It also gives the designer a flavour of the competitors. For instance, a furniture designer working with the sales team for a small furniture retailer would gain an understanding of the competitors, of the environment in which the furniture was being sold and of the type of customer. Even though market research could have supplied customer data, it is invaluable for designers to use their own senses to aid the intuitive nature of their creativity. Similarly, once book designers have spent some time on the road, or at a conference with the publisher's representative or commissioning editor, they gain an understanding of both the type of authors and their communication needs. For instance, many authors now use word processors or even desktop publishing; designers could help authors by supplying templates from which the authors could work, thus cutting out much of the typographical and layout work involved in preparing for production.

'Added value' is what design is frequently trying to achieve. Once the designer has developed a concept, it is useful for sales managers to attend the concept presentation, where they can learn from the designer what added value has been designed into the product. The designer, in his or her explanation of the development, can provide interesting information about the product which the sales personnel can use in their discussions with customers.

The sales personnel can help in preventing product failure by providing information to the designers on a competitor's product that had received an adverse reaction from consumers. Of course, as with all functions, the relationship between sales and design will vary greatly, depending on the size of the organisation. However, communication must take place, and developing a forum for direct communication between design and sales personnel can be very beneficial to product development and design.

Human Resource Management and Design

Human resource management involves bringing together people with the appropriate skills in a suitable environment and motivating them to do the best job they can.[15] Design relates to this function in many ways but the factors discussed in the following subsections are probably the most significant.

Design skills and awareness

In order to increase awareness of the value of design, human resource managers should consider how aware other management functions are of the role and value of design within the organisation, and ensure, through continual staff development and training, that design awareness is maintained and developed among all employees, particularly in the management functions. In planning the use of designers, human resource managers, along with other senior managers, have to assess the most appropriate method of employing designers and the skills needed by the organisation. They have to decide, for instance, whether to outsource design skills or to build up a design team. It is important, therefore, that they understand the contribution that design makes to the organisation.

Motivation and team building

Most organisations use teams for some aspects of design, whether it is a small team developing a new leaflet or a major new product team. The management of such teams is crucial to their success. Many members of multidisciplinary teams tend to owe their allegiance in the first instance to their own function, which can cause friction among the team members. Indeed, design, if it does not have a large functional role in the organisation, may not be included in the team until the design brief has been decided. Not only is this inappropriate, it also builds up barriers, in that the designer feels undervalued or considers that his or her contribution is seen only as "icing on the cake". For example, in book cover design giving a brief that basically says, "Just do a cover; here's the title" will result in a design that has little relevance to the contents, the consumer or the market (unless the designer understands more about the book). Team building to ensure that all functions work effectively is very important.

Communications and corporate climate

Most employees need to understand the aims and objectives of the organisation, in order to contribute effectively, that is, to know that "they are all rowing in the same direction". Communicating the corporate strategy – building up a climate in which people feel part of the success – requires continuous communications, both internally and externally. This can be achieved by using design, whether it is for a corporate video to report good practice case studies, or for a strong and effective corporate image or for the company newsletter. Effective communication design is essential, and therefore any human resource manager who is responsible for communications must engage the aid of a designer or design team to carry out the work.

Designing the organisation

Clipson[16] suggests that many corporations do not have an organisational structure and process that allows the lateral integration of marketing, research, design, engineering, finance and manufacturing. In many studies of successful product development, this has been found to be a crucial factor. Successful design does not take place without a well-structured but flexible environment. Developing and maintaining the right environment for innovation and creativity must be to some extent the responsibility of human resource managers.

DESIGN AND OTHER ORGANISATIONAL ISSUES

Design, Creativity and Innovation

Let us explore further the management implications of creativity first raised in Chapter 2. Most organisations are looking for innovation and new product development with which to continue to compete in the market-place. This requires a creative environment, one which encourages and stimulates new ideas. Creativity, innovation and design are interconnected, but one should be clear about what is meant by each:

- Creativity is the generation of novel association, of new ideas and of invention.
- Innovation is concerned with the implementation of creative ideas.
- Design is primarily involved with the delivery of ideas through to the market-place.

As part of their education process, designers develop skills in creativity (i.e. original thinking), in idea generation, in problem solving creatively, and in innovation and design (i.e. taking ideas through to a finished outcome). It should be remembered that creativity has little correlation to IQ and academic prowess, and that most people are uncomfortable with creative tasks. Creative thinking is an attitude of mind which requires developing. The driving force behind creativity in design comes from a sense of dissatisfaction and a desire to change something, which perhaps most adolescents adopt and is the reason why their taste in music, fashion and lifestyle tends to change with each generation. Designers are encouraged to continue this passion for the new, the alternative, the better and the different.

Innovation occurs in two ways, either radically, with new ideas, new materials and new technology, or incrementally, through known design modifications. Designers play an important part in the realisation of the radical invention into the market-place. As Walsh[17] suggests, design also contributes to the "swarming secondary innovation" – those competing designs that develop through product differentiation, designing for more efficient and effective use of materials, and for ease of manufacture.

Most companies do not rely on radical innovations; they rely on incremental innovation, none more so than Japanese companies, which demonstrate so well the use of frequent redesign and modification to enhance performance and quality, to reduce costs and to target sectors of the market. Perhaps one of the most frequently used examples is the Sony Walkman, which has undergone thousands of minor design modifications in order to retain and develop its market share. It is usually much more cost effective for organisations to innovate incrementally than to innovate radically. Even those firms which are successful at innovating radically do not do so very often.[18]

Organisations need to be aware of how they can harness the creativity and channel it through effective innovation. This means creating an environment where all functions contribute to that process, but particularly where design skills can be applied. Much research has gone into identifying contributors to creativity and innovation. In a study carried out in the USA, Burnside found organisational obstacles and stimulants to creativity.[19]

The four main organisational obstacles to creativity are:

- Insufficient time: either not having enough time to consider alternative approaches to the work or not enough personnel for the work that needs doing.

- Evaluation pressure, involving either a negative climate or one which pressurises for anything whether the quality is good or not.

- Status quo: this involves a reluctance to change within the organisation, management wanting to carry on the way they always have, avoiding any controversial ideas.

- Political problems: general territory protection within organisations, "empire building" and protection which results in a lack of co-operation between departments.

These obstacles apply equally to a team of designers or to a multifunctional development team. Stimulants to creativity can also apply to both designers and multifunctional teams. In fact, it is essential to the success of a team that stimulants to creativity are in place. Designers generally are able, because of their training and education, to create such an environment for themselves, but are more able to work successfully in a team when such stimulants are replicated in an organisational environment. Burnside's stimulants to creativity include:

- Coworkers: willingness to help each other, trust and commitment.

- Resources: having the most appropriate resources available, including facilities, equipment, information, funds and people.

- Challenge: feeling they are working on an important task, where their skills are most needed and challenged.

- Freedom: having a sense of control over the task and ideas.

- Supervisors/supportive managers who communicative clear goals are essential to a creative environment.

- Creativity supports: encouragement for creativity from senior management.

- Recognition: effort must be rewarded and recognised.

- Unity and co-operation: a shared vision with a co-operative culture and climate.

Inhibitors of individual creativity, identified by Heap,[20] occur with a lack of fluency in the language of the problem (i.e. not having the knowledge skills and abilities that may be applicable to a certain problem or situation), and with evaluating ideas to quickly (i.e. being judgmental, disregarding what might be silly ideas too quickly). Our own concept package, in terms of *what is the right answer*, often inhibits creativity; for example, we may associate black with evil or death and therefore be prevented from being creative with this colour in such circumstances as a wedding, for instance. Social pressures also inhibit our creativity; wanting to adhere to the norm may prevent our natural creativity. Short-term expediency, such as having time pressure to produce results, and never having a breathing space to think, also inhibits creativity. Designers working in multifunctional teams can often stimulate creativity, overcoming such inhibitions in others by their own example.

The organisation and innovation

Creativity alone will not result in innovation; the organisation has to encourage an innovative environment. Certain factors that have been identified as *contributors* to innovation success include the following:[21]

- Organisational structure: teams and matrix organisations are found to be successful contributors to innovation.[22, 23]

- Discretion or freedom of time and choice in a consultative and supportive environment have been found to support innovation.[24, 25]

- Leadership: much attention has been paid to leadership; researchers have not identified a single style but have identified the need for participative and collaborative leadership.[26]

- Feedback, recognition and social support have been identified as facilitators of creativity for employees.

- Idea champions and change agents: innovation cannot rely on top-down intervention; in studies reported by Bouwen and Fry it was observed that innovation required the extraordinary effort of an individual idea champion.[27]

Interventions that have been found to contribute to organisational innovation have been categorised by Farr.[28] These include:

- Creating change in beliefs and expectations, by constantly communicating successful innovation using visual means such as photographs and quotes from those involved with the innovation.

- Influencing the salience of alternative beliefs; making it known that doing things differently is as salient as following existing procedures. Using training sessions to project future situations, which include those employees who would be involved in change. Asking them to imagine the change and to explain how it was successfully implemented and the positive benefits that were derived from its use.

- Attitude change and persuasive communications: attitudes can be strengthened and changed by repeated expressions of an attitude or policy such as mission statements. Also, recipients of change are more likely to accept it if they are actively involved in the change process.

- Minority group influence: minority groups often do more thinking about their positions on a topic, and this thinking is more divergent than that produced by majority groups, therefore innovation may be improved if groups addressing a problem or issue are intentionally composed of several "minority" groups.

- Organisational development: theories in organisational development contribute to developing innovative environments – issues such as espoused theories versus theories in use. This occurs where senior management will support statements that support innovation; however, these individuals may behave differently and their pattern of behaviour will be followed by others in the organisation.

- Providing perceived payoff from change: feedback from peers and superiors is generally agreed to encourage and stimulate ongoing performance and innovation.

- Creating the capacity to generate new and useful ideas: training and practice are essential for ongoing individual creativity: "Performing a challenging and enriched job which requires thinking and decision making on a daily basis may also strengthen ones' capacity for generating more solution alternatives".

We have, therefore, the situation where design is a contributor to the act of innovation and creativity. Designers can also contribute to the creation of an innovative climate, because of their education and method of work. However, they cannot work alone and the organisation must develop initiatives to further a creative and innovative culture.

Design and New Product Development

New product development (NPD) and design is essential for both corporate and economic survival in all industrialised nations. In Britain, the cradle of the industrial revolution, we have seen relative decline in industrial output over two decades. Between 1965 and 1987 our total market economies fell from 5.8% to 4.6%, and our share of trade from 20% of total world trade to 8%.[29] Similarly, the US's share of world output has declined, and the US has been overtaken as the world's largest exporter by Germany and Japan. In order to recapture our share of the markets, we must develop new products for the global market.

NPD is important in its role in exploiting new technologies; here again, Britain has been lagging behind. A study a few years ago by Japan's Ministry of International Trade and Industry (MITI) found that 55% of all commercially important innovations made in the world since the war had originated in Britain. Britain has a reputation for invention and innovation, but seems incapable of commercial exploitation of the technology, which is reflected in its manufacturing growth rate as compared to those of other countries. Indeed, studies indicate that many British designers work abroad and up 73% of design consultancies work for foreign clients.[30]

NPD has attracted the keen attention of many management disciplines. It is obviously a key issue for management, and many studies have identified factors that affect the success or failure of a new product. Table 5.2 provides an overview of the factors contributing to success or failure.

It is apparent from the table that much emphasis has been paid to the need for marketing, design and technology functions to integrate and co-operate on new product development, and for "products to have a synergy with companies' technical and marketing expertise".[34] Internally integrating functional divisions, stage overlapping and intensive communication, mutual trust and goal sharing, and low specialisation without losing technological expertise are all recommended Japanese practices. Madique and Zirger found that success occurs when "the create, make and market

Table 5.2 – Factors affecting new product development success and failure

---

• **Organisational strategy** All of the evidence points to "strategy" as an important factor in new product design and development. Unless the corporate strategy is clearly defined, based on sound data, and is accurately translated into market, design and technology strategies, NPD is likely to fail.

• **Organisational structure** Culture and climate – Structure is something that occurs in every study on NPD; how key personnel are organised for the new product design and development process and how they are supported, monitored etc. is vital to the success of any programme or project.

• **NPD strategy** Almost all of the work in the area of new product design and development has indicated that a strategy and NPD plan, at both programme and project level, is essential to success.

• **NPD process** Much attention has been paid to the NPD process, to determining the appropriate stages[31] and how to co-ordinate them: product planning, idea generation, idea screening, market research, product screening, market testing, business analysis, product development and product launching.

• **Key functions** Apart from top management, the literature seems to indicate that there are three key functions in the new product design and development process: marketing, design and technology.

• **Marketing** Many studies of NPD success refer to some aspects of the marketing function as a determinant of success. For example, issues such as a "well defined market need",[32] "attention to marketing and publicity",[33] early market recognition, in-depth understanding of the market-place and reading consumer needs are all factors related to success and are part of the marketing function.

• **Design** Many bodies such as the Confederation of British Industry (CBI) and the DTI have now identified design as critical to the product development process.

• **Technology** Both in terms of the materials and processes, and the people responsible for production and manufacturing, technology is the third key function in the successful development and design of new products.

• **Finance** Investment in design, as well as repeat checks on costs, profit margins and return on investment, is essential to successful NPD. A current issue in terms of finance is that of short-termism: the Germans and the Japanese – unlike the Americans and the British – tend to invest on longer timescales, allowing for experimentation and innovation.

• **Factors intrinsic to the industry** Although success factors may in many cases operate over a number of industrial sectors, there are particular features of NPD that are intrinsic to an industrial sector and these must be taken into account. For instance, in the newly established fast growing firms, one finds product innovation pervading all operations, whereas is large established manufacturing firms, there is more difficulty. These latter firms have grown and prospered on the basis of developing yesterday's products, and now have to safeguard their futures through continued product innovation. These firms may require a different approach to using design in NPD.

• **External factors** There are a number of factors that are often out of the control of an organisation, which can affect the success or otherwise of a new product, such as (i) the economic climate, the ability of the consumer to buy; (ii) the market, including market size, competitors and changes in the market; and (iii) environmental issues, including environmental legislation; market forces in this area are now important issues in the acceptance or uptake of a product in the market, as well as a determinant of cost in design, materials and manufacture.

functions are well interfaced and coordinated".[35] A research group at the University of Strathclyde[36] found that company and product success is achieved by companies that combine technical excellence with sound marketing, when engineering and aesthetic design are represented on the board. Thomsen of Braun AG[37] recommends the early involvement in NPD of marketing, design and engineering as a strategy for the 1990s. However, a number of problems of communication, co-operation and management between these functions have been identified, particularly with regard to the design function and its relationship with the other two. How design is perceived, what its role is in an organisation, who is responsible for it and how it is managed and interfaced with marketing and technology during the new product development process is critical to success.

NPD is an issue that brings together many of the organisational functions with design. The factors we have identified as contributing to success or failure are similar to those affecting innovation creativity and, indeed, management practices in general.

Design and Quality

Quality and design are inextricably linked; for an organisation to provide any kind of service and/or product, quality must be "designed in". Like design, the term "quality" is used in many different ways: "a quality job", "top quality", "a quality service". In industry, the term has been used in a qualitative way to build up a company image – e.g. Esso's slogan, "Quality at work" – and also in a quantitative way to assess the conformity and tolerances of manufactured goods.

Most experts recognise that this does not go far enough, Dale and Cooper[38] suggest that most quality gurus now consider quality as satisfying customers' expectations and understanding and anticipating their needs. This, of course, includes quality of design and quality of conformance, but goes much further in attempting to define customers' needs, expectations and desires, now and in the future.

The role of the "quality" function is therefore, in part, to determine the quality features of the product or service required by customers, and the role of design is to help to translate those features into reality, whether this involves providing a comfortable waiting room and seating in a hospital, designing a user friendly vending machine, or providing financial services literature which is attractive, informative and understandable for customers.

Some organisations have quality managers or directors who are responsible for defining quality strategy, standards and policies within the organisation. Many organisations are trying to achieve total quality as a goal, by building a "quality culture" through communication and training. It is important that the design function, or, indeed, external design consultants, are made aware of the quality objectives within the organisation. We have already discussed how important it is for designers to work with marketing and sales to understand the customer, with production and finance to achieve targets on budget, and with production to ensure manufacturability. Total quality management involves everyone in the organisation concerned with providing services or products meeting the needs and expectations of the customers. Some companies now go as far as saying they want to do more than meet the needs; they want to "delight" the customers. Design is very much part of delighting and pleasantly surprising the customer. All of these functions need to work together to achieve total quality and continuing improvement.

Perceptions of quality in products are often design-related, as identified in a study undertaken by Gallup for the American Society for Quality Control (ASQC), which involved telephone interviews of 1050 adults in 1988, reported by Ryan[39] and Hutchins.[40] It was found that:

1   People consider the following important when they purchase a product: performance, durability, ease of repair, service availability, warranty, ease of use, price, appearance, brand name.

2   People will pay a premium for what they perceive to be higher quality.

3   Consumers are willing to pay substantially more for better intrinsic quality in products.

4   The factors that make for higher quality in services are courtesy, promptness, a sense that one's needs are being satisfied and the attitude of the service provider.

Design contributes to all of the first three factors and, indeed, unless the service provider has appropriate and well-designed back-up – whether they are good working conditions or appropriate information – they would not be able to fulfil the fourth item on this list.

Quality is created in the design stage of both the product and the process; the majority of quality related problems are caused by poor or unsuitable designs[41] Quality must be designed in. This begins at the idea and the brief development; the quality criteria on which the product is to be judged should be planned. This includes not only the product's configuration in terms of materials and machines but also the control over the product design development and production process. We return, therefore, to the need to form teams, for those teams to understand their role and responsibility and for the quality criteria to be set out from the onset of any project.

Under total quality management everyone in the organisation is involved in continually improving the process under his or her control. Suppliers and customers are integrated into the improvement process; they can contribute to the design process in particular. An understanding of the supplier helps designers to understand what they are working with, whether it is components, materials or other services. For instance, in the development of the Boeing 747, a particular company that was to supply pressurised heat treatment to the wing sections had size restrictions in its treatment unit.

The designers found this out too late in the development process, and had to supply the wings in a knocked down form.

Design and the Tools

Many quality management tools relate to design and the design function to some degree. Of the major tools identified by Dale and Cooper[42] (Table 5.3), two in particular have relevance to design.

Table 5.3 – Quality management tools

- Checklists, bar charts, histograms, graphs
- Flow charts
- Pareto analysis
- Cause and effect diagrams
- Scatterplots and regression analysis
- Design of experiments
- Quality function deployment
- The seven new quality control tools
- Departmental purpose analysis
- Mistake proofing
- Failure mode and effects analysis

Quality Function Deployment (QFD)

QFD was developed in Japan and is used by many Japanese companies. It seeks to identify those features of a product or service that satisfy the real needs and requirements of the customer. This usually involves discussions with the customer to obtain in descriptive terms how the customer feels about the product or service. This is then translated into design requirements and deployed through each phase of the manufacturing cycle to ensure that what is delivered truly reflects the needs of the customer. It is a process that both marketing and design can use when developing a design brief or specification.

QFD is an industry-initiated process, the primary aim of which is to capture and convert the "voice of the customer"[43] into the product and process requirements that profitably deliver the identified customer needs and wants. QFD manages across individual functional aspects of NPD, providing mechanisms that weave the individual functions into a coherent process.[44]

In QFD, the cross-functional teams use a series of interaction matrices to translate from customer needs to process specification; however, research in the USA[45] has identified that success only occurs if QFD is seen as a means to an end and that there is already high cross-functional integration. It does not work when it is used by management to dictate to staff or when team members are strangers and are isolated as functional groups.

Failure Mode and Effects Analysis (FMEA)

FMEA was developed in the aerospace and defence industries. It is a systematic and analytical planning process for identifying what problems may occur in the product service and process design stages. It starts by focusing on the function of the product, identifying potential failure and what effects that may have, assessing current controls and allocating a risk priority number, followed by recommending corrective measures and monitoring these as they are put into place. FMEA design addresses issues in terms of what could go wrong with the product, and also assists in the identification or confirmation of critical product characteristics design. The FMEA process considers the problems that may occur if there is non-compliance with the specification or design intent. FMEA is recommended by many experts in quality; however, its use must be by informed and well-trained personnel working in teams.

Information Technology and Computer Aided Design

Information technology and computer aided design applications are also tools that have been identified as aiding communication between mangers and designers. In recent research[46] the use of CAD in the early modelling stages of product packaging, textile design and interior design has been identified by designers, marketeers and engineers as making a great contribution to communication, understanding and decision making, and to reducing time to market.

There is a need, in design management terms, to assess many of these tools and determine to what degree they can be used in design disciplines, other than product design. It is clear that there may be lessons to learn and aspects that could be applied to a range of design disciplines and design problems, both in product, environmental and communication design. Managers might find that they aid the interface between design and other functions, and thus contribute to the overall business of the organisation.

Conclusion

Earlier chapters emphasise how design relates to the organisation in both value and strategic terms; this chapter illustrates how design interfaces with all organisational functions, tools and processes. Indeed, "silent design"[47] is undertaken in every organisation. However, in many organisations design is not seen as a core activity. It is now important to take advantage of the skills that designers have, to harness design and manage it effectively. In understanding design's relationship to all organisational functions and activities, design can be channelled appropriately to achieve corporate objectives.

Summary

• **Design is a core aspect of every organisation's business; it should be a concern of every function.**

• **Design and R&D**

R&D feeds design with information on new technologies, new materials and processes. It can guide R&D on potential research directions for new products.

- **Design and marketing**

Marketing and design are interdependent, although little has been published in the marketing literature. Design is related to every aspect of the marketing mix: in "Product", design influences quality, function, service, usability, appearance and other features; in "Price", the way a product is designed can affect the cost of manufacture and distribution, and also add value; in "Place", designers are involved in packaging and distribution and they also design outlets, for example retail stores, exhibition stands, leisure facilities etc.; in "Promotion", design always has a key role in the production of advertising, support literature, point of sale displays etc. The critical nature of the design–marketing interface means that market research must be undertaken in such a way as to inform designers both quantitatively and qualitatively about the end users of their design, e.g. supply market sizes, customer profiles and lifestyle information.

Communicating market information, determining the design brief and evaluating design concepts are critical to the success of most design projects. A number of tools are available to improve this process, e.g. the use of mood boards, scenarios and semantic differentials.

- **Design and production**

In every discipline design concepts must be transferred from the drawing board into reality. This involves a production process, therefore it is inevitable that there must be an interface between designers and production. The interface must begin at the briefing and concept stage, and continue through development to production. This enables the production specialist to contribute knowledge and experience at the beginning, thus reducing the risk of problems later in production. Designers must also be kept aware of all of the production issues, which will aid economic and efficient manufacture or assembly. The communication process between both functions must also involve efficient and clear transfer of design instructions and specifications to enable effective manufacture.

• Finance and design

In order to increase the added value element of their products or services, companies need to invest in design. Research has found that investment in design is profitable. Investment in design benefits not only the company and its core product but also enhances employee effectiveness and public perceptions of the organisation, its philosophy and its effectiveness.

During the design process the finance function should be involved from concept to launch, in terms of forecasting sales and profits, costing projects, allocating resources, monitoring project expenditure and authorising expenditure. In order to resource and monitor design effectively, however, the finance function must understand the value of design to the company and also the activities involved in the design process.

• Design and sales

Sales personnel are frequently the closest to the customer and the competitors, therefore they can supply design with valuable information, contributing to the design and development process. Sales also require support and back up through point of sale literature and corporate image promotion; designers need to be aware of the requirements of sales staff. Designers are frequently the most knowledgeable personnel on the product design features, therefore communicating this information to sales personnel can aid their own ability to communicate this clearly to the customer.

• Human resource management and design

The human resource management function can aid design effectiveness within an organisation by:

1 Developing skills, knowledge and understanding of design.

2 Including design early in project teams and motivating and building teams that will work together effectively, removing functional barriers.

3   Using design in corporate communications and communicating the value of design throughout the organisation.

4   Designing the organisational structure to encourage the integration of design with other functions and provide the flexibility needed for innovation and creativity.

• Design and other organisational issues

There are a number of other issues with which design is related.

Creativity and Innovation

Although designers themselves have highly developed skills in creativity and innovation, it is important that the organisation creates an environment that encourages and stimulates these processes. Contributors to innovation include organisation structures that encourage teams, a supportive climate which allows discretion and freedom of choice, a participative leadership style, feedback and recognition, and the use of idea champions. Interventions that contribute to innovations include creating change in beliefs and expectations, using persuasive communications, using minority groups to influence change, and training and practice in creativity.

New Product Development

Research suggests that there are three key functions in new product development: marketing, design and technology (people, materials and processes). How they are managed and how they interface with one another is critical to the success of new products.

Design and Quality

Designers are involved with all perceptions of quality, including product performance, appearance, price, delivery, repair and service. Quality is often created in the design stage of both products and process: the majority of quality related problems are caused by poor or unsuitable designs. It is important that everyone in the organisation is involved in continuing the quality process under his or her control and that everyone contributes to the design process. This includes suppliers and customers, both internal and external to the organisation.

Design and the Tools

A number of management and quality tools are used in organisations, some of which have an influence on or are influenced by design. Particular examples include quality function deployment and failure mode and effects analysis.

References
1 Morita, A. (1992) *"S" does not equal "T" and "T" does not equal "I"*, The First United Kingdom Innovation Lecture, The Royal Society, London.
2 Ibid.
3 Kotler, P. and Rath, G.A. (1990) Design: A powerful but neglected strategic tool, *Journal of Business Strategy*, **5** (2).
4 Service, L., Hart, S. and Baker, M. (1987) *Design for Profit*, The Design Council, London.
5 Bruce, M. and Roy, R. (1991) Integrating marketing and design for commercial benefit, *Market Intelligence and Planning*, **9**(5), pp 23-8.
6 Kotler, P. and Rath, G.A. (1990) Design: A powerful but neglected strategic tool, *Journal of Business Strategy*, **5**(2), 1990.
7 *Marketing Week* (1993) MFI unveils major store revamp, **27** August.
8 Clarke, K. (1991) Product concept development in the automotive industry, paper presented at the 3rd International Conference on Design Management Education and Research, The Design Management Institute, Harvard, May.
9 Woodhuysen, J. (1990) The relevance of design futures, in Oakley, M. (ed.) *Design Management*, Basil Blackwell, Oxford.
10 The Design Council (1991) *Design for Effective Manufacture, A Management Overview*, DTI, London.
11 Davies, R.F. (1982) Investigating the effect of computer aided design on the work of the typographer, PhD thesis, Manchester Polytechnic.
12 Whitney, D.E. (1988) Manufacturing by design, *Harvard Business Review*, July/August, 83–91.
13 Potter, S., Roy, R., Capon, C.H., Bruce, M., Walsh, V. and Lewis, J. (1991) *The Benefits and Costs of Investment in Design*, Using Professional Design Expertise in Product, Engineering and Graphics Projects, Open University/UMIST Design Innovation Group, Report DIG-03, July.
14 The Design Council (1991) *Managing the Financial Aspects of Product Design and Development*, A Management Overview, DTI, London.
15 Cooper, C.L. and Robertson, I. (1987) *Human Behavioiur in Organisations*, Blackwell, Oxford.

16 Clipson, C. (1991) Innovation by design, in Henry, J. and Walker, D. (eds) *Managing Innovation*, Sage, London.

17 Walsh, V. (1991) *Design, innovation and the boundaries of the firm: implications for management*, paper presented at the colloquium on Management of Technology – Implications for Enterprise Management and Public Policy, organised by Grandes Ecoles Francaises, MIT/University of California at Berkeley, 27–28 May.

18 Freeman, C. (1982) *The Economics of Industrial Innovation*, Francis Pinter, London.

19 Burnside, Robert M. (1990) Improving climates for creativity, in West, M.A. and Farr, J.L. (eds) *Innovation and Creativity at Work*, John Wiley and Sons, Chichester.

20 Heap, J. (1989) *The Management of Innovation and Design*, Cassell, London.

21 King, N. (1990) Innovation at work: the research literature, in West, M.A. and Farr, J.L. *Innovation and Creativity at Work*, John Wiley and Sons, Chichester.

22 Kanter, R.M. (1983) *The Change Masters*, Simon and Schuster, New York.

23 Lovelace, R F. (1986) Stimulating creativity through managerial intervention. *R&D Management*, 16 161-174.

24 Glassman, E. (1986) Managing for creativity: back to basics in R&D, *R&D Management*, **16** 175-183.

25 Peters, T.J. and Waterman, R.H. (1982) *In Search of Excellence: Lessons from America's Best Run Companies*, Harper and Row, New York.

26 King, N. (1990) Innovation at work: the research literature, in West, M.A. and Farr, J.L. *Innovation and Creativity at Work*, John Wiley, Chichester.

27 Bouwen, R. and Fry, R. (1988) An agenda for managing organisational innovation and development in the 1990s, in Lambrecht, M. (ed.) *Corporate Revival*, Catholic University Press, Leuven, Belgium.

28 West, M.A. and Farr, J.L. (1990) *Innovation and Creativity at Work*, John Wiley, Chichester.

29 Policy Studies Institute (1991) *Britain in 2010*, Policy Studies Institute, London.

30 McAlone, B. (1987) *British Design Consultancy Report*, The Design Council, London.

31 Kotler, P. (1986) *Marketing Management, Analysis, Planning and Control*, 3rd edn, Prentice Hall, Englewood Cliffs, New Jersey.

32 Townsend, J.F. (1976) Innovation in coal machinery: The Anderton Shearer Loader – the role of the NCB and supply industry in its development, *Science Policy Research Unit Occasional Paper*, series no. 3, University of Sussex, Brighton.

33 Rothwell, R. (1972) 'Factors for success in industrial innovations', *project SAPPHO: A comparative study of success and failure in industrial innovation*, Science Policy Research Unit, University of Sussex, Brighton.

34 Hopkins,D. (1981) New product winners and losers, *Research Management*, **24**(3).

35 Madique, M. and Zirger, B. (1972).

36 Service, L.M., Hart, S.J. and Baker, M.J. (1987) *Profit by Design*, The Design Council, London.

37 Thomsen, T.H. (1990) Financial Times Report, London.

38 Dale, B. and Cooper, C. (1992) *Total Quality and Human Resources*, Basil Blackwell, Oxford.

39 Ryan, J. (1988) Consumers see little change in product quality, *Quality Progress*, December, 16–20.

40 Hutchins, S. (1989) What customers want: Results of ASQC/Gallup survey, *Quality Progress*, February, 33–36.

41 Dale, B. and Cooper, C. (1992) *Total Quality and Human Resources*, Basil Blackwell, Oxford.

42 Ibid.

43 Griffin, A.J. and Straus, A.Z. (1991) *The voice of the customer*, University of Chicago Working Paper.

44 Huser, J.R. and Clausing, D. (1988) The house of quality, *Harvard Business Review*, May/June, 63–73.

45 Griffin, A.J. (1992) Evaluating QFD's use in US firms as a process for developing products, *Journal of Product Innovation Management*, **9**(3), September 1992.

46 Davies, R.F. and Cooper, R. (1992) *Diagnosing the sources of success/failure in new product development*, Marketing Education Group Conference Proceedings.

47 Gorb, P. and Dumas, A. (1987) Silent design, *Design Studies*, 150–156.

6 Design Audits

"Few functions are spoken about more and understood less than auditing. It is often the last refuge of those who don't really know how to run a prevention orientated life. Audit is the Bat Masterson of business. When you get into trouble, just call old Bat. He'll find all the bad guys and drag them to justice. And even if he fails to find the real ringleaders, you still look good. After all you called in the law didn't you?"

Philip B. Crosby[1]

In the event of major disasters or even minor problems, there is frequently a call for an "enquiry" to examine all aspects of the situation. As "design" becomes recognised as a key competitive weapon, managers are implored to examine their own corporate use of design in an attempt to address problems in corporate competitiveness.

The term "design audit" has become popular for such an activity. However, what design audits are, who conducts them and what they audit are questions that have not been addressed in the literature. This chapter attempts to do so by examining audits in general and assessing examples of design audit practice.

The Origins of Audits

For most people the term "audit" is synonymous with finance: according to the *Oxford English Dictionary*, as a noun

Chapter Map

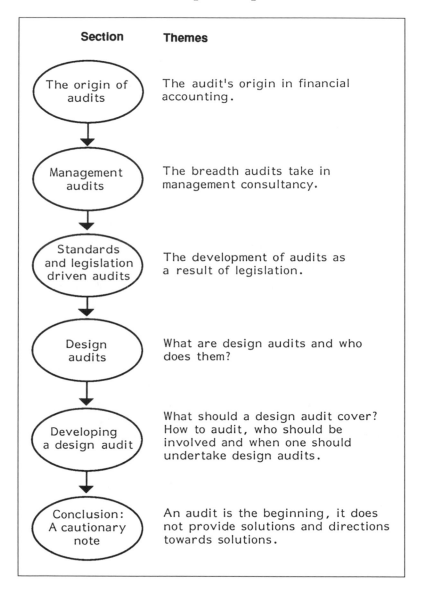

Section	Themes
The origin of audits	The audit's origin in financial accounting.
Management audits	The breadth audits take in management consultancy.
Standards and legislation driven audits	The development of audits as a result of legislation.
Design audits	What are design audits and who does them?
Developing a design audit	What should a design audit cover? How to audit, who should be involved and when one should undertake design audits.
Conclusion: A cautionary note	An audit is the beginning, it does not provide solutions and directions towards solutions.

it means "official examination of accounts"; as a verb "to examine (accounts) officially". The Auditing Standards and Guidelines,[2] approved by most accounting bodies, define clearly what is meant by audit:

"An audit is the independent examination of and expression of opinion on the financial statement of an enterprise by an appointed auditor in pursuance of that appointment and in compliance with any relevant statutory obligation."

In accounting, therefore, clear procedures have been established in order to undertake an audit. There is a statutory requirement for incorporated companies to have internal and external audits, and for accounts and information systems to be available for inspection. The responsibility for preparation of the financial statements and the presentation of information rests with the management of the enterprise (in the case of a company, the Directors); the auditor's responsibility is to report on the financial statement as presented by management.

Auditing standards prescribe the basic principles and practices that members are expected to follow in the conduct of an audit. However, even in financial auditing the guidelines suggest that:

"it would be impracticable to establish a code of rules sufficiently elaborate to cater for all situations and circumstances which an auditor might encounter. Such a code could not provide for innovations in business and financial practice. In the observance of auditing standards, therefore, the auditor must exercise his judgment in determining both the audit procedures necessary in the circumstances to afford reasonable basis for his opinion and wording of his report."

There is, then, a degree of latitude in terms of how a financial audit is carried out. Today, the term "audit" has become popular in business to mean any type of examination. It is used in connection with other management issues such as quality, skills and stress. It tends to represent the desire by management to make an objective analysis of the current position within the organisation, in terms of a particular topic, whether economic, ergonomic or social. The methods used to undertake such audits are even less clearly defined than for financial audits.

Management Audits

In the United States and now in Europe the term "management audit" is quite commonly used. Thomas Wheelen and David Hunger[3] reported that in the United States the National Association of Regulatory Utility Commissioners analysed 31 management audits that had been completed or were in progress, and reported that the agencies using management auditors were pleased with the results and intended to continue using them. Often these audits recommended changes in the operating practices of management, and suggested areas where substantial reductions in operating costs could be made. The term "management audit", they suggest, is used in the United States to describe a list of questions that forms the basis for an in-depth analysis of a particular area of importance to the corporation – for example, a sales force audit, a social audit, a forecasting audit, a technology audit, a human resource audit. The complaint made by Wheelen and Hunger was that rarely did audits go beyond functional areas. They went on to suggest that a "strategic audit" was key to the well-being of an organisation, providing a framework from which organisations should develop their own questions.

In the United Kingdom, Gerry Johnson and Kevin Scholes[4] consider the importance of audits in relation to strategy. They cite the example of the Audit Commission's report of 1983, which used a questionnaire to enable Local Authorities to assess the interaction of several factors in their organisation. The questions covered areas such as vision, strategy, structure, systems, style, skills and staffing. Johnson and Scholes go on to discuss the importance of two other types of audit: the environmental audit and the resource audit. The environmental audit refers to the need for organisations to understand the environmental influences important to it, and the authors provide a summary of some of the questions to ask about likely key factors at work in the wider environment. These questions are fairly wide-ranging, covering economic environment, capital markets, demographics, socio-cultural factors, technology, labour markets, competitors, government, ecology and suppliers. In terms of the resources audit, Johnson and Scholes suggest an audit of the internal capabilities of the organisation in terms of the following:

• **Physical resources**: an assessment of a company's physical resources must stretch beyond a mere listing of the number of machines or production capacity, and ask questions about the nature of these resources – age, condition, capability and location of each resource, for example.

• **Human resources**: the analysis of human resources must examine a number of questions. An assessment of the number and types of different skills within an organisation is clearly important, but other factors, such as the adaptability of human resources, must not be overlooked. For example, if a company is likely to face a period of difficulty or retrenchment then it is important to know how able the people are to cope with a situation where traditional boundaries and demarcation lines will have to change to ensure economic survival. As with physical resources, the location of key human resources could be important. A multinational company may be concerned that all its skilled operatives are in high-wage countries, making it difficult to compete in world markets.

• **Financial resources**: analysis of this would include the sources and uses of money within the value chain, such as obtaining capital, managing cash, controlling debtors and creditors, and the management of relationships with suppliers of money (shareholders, banker, etc.).

• **Intangibles**: one mistake that can be made in a resource analysis is to overlook the importance of intangible resources. There should be no doubt that these intangibles have a value, since when businesses are sold part of their value is "goodwill". in some businesses, particularly services such as solicitors, retail shops and the catering industry, goodwill could represent the major asset of the company. It may result from brand names, good contacts, company image or from many other sources.

We have a sense, therefore, that the use of the term "audit" has become wide-ranging, and encompasses every aspect of an organisation. However, in order to undertake an audit, a methodology must be created. Management consultancies frequently offer their services to create and undertake specific audits; for example, an operational audit. This might involve a "troubleshooter"-type approach, examining aspects of the management of the company. The British Department of Trade and Industry, for instance, in their "Managing in the '90s" programme, produced an innovation self-assessment guide and workbook. Using a process of self-assessment and innovation scorecards, it leads firms through six steps:

1 Team formulation

2 Initial assessment

3 Choice of focus

4 In-depth assessment

5 Benchmarking

6 Action: closing the gaps

The aim of this is "to help businesses to develop and improve their innovation performance and hence their overall competitive edge. The guide provides a framework to enable firms to assess their innovation processes and performance".[5]

There are also simple guidelines to audits, for instance, Majaro's[6] creativity and innovation audits for managers and functions, which lists the criteria and even the questions to ask (Figure 6.1).

Standards and Legislation-Driven Audits

Quality audit and environmental audits tend to have evolved from international or British standards or legislation, and are also driven in part by popular demand in terms of "caring for the customer'.

Quality audits

Many companies – those who wish to trade in Europe, for instance – must meet the quality standard BS5750 or ISO9000.[7] To pass an ISO9000 audit, the quality system must work as stated and documented by the company. The external auditor not only audits documentation, systems and procedures but also ensures that the internal quality audits

Figure 6.1 – Example of Majoro's quality audit

2 AUDITS

In this section you are asked to answer a number of questions regarding aspects of creativity in your organisation. The questions are phrased in such a way that either 'Yes' or 'No' is the obvious answer. However, since the situation in any organisation is rarely so black or white, there are a range of possible answers along the spectrum between 'Yes' and 'No', indicating various shades of grey, as shown below.

Creativity Audit at Corporate Level

Select your score for each question and enter it in the box provided.

Your Answer	No	Rarely	Sometimes	Often	Yes
Points	0	1	2	3	4

1	Does the organisation's Mission Statement mention 'creativity', 'innovation' or both as being part of the corporate ethos?	
2	Is top management involved and actively interested in the process of generating ideas?	
3	Is the organisational climate supportive of the idea-generation process?	
4	Can staff approach top management with ideas and get a fair hearing?	
5	Do people in the organisation talk about 'creativity', 'ideas' and 'innovation'?	
6	Do people in the organisation know where to take their ideas?	
7	Does the organisation undertake regular training or idea-generating exercises in order to stimulate the overall climate for creativity?	

Source: Reproduced with kind permission of Butterworth-Heinemann Ltd, from *The Creative Marketer* 1991.

procedures but also ensures that the internal quality audits have been performed in accordance with a documented procedure to verify whether quality activities are performed as planned. An external quality audit covers a number of areas, such as management responsibility, contract review, document control, purchasing, process control, design control, control of non-conforming product, corrective action, handling and storage.[8] Internal quality audits are expected to uncover potential danger spots, eliminate waste and verify that corrective actions have occurred. The management and quality guru Philip Crosby[9] describes a quality audit as a planned examination of a function, carried out either by determining conformance to procedures in process or by critical analysis of the product or service that is the result of the process. In quality terms, Crosby gives a few basic rules for a successful audit:

- *Be specific about what you want audited and against what criteria the audit is to be accomplished*

- *Select individuals to conduct the audit who couldn't possibly be interested in the outcome one way or the other*

- *Brief the audit team carefully and give them time to write a proper report*

- *Do not tell them in any manner what kind of results you expect to find*

- *Remember the findings will point only to the front line troops. The real cause of the problems lies behind the findings*

The more procedurally-driven quality audits have arisen out of a desire to conform to a standard of Quality Assurance. More comprehensive quality audits tend to have originated from the internal drive towards "Total Quality", aimed at assessing both external and internal relationships in an organisation with regard to attaining customer quality needs.

Environmental audits

In the United States, auditors are advised to audit for violations of environmental laws. Cornall and Apostolou[10] advise that auditors should:

"design their audits of client companies, to consider the financial statement impact of costs of noncompliances with environment laws, the procedure recommended includes; holding discussions with management, reviewing documentation, obtaining written management representations and sending attorney letters. If environmental problems are discovered, the auditor should determine if the client has accrued for estimated loss contingencies for the clean up and remediation. If the client has not done this the auditor must determine the impact of these cost on the audit."

This financial/environmental legislation driven audit is rather narrow, and as environmental laws have become more complex and the environmental lobby greater, some companies have taken a wider remit when conducting environmental audits.

Tusa[11] recommends that the development of an environmental audit programme should include:

1   Corporate goals and philosophy

2   The type, tools and reporting methods of the audit

3   Selecting of the audit team

4   Pre-audit preparation and implementations of the audit

The tools to be used would include an audit notification form, a manual, a checklist and a report form.

As part of their environmental responsibility programme, a UK clearing bank, the National Westminster Bank carried out a full review of its current performance. It did this through a two-year audit programme, focusing on six key areas:

- Property and facilities management: addressing matters such as estate management; new development and refurbishment; construction materials and utility equipment specification; internal specification; fixtures management; health and safety; water; energy; building and furniture waste.

- Office services and staff practices: the audit examined communications; waste segregation and collection; consumables, distribution and storage; photocopier specification, purchasing, location, use, delivery and disposal; personal computing; cleaning; catering and vending in terms of maintained services, direct staff use of facilities (e.g. kitchens), consumption, disposal; microfilm production and development; information technology systems procurement, design and use.

- Paper, printing and plastic: the audit investigated specification; raw material and printing equipment purchasing; internal ordering; use and storage; waste collection and disposal in terms of paper, chemicals and plastic.

- Transport and distribution: the scope of the study embraced distribution of internal mail; stationery; waste collection; external mail; clearing; bank vehicles; staff commuting; business travel.

- Corporate policies and practices: the study addressed executive direction; marketing and public relations; training; encouragement of staff activities; sponsorship; communications strategy.

- Business activities: each audited unit considered its core business activities for direct and indirect environmental impact. Business opportunities and threats were also considered.

The audits were undertaken in phases. The first was undertaken by a joint team of trained managers from the bank and from the consultancy Coopers & Lybrand: "The involvement of Coopers & Lybrand ensured both an independence of view and a transfer of skills and experience from the consultants to our own staff".[12] The succeeding UK audits were lead by bank staff, with Coopers & Lybrand monitoring "to confirm the quality of both the audit and its output". For overseas audits, a detailed pack was provided to the Environmental Co-ordinator in each unit and the audit conducted by National Westminster Bank staff, "with training, support and quality control provided by Group Environmental Management Services". Each business unit was audited against environmental "best practice" and recommendations were made. A sample of the findings were presented in their 1993 Environment Report. For example, the investigation into property and facilities management found that no environmental criteria were used in the selection process for the authorised supplier list and no formal policy or standards for furniture replacement and disposal were in place.

On completion of such audits a timetabled action plan with targets is produced, with the objectives of delivering improvements. To monitor their progress, the bank has in place an ongoing review, management and control system, "to ensure that we achieve our policy goals, objectives and chosen annual targets."

This National Westminster Bank example illustrates an environmental audit that goes beyond legislation requirements; indeed, it attempts to address environmental issues from the philosophy of social responsibility and marketing acumen.

Social audits

"Social accountability" encompasses even wider issues than those of environment; it means that consideration will be given to non-economic and non-financial variables, such as the quality of the environment, working conditions and equality of opportunities. However, only when there is already a high level of material welfare can such issues be considered. Social audits are therefore generally confined to companies in the highly industrialised economies of North America and Western Europe.[13]

What is audited, therefore, depends very much on the goals and philosophy of the company, and one cannot determine the parameters of the audit unless these have been defined. An organisation may, for instance, want to address and improve its position with regard to equal opportunities, and will use an audit to assess its current position.

In summary, then, an "audit" suggests going in, often unannounced, to examine some aspect of an organisation's affairs. The size and complexity of the audit will depend on the organisation and its objectives. Management audits[14], for instance, have expanded beyond the traditional concern of adequacy of the internal control system to include evaluation of efficiency of operations and the quality of the management information system. It is important, therefore, to define the focus of audits, particularly because their remit can expand throughout every aspect of the organisation and beyond, into factors in the environment, whether economic, political or social.

Design Audits

Design audits suffer from the same problems as any other audit; that is, how does one define the boundaries of a design audit, what are the criteria for assessment, how should it be implemented and by whom?

Olins,[15] in describing a former colleague's "journey", explains a process that many designers would see as an unstructured design audit.

"Michael Wolff's journey encapsulates the various points of contact which take place sequentially between an organisation and those who come into contact with it ... The 'journey' starts with the critical telephone conversation or other initial point of contact. It takes into account both how long it takes to answer the 'phone and in what manner it is answered. It moves on then to the correspondence. Naturally it takes into account the content of the letter, but it also takes account of its form – the time taken in response, the politeness, clarity and level of literacy of the reply as well as the physical qualities demonstrated by the letterhead. The next act in the journey might well be "the meeting", which geographical area, which part of the town, what kind of signs, what kind of building, the reception area, its appearance, size, cleanliness, comfort."

This journey continues through every aspect of product environment and communication within a company. It provides a story of the use and concern for design. It could be seen as the basis of an audit, although an unstructured one, the aim of which is to record the present situation. It is something that is done frequently by designers on contact with a company, yet they rarely record or measure their journey in any methodological manner.

Despite the breadth many management professionals and academics have given to audits, this is one audit that is noticeable by its absence in most texts. Auditing design is rarely mentioned, except for minor reference in strategic audits. The most common reference to audit among the design profession is that of a "communication audit", as related to corporate identities. Most corporate identity designers consider it important to understand the company at a number of levels: firstly, to understand the corporate philosophy and strategy; secondly, to understand how the company operates, and finally, to understand how it communicates and to whom. Communication audits are generally designed to assess these levels, and are undertaken to varying degrees of depth. For instance, corporate philosophy may be established through reading documentation, through interviews with senior management, or through a series of interviews at all levels of the organisation. Corporate operation may be similarly assessed, while the means of communication may be audited by collecting examples of every visual manifestation of the company image, from letterheads and advertising brochures to vehicles, uniforms, interiors and signs. An audit of these will consider a number of criteria, including application and consistency, the "message" presented, and its interpretation and function.

Design audits in a more general sense have not been developed to any great degree or, indeed, in any manner of consistency. General checklists on design and business "best practice" are available, and provide the basis on which audits could be developed. For instance, the Design Council has, in conjunction with the Department of Trade and Industry (DTI), published a large number of documents addressing aspects of design management. Many of these provide checklists of issues to be addressed. For example, the DTI booklet Design and Business Performance: A Chief

Executive's Handbook[16] provides the following checklist under the section entitled "Creating the right organisation":

- ensure that you have the right skills available
- choose the right team structure
- check that you have the specialists that rapid development of new technology will demand in nearly all areas of product design
- involve all project team members, in-house or external, from the outset
- keep your staff well trained in all your activities
- ensure the efficient management of information and understand how EDM can be used to control and manage all product information
- encourage effective collaboration and mutual commitment and resolve any language and culture problems."

It would be relatively easy to change these instructions to questions, and by adding a scale of 1 to 5 to assess the degree to which each is done, you might then have the basis from which a simple audit process could be developed: for example,

Do you have the right design skills available?

No 1, 2, 3, 4, 5, **Yes.**

This approach was suggested by Kotler and Rath,[17] urging marketers to assess corporate design sensitivity and measure design management effectiveness. In their audit, they used five questions for each topic and, scoring the answers, providing the company with an overall design sensitivity and design effectiveness rating (Table 6.1, see pp. 202-3).

The Kotler and Rath audits, although limited in nature, are broader than that of Oakley.[18] For instance, the latter views design audits as serving much the same purpose as financial audits – "basically to review the return (or potential return) being achieved on the resources employed, to check whether the level of resources is adequate for the tasks involved and to highlight relative successes and failures". He identified two kinds of design audits that should be conducted.

Firstly, a regular across-the-board audit of all design projects and design results should be undertaken every six or twelve months. This type of audit would, he envisaged, examine the design activities, calculate the time and cost and relate these to the success of the design results – in essence, look at the bottom line. Oakley did warn of the rather simplistic nature of such an audit, but recommended its use with degrees of margin as a means of collecting data and indicators, which could prove beneficial in forward planning. This design audit should evaluate the factors that have influenced success and failures, which might include:

1   Presence or absence of a competent project brief

2   Correct prediction of resources required

3   Competent management of project (including the ability to work within time and costs restraints

4   Quality of working relationship between designers and others, both inside and outside the company

5   Availability of skills and effective deployment

6   Ability to respond to any changes in specification

7   Whether progress reviews are held at appropriate times and correct decisions taken about further work, new directions or abandonment

8   General quality of project management

9   Performance of outside design expertise, if used

10 Support, interest and influence of top management

Secondly, pre-project audits should be undertaken before the start of all significant design projects, to compare the resources needed with those available and to assess the chances of a successful outcome. In addressing or formulating design policy for using in-house or external design staff, Oakley recommends that the pre-project audit identify skill levels and training needs.

Table 6.1 – How a corporation's design sensitivity and design management effectiveness can be measured

Companies need to review periodically the role that design plays in their marketing program. At any point in time, company management will have a certain degree of design sensitivity. A design sensitivity audit (exhibit 1) consists of five questions that will indicate the role design plays in a company's marketing decision making. A design management audit (exhibit 2) asks five more questions that rank how well management uses design. Each is scored 0, 1, or 2. A corporation's design sensitivity will range from 0 to 10, and its design management will also range from 0 to 10. Companies with a combined design sensitivity and design management effectiveness rating of anywhere from 14 to 20 are in fairly good shape. Those less than 8 should examine whether they are missing a major opportunity by not making more use of design thinking in their marketing strategy.

Exhibit 1

Design Sensitivity Audit

1   What role does the company assign to design in the marketing decision process?
(0) Design is almost completely neglected as a marketing tool
(1) Design is viewed and used as a minor tactic tool
(2) Design is used as a major strategic tool in the marketing mix

2   To what extent is design thinking utilized in product development work?
(0) Little or no design thinking goes into product development work
(1) Occasionally good design thinking goes into product development work
(2) Consistently good design thinking goes into product development work

3   To what extent is design thinking utilized in environmental design work?
(0) Little or no design thinking goes into environmental design work
(1) Occasionally good design thinking goes into environmental design work
(2) Consistently good design thinking goes into environmental design work

4   To what extent is design thinking utilized in information design work?
(0) Little or no design thinking goes into information design work
(1) Occasionally good design thinking goes into information design work
(2) Consistently good design thinking goes into information design work

5   To what extent is design thinking utilized in corporate identity design work?
(0) Little or no design thinking goes into corporate identity design work
(1) Occasionally good design thinking goes into corporate identity design work
(2) Consistently good design thinking goes into corporate identity design work

Exhibit 2

Design Management Effectiveness Audit

1   What orientation does the design staff follow?
(0) The design staff aims for high aesthetic ideals without any surveying of the needs and wants of the marketplace
(1) The design staff designs what marketing or consumers ask for with little or no modification

(2) The design staff aims for design solutions that start with an awareness of consumer needs and preferences and adds a creative touch

2   Does the design staff have an adequate budget to carry out design analysis, planning and implementation?
(0) The budget is insufficient even for production materials
(1) The budget is adequate but typically cut back during hard times
(2) The design staff is well budgeted, especially on new product development projects

3   Do managers encourage creative experimentation and design?
(0) Creative experimentation and design are discouraged
(1) Designers are occasionally allowed creative freedom, but more typically they have to design within tight specifications
(2) Designers have creative freedom within the limits of the project parameters

4   Do designers have a close working relationship with people in marketing, sales, engineering and research?
(0) No
(1) Somewhat
(2) Yes

5   Are designers held accountable for their work through post-evaluation measurement and feedback?
(0) No
(1) Designers are accountable for cost overruns in the production process
(2) Design work is evaluated and full feedback is given to the designers

Source: Kotler, P. and Rath, G.A. (1990) Design: A powerful but neglected strategic tool, *Journal of Business Strategy*, **5**(2).

The Council for National Academic Awards[19] have made recommendations that an "audit" of design activities might involve:

"assessing the results achieved in the past and the present capabilities of the design department ... strategic planners must review conditions in the market place and the overall business environment, as well as the particular firm. The analysis must not concentrate on present events only; predictions are essential to ensure that future work will be compatible with attitudes and perceptions prevailing at the time of the launch."

In comparison, Topalian's[20] approach to audits is much more comprehensive, suggesting that corporate design audits "denote the formal and comprehensive examination of what goes on design wise within industrial and commercial organisations". Topalian suggests a framework (Table 6.2), which "should provide a sensible guide to an organisation's involvement with and attitude towards design, as well as its approach to managing design". This extensive checklist, Topalian recommends, "should not be audited together, but normally unfold over a sensible period of self-examination by in-house staff, supplemented by the advice of external specialists and feedback from other interested parties such as consumers, suppliers and stockists".

Table 6.2 – Topalian's checklist for corporate design audits

Design policy audit

Any examination of corporate design objectives should start with corporate design objectives and strategies and their link with corporate plans. There should be an overall assessment of the recognition and status of design within the company, together with a statement of strengths and weaknesses in the field.

Design activities audit

The range of design activities undertaken by or on behalf of the company should be listed, stating the scope, importance to the company and where and how undertaken.

Product design audit

For every product, the audit should cover objectives set, fitness for purpose and performance, sales and financial record, importance to company, materials and components used, aesthetics/styling, manufacture/assembly, packaging and after sales support, marketing and distribution.

Design services audit

Assistance/backup provided by design specialists in the planning, organisation and control of design activities, internal/external consultancy in say, educating target audiences: information service on design matters.

Visual identification audit

Survey of elements of corporate identification (symbol/logotype/corporate colours etc.), areas of application; discipline with which identification system is used; evaluation of overall visual identity and corporate image.

Audit of target audiences of design function

"Clients" of design function and other interested parties, inside and outside the company; principal points and nature of contacts.

Audit of personnel involved in design activities

Range of individuals, whether design specialists or not, in-house or external to company; qualification, skills and experience; recruitment/selection procedures; training of non-design specialists in design matters and design specialists in company/business matters; sources of outside advice.

Design facilities audit

Range and quality of equipment; space allocated; ancillary support available etc.

Work environment audit

General survey of internal and external environments (interiors, architecture, landscaping, location, amenities)

Design management system audit

Design management; chain of command; method of planning, monitoring, organisation and control; keeping up-to-date with design trends and technical developments; nature of decision-making and leadership; where responsibility rest; the link (if any) between design management and management of communications generally.

Design discipline and procedures audit

Survey of guidelines on preferred practice, for example, the setting up of design project proposals, selection of designers, documentation/control/evaluation systems, publication of achievements through design within and outside company.

Corporate design standards audit

Range of quality standards, whether self generated or externally imposed; documentation and communication of standards; sanctions applied to ensure conformity; review and development of standards.

Design funding audit

Capital and operating budgets allocated specifically to design activities; proportion of advertising budget which is actually spent on design work; position of design in investment in design; return on investment compared with other functions; ideal level and distribution of investment in design.

Design department audit

Terms of reference/objectives set; status in company; physical location; staffing; relationship and interaction with other departments; skills/services/facilities offered; activities undertaken; principal "clients" outside the company; contribution to corporate success.

Source: Topalian, A. (1984) Corporate identity: beyond the visual overstatements, *International Journal of Advertising*, 3, pp 55–62

Topalian gives us a range of subjects to be audited, but how should these activities be measured and tested, and against what criteria? Borja de Mozota,[21] in her recommendations, suggests a similar broad sweep of corporate activity in audits, but links them specifically to design strategies and to costs through the use of a design audit summary chart, along the lines of Table 6.3.

Table 6.3 – Design audit summary (percentages)

	Graphic	Package	Product	Architecture
Strategy/design mix Ratios of design investments	*30%*	*10%*	*40%*	*20%*
• If cost domination strategy: evaluation of cost reduction by design			*10%*	
• If marketing differentiation strategy: evaluation of quality and image upgrading possible	*10%*			

Adapted from: Borja de Mozota, Brigitte (1990) Design as a strategic management tool, in Oakley, M. (ed.) *Design Management: A Handbook of Issues and Methods*, Basil Blackwell, Oxford.

Another approach to design audits which may apply a degree of rigour and consistency to their development is to use the most appropriate British Standard as a basis, as has been the case with quality and environmental audits. This is the method used by The Design Council and, in particular, in the audit process developed by Bill Morton as Director of the Design Council for the North of England. This Design Council Design Audit takes the three levels used by BS7000 – corporate level, project level and design activity level – and five topics: objectives, planning, communications, implementation and evaluation. Using methodologies arising from other measurement activities such as job assessment, questions are developed for each level and topic, with answers scored on a scale of *a* to *e*, where *a* represents a clearly unacceptable situation and *e* is the ideal; *c* is usually the minimum acceptable standard of achievement (Table 6.4). The audit process entails a trained professional carrying out an audit throughout a company using the audit questionnaire. The final audit report includes statements relevant to each question and scale with accompanying comments from the auditor. This tool aims to enable the company to identify key issues, and the most important variables in the standards of managing product design at every level.

Table 6.4 – Sample questions used in the Design Council audit based on BS7000

Corporate level management

Topic	Question	Response	Comments
Objectives	Are the company's objectives clear?	a b c d e	

a No objectives exist other than to "stay in business" by any means available. Senior offices give conflicting interpretations of objectives

b The chief executive gives a coherent but questionable oral description of Company objectives. Other senior officials do not confirm these objectives. There are indications that objectives may change unnecessarily according to circumstances.

c The chief executive gives a clear description of Company objectives which defines the market position and corporate identity that are sought and the "business that the company is in". Reference is made, as appropriate, to industry leadership benchmarks.

d As (c) with the addition that all senior staff officers understand and accept these objectives and can make sensible interpretations of them within their own areas of responsibility.

e As (d) but the quality and clarity of the objectives indicates notable leadership and unity of purpose.

Project management

Topic	Question	Response	Comments
Project plans	Do all the designers involved in any project know for what and to whom they report and how they should relate to other functions within the organisation?	a b c d e	

a Designers know to whom they report organisationally. There is no functional reporting.

b As (a) but a particular manager has clear project responsibility and designers communicate with him as appropriate on project matters.

c As (b) but designers have clearly defined reporting links to project managers and to other functions (e.g. production) as appropriate, and participate in multi-disciplinary teams.

d As (c) but designers have a clear understanding of how their work bears on the roles of other functions and can therefore take intelligent actions to assist other functions to achieve Company objectives.

e As (d) but designers' understanding of other functions is sufficient to permit designers to play a full and constructive role in new management techniques, e.g. simultaneous engineering. There is evidence of matrix management.

The design team

Topic	Question	Response	Comments
Plans	Are budgets raised?	a b c d e	

a The design function is regarded as an overhead of some other function and does not have a budget.

b A budget is imposed on the design function.

c A budget, including a separate budget for capital equipment, is raised in collaboration with the design manager.

d As (c) but there is a recognised budget planning cycle.

e As (d) but both budgets are monitored at least quarterly.

The Design Council audit procedure has been developed in the UK, and is one of the first most structured and methodological approaches that has been implemented. It is also being developed by design councils throughout Europe, including Spain, Portugal, France and Ireland, working with five industrial sectors in order to develop a consistent European design audit.

The Irish Trade Board's Design and Product Development Department has also undertaken design audits. Their aim in using "design audits" is to assess the effectiveness of a firm's existing use of design, and to make recommendations for improvement. Consultants are used to do the work and are provided with a Design Audit Workbook (Table 6.5), which outlines how interviews with a firm's senior management should be carried out and what topics should be covered. Checklists are also provided, indicating the subjects to be covered during the audit. In addition, the structure of the design audit report to be provided to the Board of Trade is detailed in four sections: Corporate overview, Design review, Recommendations to the firm, and Cost projections (in terms of implementing recommendations). In comparison to the British Design Council's approach, this is less structured, and, according to the Irish Board of Trade, possibly more flexible. However, it does rely heavily on the skills of the consultants used, who may be more subjective in their findings than they would using more quantitative measures.

Another technique used often by marketing may be equally useful in design audits to analyse the data collected; that is, the use of SWOT (strengths, weaknesses, opportunities and threats). Internal factors are measured in terms of strength and weakness to the organisation, organisational strategies and position relative to competitors, and external factors are measured in terms of opportunities and threats presented by the external environment and the competition. A flow chart by Lusch and Lusch[22] shows the relationship quite succinctly (Figure 6.2).

Table 6.5 – The Irish Board of Trade design audit workbook

Overview of issues covered

Section 1 Corporate Overview

The firm – its turnover, number of employees, etc.

Type of business – general description of products and markets

Distribution – agents, distributors, retailers, etc., the route to market

Business objectives – intentions for new and existing products and markets

Other relevant information

Section 2 Design review – products

Detailed description of products, varieties and qualities

Processes involved in each stage of production, unique processes or technology

Attitude to quality, quality control procedures and quality standards, etc.

In-house or consultant designers used

Method of introduction of new product designs

Design review – packaging

Packaging: types, materials, and in-house paint and machinery used

Suitability for type of product, protection, display, etc.

Manufacturers and suppliers of packaging and labels

Designers used for packaging and other related products

Design review – graphics

Corporate and brand identities, their quality and appropriateness

Brochures and other printed material, both corporate and product

Housestyles and stationery, quality and suitability

Designers used for identities, brochures and other products

Other design information

Comments on firm's design policy, if any

Persons responsible for design projects

Status of design projects in hand, product, packaging and graphic

Design related research undertaken in the past, in hand or planned

Any past assistance for design from State or other agencies, grants etc.

Figure 6.2 – SWOT analysis

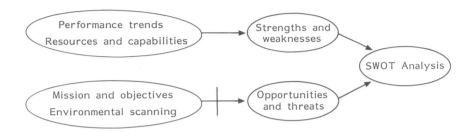

It must be remembered, however, that a SWOT analysis only supplies lists of strengths, weaknesses, opportunities and threats, without any prioritisation or comparison, against strategic goals.

Design audits, as we have seen, can cover a broad spectrum of activity throughout an organisation. However, there is frequently a need to focus on one aspect. There are tools that can aid such analysis. For instance, to audit a product, tools such as Value Analysis have been developed. Value Analysis[23] entails a team representing various functions, following a procedure which involves:

1 Familiarisation with the product components, drawings, manufacturing costs

2 Investigation of the value of each component in terms of its function and contribution to the whole; exploration of new ideas for improvement in component product and cost

3 Exploitation, which involves the development of a number of cost saving modifications

There are other methods used mainly in manufacturing industry to assess a product and aid in the development process, such as Design for Assembly (DFA): although not specifically defined as an audit, they do examine, in a structured and methodological manner, the design of a product. There are a number of such tools of varying complexity, using software and generally known as computer integrated manufacture (CIM). The reader is advised to turn to specialist advice and guidance on the use of such tools.

Design audits can cover the strategic, the management and the skill factors related to the use of design by an organisation. They can also cover the sensory, aesthetic and functional result of design decisions: the products, the brochures and the environment. In addition, by addressing Dumas' assertion of "silent design" (i.e. that design decisions are made by everyone in the organisation), one might decide to audit the level of design awareness/design understanding among the employees, the breadth of design decision making throughout the organisation and the culture of the organisation with regard to its orientation towards the value and support of design. The potential breadth and depth of "design audits" means that, to be effective, they require thorough planning in terms of deciding what to audit, the aims and objectives of the audit, how to audit, who should do the audit and when to audit.

Developing a Design Audit

An audit, like any other examination, is basically a research activity, involving asking questions, searching for answers and testing the reliability of those answers in order to gain new knowledge and move forward. Like research, a methodology needs to be created. Most methodologies for research borrow from other disciplines in order to develop their own specific approach to the activity.

The following discussion is not intended as a prescription for undertaking audits, rather as a *guide* to the issues that need to be considered when planning design audits.

What to audit

As we have described in previous chapters, the term "design" is used in a multitude of ways and relates to all the activities of the organisation, so where does a design audit begin and end? What does it encompass?

There are four levels (Figure 6.3) at which one might address design audits:

1 Environmental issues which impact corporate strategy and design strategy such as legislation, market trends and competitor trends.

2 The corporate culture, the levels of design awareness, including values and vision, the design strategy (implicit or otherwise) and the silent design decision making.

3 The "management" of the design and design projects, and the design processes and design skills available.

4 The physical manifestations of design; the product/service, place and communication in all of the organisation's activities.

Clearly, what one audits is dependent on what is important to the business, and also on the resources available to support an audit programme. Although all levels are important, it may be appropriate to conduct audits at every level incrementally (Figure 6.3).

The aims and objectives

Not only must one define what the audit will cover, but clearly there must be aims and objectives. Again, these must be generated by each organisation, for example, potential aims might be:

- Advise and direct strategic change (e.g. noting competitor activity and market forces might suggest the need for repositioning the whole company through a corporate identity change).

- Improve overall standard of product design as compared to competitors (the design audit, having assessed the products and benchmarked against competitors, can inform an improvement process).

- Develop a design policy manual.

- Monitor policy implementation (having set a policy, the audit periodically monitors the level of policy implementation throughout the organisation).

- Improve design standards (e.g. having set targets for design standards or policy, the audit monitors current position in order to inform and advise on methods for improvement).

Figure 6.3 – The levels an organisational design audit might address

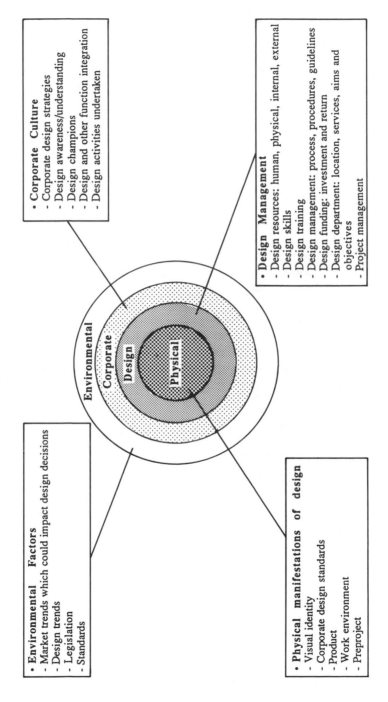

• Corporate Culture
- Corporate design strategies
- Design awareness/understanding
- Design champions
- Design and other function integration
- Design activities undertaken

• Design Management
- Design resources: human, physical, internal, external
- Design skills
- Design training
- Design management: process, procedures, guidelines
- Design funding: investment and return
- Design department: location, services, aims and objectives
- Project management

• Environmental Factors
- Market trends which could impact design decisions
- Design trends
- Legislation
- Standards

• Physical manifestations of design
- Visual identity
- Corporate design standards
- Product
- Work environment
- Preproject

Environmental

Corporate

Design

Physical

The organisation must also know what it will achieve from an audit process. The outcome should be defined not only as general objectives (e.g. understanding the standards of design management within the organisation), but also more specifically (e.g. receiving a report with conclusions and recommendations), and will possibly include the methods for implementing recommendations.

How to audit

How to carry out an audit depends quite obviously on what is being audited. For instance, if one was concerned with product design management, one might choose the Design Council approach, using the BS7000 standard against which to benchmark the activity. If one was concerned with a product, one might use the relevant tools such as Design for Manufacture, or Value Analysis. However, if these are considered too prescriptive for the subject, then a methodology must be used that is appropriate. Methods include developing a checklist of issues (Table 6.6) or questions to ask, questionnaires and interviews, both structured and unstructured. There are also observational techniques, as in the "Journey" method, recording all relevant design activities and measuring them using a predetermined criteria, for instance, of what is acceptable, good or poor.

Table 6.6 – Design audit, example of benchmarking checklist

Issue	Current position	Competitor position		
Corporate identity		1	2	3
(1) Level of implementation				
(2) Level of consistency of application				
(3) Ability to communicate corporate philosophy				
Score: 5, excellent; 4, good; 3, adequate; 2, poor; 1, inadequate				

In all of these methods of collecting the data, it is the criteria used in the analysis which becomes important; for instance, on what level do you assess the design of an ice cream pack?

On reflecting brand value, customer interest, functionality, cost, or on environmental and aesthetic qualities? Similarly, how would you judge a marketing manager's understanding of design, his/her knowledge of the design process, knowledge of the skills involved, or understanding of design terminology. What level of understanding would you accept as satisfactory? It is crucial, therefore, that the method of collecting data is appropriate, and the criteria for evaluation of that data is clear.

Who conducts the audit?

The choice of auditor is crucial to the success of the audit process. Advice currently ranges from choosing someone who has no vested interest in the outcome of the process, through to using someone who not only knows how to carry out an audit but also what questions to ask, to using a design manager with an understanding of the design process. The choice should be made on the basis of the audit subject, the aims and objective and how the audit is to be undertaken.

External auditors (i.e. using an independent specialist) are often appropriate when the aim of the audit is to assess current overall position against competitors (often carried out as a benchmarking activity). Internal auditors can also undertake this activity, but it might be advisable to include an external member to lead the team to ensure objectivity.

Internal audits should be undertaken by a team, perhaps most effectively where the team incorporates all key functions, including design. This enables a broad perspective on the topic to evolve. Internal audits are appropriate for audits at all levels, but particularly in "physical" design audits. Internal audit teams can also be developed to take over from the external team, as was the case with the National Westminster Bank environmental audits described earlier.

In assessing design, there are a number of different stances that can be taken: the philosophical view, the strategic view, the system or tactical view. A frequent criticism of consultancies offering audits is that they will undertake reviews of the system or tactical approach, and then dress it up with philosophy, without being able to identify or influence the deep-rooted ethos within the organisation. It is important, therefore, when using design consultancies to brief them clearly in terms of the aims and objectives of the audit.

When to audit

When to audit again depends on the type of audit. If the audit is one related to strategy and change, this may entail a one-off audit or one that occurs in relation to periodic strategic planning. If the audit is aimed at reviewing policy implementation, annual audits would be appropriate. If the audit is aimed at reviewing design management, it could occur at any time according to management needs. If the audit is related to the design of the "product", pre-project audits should occur before the onset of new product development or whenever a business identifies a weakness in the "product". Post-project audits may be used to evaluate the level of success achieved by a project or a product.

Using the audit findings

The audit is only the beginning of a process; plans must include a process to consider the findings and their implications for the organisation, its resources and its products. Managers must be made responsible for acting upon the recommendations. This may involve anything from empowering individuals or teams with the authority to implement change in any area, to recruiting a design consultancy to make design recommendations for products, communication and environments, or developing programmes of design awareness building throughout the organisation.

Checklist of questions to ask when considering a design audit

- What is the subject of the audit?
- What are the aims and objectives?
- Who is responsible for commissioning the audit?
- Who will undertake the audit?

- What questions will be addressed?

- How is the data to be collected?

- What criteria will be used to determine level of achievement, e.g. poor, good, adequate, or numerical scoring, and what do they mean?

- When will the audit be undertaken?

- What outcome is expected from the process?

- How are the findings to be used or implemented?

- Who is responsible for acting on the recommendations?

- How much will the audit cost?

- How will the audit be evaluated?

Conclusion: a cautionary note

There are basically two types of audit, one which is grounded in some standard or legislation, and one which arises out of a philosophical stance, a social concern or a management theory. There are fundamental differences between these two types of audit. The latter approach considers the issues and then develops criteria against which the organisation/functions are audited, using the results to inform and direct the management. The former approach is chiefly concerned with quantification and standardisation, assuming that once something can be quantified against external predefined standards, it will be forced to improve or to maintain standards. However, this type of audit can create a dependency on procedures and processes and, it is argued, inhibit a creative, innovative or questioning response, which takes an organisation forward. In quality terms, we are addressing the BS5750 quality assurance driven approach, against that of generating a quality ethos, through the philosophy of empowerment and total quality management. In design terms, it is the issue of using a design audit, such as that based on BS7000 to drive improvements in design, or to develop an audit whose criteria is grounded in the organisation's design philosophy and strategy, to inform and direct design management.

Is one method of audit inconsistent with the other? Achieving a level of product design management which is consistent with BS7000 may help to improve the standard of that activity, but introducing a design-centred ethos into an organisation may require a more creative approach to managing people and resources. Therefore, using audits will help organisations to define current practice and benchmark themselves against other organisations, but relying on audits to measure practice, stimulate improvements in practice and for overall change is inappropriate. Organisational change requires more than the use of audits.

Summary

- Audits origins are synonymous with finance and the "independent examination of and expression of opinion on the financial statement of an enterprise", and although there are principles and practices for financial audits, there is still a degree of latitude to be exercised by the auditors.

- Audits are now common in other areas of management, for instance strategic, marketing and innovation audits.

- Some audits occur as a result of legislation or standards; for example, quality audits are derived partly out of the need to meet BS5750. Similarly, environmental audits have arisen due to environmental laws and societal pressure on organisations.

- The use of the term "audit" does refers today to an examination of some aspect of an organisation's affairs, in order to determine current practice and make recommendations for change or improvement.

- As with other types of audit, there is no formula in existence for undertaking design audits. Indeed, neither the scope nor the process has been defined clearly. A number of individuals, bodies and consultancies offer their own approaches, which vary from a mechanistic examination of the cost of using design, to a subjective examination of all organisational activities that involve design.

- The development of a design audit must address what to audit. There are four levels: environmental (legislation, market trends, competitors), corporate culture (design awareness, values and vision), design management, and physical and visible design.

- The aims, objectives and criteria for design audits must be clearly established before the onset of an audit.

- Design audits can be undertaken by external auditors, an internal team or a combination of both. The choice depends on the type of audit, and on whether there is a need to ensure complete objectivity.

- The nature of the audit goes some way towards determining the timing of it. For instance, a pre-project product design audit will obviously be before a new product development begins; a strategic overview would be a one-off audit, undertaken prior to any policy making programme.

- Design audits must be planned and undertaken with a great deal of care and consideration, using a checklist of issues to be considered.

- Design audits do not create change; rather, they measure current practice. It is up to the organisation to implement through good management practice the improvements and changes determined necessary.

References

1 Crosby, B. (1979) *Quality is Free*, McGraw-Hill, New York.
2 The Institute of Chartered Accountants (1985/86) *Auditing and Reporting*, The Institute of Chartered Accountants, London.
3 Wheelen, T.L. and Hunger, J.D. (1990) *Strategic Management*, 3rd edn, Addison-Wesley, Reading, Massachusetts.
4 Johnson, G. and Scholes, K. (1989) *Exploring Corporate Strategy: Text and Cases*, Prentice Hall, Hemel Hempstead.
5 Department of Trade and Industry (1993) *Managing in the '90s, Innovation – Your Move: Self Assessment Guide and Workbook*, DTI, London.
6 Majoro, S. (1991) *The Creative Marketer*, Butterworth Heinemann, Oxford.

7 Stern, Gary M. (1992) Sailing to Europe: Can auditing play a role in the new international quality standards? *International Auditor*, **19**(5) Oct, pp 29–32.

8 Jackson, Susan (1992) What you should know about ISO 9000, *Training*, **29**(5) May 1992, pp 48–52.

9 Crosby, B. (1979) *Quality is Free*, McGraw-Hill, New York.

10 Cornell, D.W. and Apostolou, B. (1991) Auditing for violation of environmental laws, *National Public Accountant*, **36**(7), Jul pp16–20.

11 Tusa, W. (1990) Developing an environmental audit program, *Risk Management*, **37**(8) Aug pp 24–29.

12 National Westminster Bank (1993) *Environment Report*, The Environmental Management Unit, London, July.

13 Shere, M. and Kent, D. (1983) *Auditing and Accountability*, Pitman, London.

14 Shere, M. and Kent, D. (1983) *Auditing and Accountability*, Pitman, London.

15 Olins, W. (1985) The mysteries of design management revealed, *Journal of the Royal Society of Arts*, January, pp 103–114.

16 The Design Council (1992) *Design and Business Performance: A Chief Executive's Handbook*, Department of Trade and Industry, London.

17 Kotler, P. and Rath, G.A. (1990) Design: A powerful but neglected strategic tool, *Journal of Business Strategy*, **5**(2).

18 Oakley, M. (1990) Assembling and managing a design team, in Oakley, M. (ed.) *Design Management: A Handbook of Issues and Methods*, Basil Blackwell, Oxford.

19 CNAA (1984) *Managing Design: An Initiative in Management Education*, CNAA, London.

20 Topalian, A. (1983) *Summary Notes on Corporate Design Audits*, Alto Design Management.

21 Borja de Mozota, Brigitte (1990) Design as a strategic management tool, in Oakley, M. (ed.) *Design Management: A Handbook of Issues and Methods*, Basil Blackwell, Oxford.

22 Lusch, R.F. and Lusch, V.N. (1987) *Principles of Marketing*, Kent Publishing.

23 Oakley, M. (1979) How to analyse value, *Management Today*, November, 171, 176, 180.

Design Management:
7 setting the agenda

"Design is a significant, potentially powerful management resource, susceptible like every other management resource to intelligent direction and control."

Wally Olins[1]

"A strategy is a pattern or plan that integrates an organisation's major goals, policies and action sequences into a cohesive whole. Policies are rules or guidelines that express the limits within which action should occur."

James Quinn[2]

"Good design management is perfect orchestration."

John Thackara[3]

A Matrix for Managing Design: Identifying Who's Involved

The preceding chapters have considered what design is; its value; strategic approaches to the use of design; design's relationship to other organisational functions and processes; and auditing design. We have tried to indicate both the breadth and depth of design in its contribution to society and more particularly to industry. It follows, then, that there are a number of ways of addressing the management of design, for example from a government policy making, a social and environmental, a design profession and educational or an organisational point of view. All four areas are valid. However, the aim of this book in the first instance is to raise management awareness, and to offer an agenda for design. This chapter will therefore concentrate on the issues related to managing design in organisations.

Chapter Map

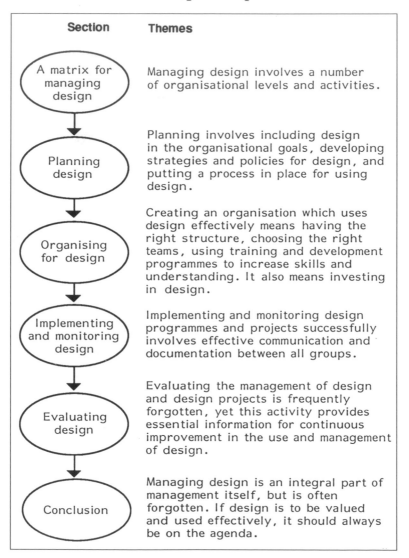

Section	Themes
A matrix for managing design	Managing design involves a number of organisational levels and activities.
Planning design	Planning involves including design in the organisational goals, developing strategies and policies for design, and putting a process in place for using design.
Organising for design	Creating an organisation which uses design effectively means having the right structure, choosing the right teams, using training and development programmes to increase skills and understanding. It also means investing in design.
Implementing and monitoring design	Implementing and monitoring design programmes and projects successfully involves effective communication and documentation between all groups.
Evaluating design	Evaluating the management of design and design projects is frequently forgotten, yet this activity provides essential information for continuous improvement in the use and management of design.
Conclusion	Managing design is an integral part of management itself, but is often forgotten. If design is to be valued and used effectively, it should always be on the agenda.

If you care to search for it, there is a plethora of disparate information on design management in various texts and journals, from all perspectives: from the doyens of the design profession; from the "enlightened" chief executives; from the rare breed of design managers and directors in industry; from public bodies such as the UK Department of Trade and Industry (DTI) and the Design Council; and from the small group of design management researchers and academics in various disciplines such as management, marketing, engineering, innovation and technology. Dumas and Mintzberg take a holistic view, where design is an intrinsic part of all aspects of an organisation, managing design through infusion[4]:

"'Infusion' – the permeation of design throughout the organisation. Infusion is informal; the ultimate intention is to have everyone concerned with design. Managers whose responsibilities touch design do not merely accept it but become part of it. Design thus becomes a way of life in the organisation."

Alternatively, Topalian's[5] view of the organisation consists of managing all aspects of design on two levels, the corporate level and the project level (Table 7.1) Another, more prescriptive, view is the *British Standard 7000, Guide to Managing Product Design*. This provides guidelines on managing product design at three levels, corporate, project and design activity level. There are also many prescriptive guides to managing projects, which are valuable in highlighting best practice and the pitfalls of project management.

As this book has indicated, design touches everyone and everything inside and outside an organisation. It is the Board and top management who set the strategic/policy direction and monitor it. It is middle/business/functional managers who contribute to policy making and manage and monitor implementation. And it is the third level, of operational managers/specialists who implement policy, while simultaneous communication passes between each group. While the external environment is a key driver for all decision making, and although the levels will vary depending on the size and structure of the organisation,

Table 7.1 – What design management encompasses: The key issues by Alan Topalian

The lack of a consensus on what design management encompasses remains a critical obstacle to establishing its credibility as a rigorous business discipline. Attempts to define the discipline in a couple of sentences are futile. Yet it is possible to "map out" the key issues that should be taken into account in professional practice as follows:

At corporate level
- Contribution of design skills to corporate profitability
- Design responsibility and leadership
- Corporate design policy and strategy formulation
- Positioning and "visibility" of design
- Degree of centralisation and integration of design
- Auditing corporate design and design management practices
- Devising and introducing corporate design management systems
- Establishing and maintaining corporate design standards
- Funding of design activities
- Legal dimension of design
- "Green" dimensions of design
- Design awareness and design management skills development programmes
- Design and the manifestation of corporate identity
- Evaluation of the contribution and impact of design

At the project level
- The nature of the design process and different types of design project
- Formulation of design project proposals and the briefing process
- Selection of design specialists
- Composition and management of "augmented" design project teams
- Planning and administering design projects
- Costing design work and drawing up design project budgets
- Design project documentation and control systems
- Design research and the generation of new ideas for investment in design
- Presentation of design recommendations
- Implementation and long-term survival of design solutions
- Evaluation of design projects

Clearly, there is considerable common ground between the management of design and that of other business disciplines. Nevertheless, success with design and the development of a distinctive competence in managing design result from an enlightened handling of the detailed differences.

Reproduced by permission of Alan Topalian. Best practice benchmarking of design management practices and performance: *The Alto Design Management Workbook*, Alto 1994.

decisions must be made, whether by one manager or several. We should look, therefore, at the management of design from each perspective.

The Design Agenda

Figure 7.1 – A design management matrix of issues to address

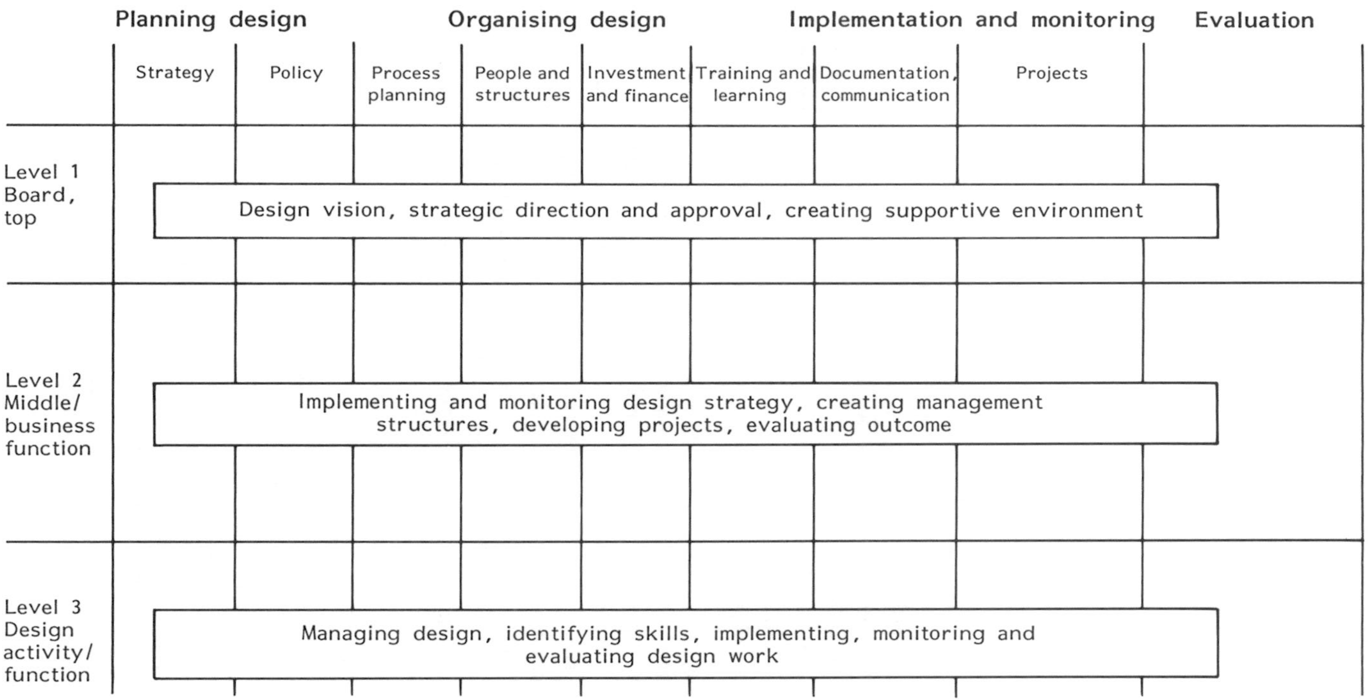

	Planning design			Organising design			Implementation and monitoring		Evaluation
	Strategy	Policy	Process planning	People and structures	Investment and finance	Training and learning	Documentation, communication	Projects	
Level 1 Board, top	Design vision, strategic direction and approval, creating supportive environment								
Level 2 Middle/ business function	Implementing and monitoring design strategy, creating management structures, developing projects, evaluating outcome								
Level 3 Design activity/ function	Managing design, identifying skills, implementing, monitoring and evaluating design work								

Management of design includes planning, organisation, implementation, monitoring and evaluation. A design management matrix (Figure 7.1) has been created, based on the levels of management and the actions they need to take. This matrix gives us the basis upon which to address the key issues involved in the management of design by an organisation. The remainder of this chapter will set out an agenda for each level of management decision making, based on the key aspects of the management process, as summarised in Figure 7.2.

Figure 7.2 – Key aspects of the management process

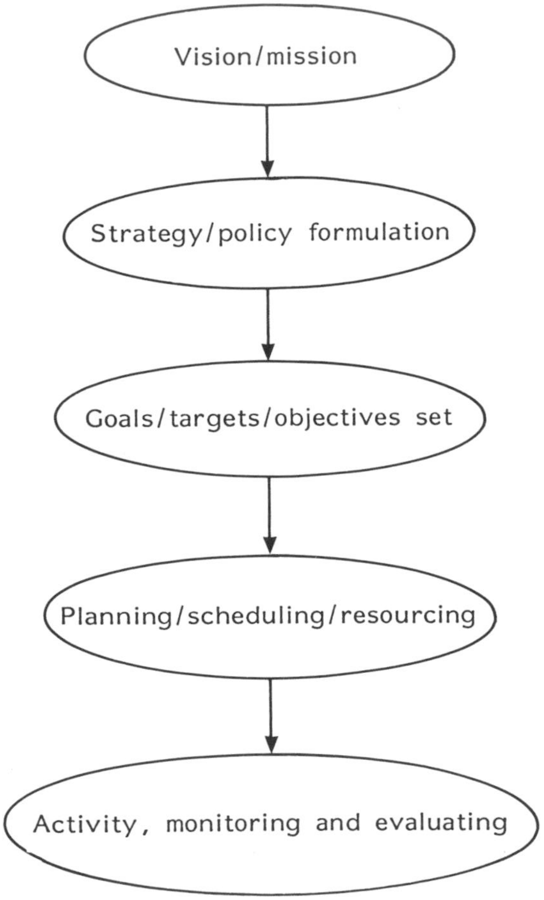

Planning Design

Strategy

Level 1: Board/Top Management Responsibilities

- Define corporate strategic objectives, including corporate design objectives
- Approve design strategy linked to marketing strategy
- Ensure design strategy covers products, communications and environment

As discussed in Chapter 4, design must be valued as a strategic resource. When setting the overall vision, senior managers must consider future trends in customer needs, design standards and design opportunities. They must use the various sources of data, such as market research, design consultants and competitor analysis, to determine their position. For example, in communicating the Body Shop strategic vision, "We will be the most honest cosmetic company", Anita Roddick also has to translate that into a strategy for design, in terms of corporate identity programme, product presentation, labelling and container design, and the working environment for employees.

A design strategy should set out how the company is going to use design to achieve overall corporate objectives. Business strategies as defined in a mission statement frequently contain a degree of generality, to enable the statement to perform an integrating function among the various stakeholders over a period of time. Design strategies should be detailed enough to complement the marketing strategy. Companies have been criticised for a lack of marketing expertise or a lack of marketing vision, or there has been what Lorenz[6] calls a "misalliance between marketing and design". Design is often treated as a *servant* of marketing rather than a partner, or has to contribute the vision lacking in marketing. Marketing must set their vision and goals for the companies as a whole, and for particular brands or product ranges. A design strategy must work to express that vision through the design of products, the corporate identity, corporate brochures, advertising, graphic symbols and the physical corporate environment itself (offices, buildings etc.). It is senior management's responsibility to set the overall corporate vision and strategy and to ensure that the design strategy is consistent with it. Marks and Spencer's mission and objectives provide an example of the design implications of setting out such a strategy. The mission statement reads as follows:[7]

"Our aim is to create an international retailing business, meeting local needs but integrated in such a way as to allow expertise and experience to be shared throughout the Group. We are building on the traditional strengths of Marks and Spencer: a reputation for high quality and good value, a first class procurement base, an excellent team of people and highly professional management."

Marks and Spencer's principal objectives are:[8]

1   To offer our customers a selective range of *high quality well designed and attractive merchandise* at reasonable prices

2   To *encourage our suppliers* to use the most modern and efficient techniques of production and quality control dictated by the latest discoveries in science and technology

3   With co-operation of our suppliers, to ensure the highest standards of quality control

4   To plan the expansion of our stores for the better display of a widening range of goods for the *convenience of our customers*

5   To *simplify operating procedures* so that our business is carried on in the most efficient manner

6   To foster good human relations with customers, suppliers and staff

Design relates to each one of these objectives, for instance:

1   High quality well designed garment and merchandise design

2   Design for manufacture in terms of designing for new technology using current R&D expertise

3   Designing-in quality

4   Store and interior design aimed at displaying merchandise effectively and for the convenience of the customer

5   Effective communications and information systems design for efficient operating procedures

6   Excellence in communications, corporate identity with customers, suppliers and staff

This example illustrates well the relationship that must be made between corporate vision and objectives and a design strategy. Following such a strategic plan, corporate objectives are necessary.

Strategy

Level 2: Middle/Functional Management Responsibilities

- Use design audits to inform strategy
- Define design strategy to achieve corporate design objectives
- Co-ordinate detailed strategy with marketing and other functions

Design management at this stage involves informing the corporate strategy from a design perspective, by undertaking *design audits*. It also involves setting design objectives for corporate communications, products and environments, having them approved by senior management, then developing strategies for achieving those objectives.

The examples in Table 7.2 illustrate how such objectives and strategies for communications, products and environments may be developed.

Table 7.2 – Development of objectives and strategies for communications, products and environments

Area	Design objectives	Design strategies
Corporate Communications	To communicate clearly and simply to all our stakeholders the values held in our corporate mission statement.	To develop a corporate identity that effectively communicates the corporate values. To communicate use and implementation of the corporate identity through a corporate design manual and training workshops.
Product design	To reflect corporate values in the design of our products. To develop a consistent "design" across the product range. To define clearly through design, the attributes of each brand.	Design products that are innovative, easy to use and maintain and which are reliable and durable. Develop a design semantic that should form the basis of the complete range of a product group. Use brand attributes as defined by marketing, as a significant element of the design brief.
Environment design	To ensure the all corporate environments reflect corporate values. To ensure all retail environments are designed to enhance employee and customer satisfaction and comfort.	Maintain regular audits of corporate environments. Develop standards for levels of work comfort, lighting, space, fitting and furniture. Develop design standards for requistion of furniture and fittings. Use consumer and employee research finding to aid the design of retail environments. Use only approved contractors and suppliers who will maintain standards of quality and consistency of design.

These are only a few suggestions of how a design objective may translate into a design strategy. Design does not, however, work in isolation. We have seen in Chapter 5 that the link between marketing and design is essential, and it is at this level of management decision making that design must interface with marketing and other functions to develop detailed design strategies, to achieve the design, marketing and overall corporate objectives.

Strategy

Level 3: Design Activity Management/Design Function Responsibilities

- Maintain awareness of design trends
- Contribute to design objectives and strategy

Designers and design managers, at the design activity level, can contribute to strategy by understanding current design trends, by an awareness of competitor design trends and by understanding the design needs of customers and consumers. This knowledge needs to be collected and communicated to other levels, via presentations and reports. This will enable the development of design objectives and strategies that are relevant and flexible, responding to changes in the market place and in design trends.

Policy

Level 1: Board/Top Management Responsibilities

- Define the meaning of design within the organisation
- Approve policies standards or guidelines on design and also on related factors such as quality, legal and environmental issues
- Approve financial systems and cost controls related to design

It is the responsibility of senior management to ensure that policies are developed on design and related issues, to enable employees to plan strategy implementation in the light of that corporate policy. It is important to remember that these policies must capture beliefs already held[9], or not transgress too far away from corporate philosophy. Policies alone, like mission statements, will not drive people into action; they represent boundaries within which employees can operate.

It is often appropriate in policy statements to indicate what the company means by design and how it affects the operation of the company, as well as the company's own philosophy towards design, across its many activities. Bang and Olufsen, the Danish electronics manufacturer, sets out such policy statements as follows: [Jørgen Palshøj (1990) Design management at Bang and Olufsen in Oakley, M., *Design Management – A Handbook of Issues and Methods*, Basil Blackwell, Oxford.]

"Authenticity

Faithful reproduction, the best sound or picture reproduction is that which comes closest to reality – as experienced by the human being and not by a measuring instrument.

Autovisuality (Harmony)

A mutual balance between functions, mode of operation and materials used. Design is a language, a communication between those who create the products and those who use them.

Credibility

In products, dealing and action. Product specifications are minimum data.

Domesticity (Relevance)

Technology is for the benefit of people – not the reverse.

Essentiality (Topicality)

Electronic products have no form given by nature. Design must be based upon a respect for man–machine relations. Simplicity in operation. Design is an expression of the time in which we live, not a passing fashion.

Selectivity

Bang and Olufsen is the alternative to mass production.

Inventiveness

As a small company we cannot carry through basic research in the electronic area, but we can implement the newest technology with creativity and inventiveness."

In addition to such design policy statements, senior management must approve design standards on a range of issues, including quality, legal and environmental issues. Much criticism has been made of those companies attempting to capitalise on green issues. Once environmental design policies have been established, senior management must agree them, but must also understand the implications, such as the costs. Indeed, determining design expenditure and implementing cost controls is another important issue for senior management to address. Frequently design expenditure is subsumed under marketing and advertising, R&D or production budgets. However, this is not conducive to understanding the costs of design, nor does it further our understanding of the value and contribution of design to company performance. If design costs are to be considered in the same way as other function budgets, financial systems must, similarly, apply, to allocate resources and monitor investment.

Policy

Level 2: Middle/Functional Management Responsibilities

- Define design policy

- Define design performance standards

- Define quality, legal and environmental standards relating to design (including materials, safety, service and design)

- Ensure consistency of policy across products, communications and environments

All managers at this level must work together to develop a design policy. It is usually appropriate that function leaders contribute to the definition of the policy, in conjunction with an experienced design manager. The involvement of quality, legal and environmental experts may also be required. In this way, the policy will be *owned* by the whole organisation rather than just the design function. The policies should be expressed as corporate guidelines to cover products, communications and environments. However, where possible they should not become so cumbersome and controlling as to inhibit rather than encourage use.

Policy

Level 3: Design Activity Management/Design Function Responsibilities

• Inform policy and define design specifics, e.g. colours, shapes, sizes, corporate identity

The design function contributes to policy development by interpreting corporate philosophy in design terms. The knowledge and experience of design held by such personnel should be tapped by higher levels to ensure relevance and feasibility of the policies being developed. For instance, a policy that states that all material used in manufacture must be environmentally friendly has be translated into more specific guidelines, taking into account the cost implications, the mission and values of the company, and the demands of the market-place. For example, simply designing literature to be printed on a coarse, grainy, slightly yellow recycled paper to a particular cost may not project the corporate values of high quality and sophistication. The design function will need to translate policies into specifications/standards, e.g. the type of acceptable materials or processes to be used in relation to corporate strategy.

Programmes and procedures

Planning programmes or procedures is the stage where the strategy and policies are translated into activities to be undertaken over a predefined time-scale. Planning consists, in this instance, of taking the overall goals and strategies and developing sub-goals and sub-strategies,[10] which can be achieved by carrying out a discrete set of activities, to which resource implications can be attached. This planning activity is iterative, and becomes more detailed and precise the closer to the activity level it gets. Plans, although important, should always remain flexible to allow for change. Changes in resources, changes in management and changes in the market-place may all impact even the most well prepared plans. Quinn[11] suggests that few, if any, major innovations result from highly structured planning processes; indeed, that innovations are best managed as incremental, goal-orientated and interactive learning processes, and not just paper plans. However, much of Quinn's work is related to smaller organisations; it is more difficult to rely on "chaos" creating innovation in larger companies, and it takes a considerable effort to change cultures. The key to successful process planning, identified in other studies,[12] is communication: excellent communications is the key to implementing plans.

Programmes and procedures

Level 1: Board/Top Management Responsibilities

- Define programmes
- Define targets

Senior management are responsible for providing direction, in terms of the programmes to be followed, in order to achieve strategic goals. For example, in order to visualise and communicate corporate objectives, a *corporate identity audit* may be required, followed by a corporate identity programme or a corporate identity revision; in order to produce new products or services to enter a new market, a new product development programme needs to be established.

Senior management are responsible for determining the overall programmes and for setting targets for successful completion of the programmes, such as the deadlines, required return on investment or market share. At this stage, the development of such plans is relevant to all functions, including the design function, which will be able to define contribution to programmes and targets.

Programmes and procedures

Level 2: Middle/Functional Management Responsibilities

- Set preferred programme/project procedures
- Define project proposal contents
- Commission and undertake audits

The programmes that have been derived from corporate strategy can vary in size, depending on the size and nature of the organisation, from an initiative to develop a series of related products and services over a number of years, to sequential programmes of environmental and building work, to a number of small new product development projects. Middle/functional managers are responsible not only for defining the particular programmes or projects, but also for the establishment of a planning procedure in the first instance.

Project procedures vary from a simple one-page guide, to a more complex project lifecycle manual, depending on the nature and size of the company and the project stages necessary. A project procedure should clarify roles, responsibilities, project objectives and stages/phases for approval. For instance, all projects will need a business proposal, which includes a marketing plan, design plan and production plan, the contents of which require definition.

In addition, the design manager should, in conjunction with other function managers, establish guidelines for the development and content of the design brief and project proposals. In order to improve the project development process it may be necessary for managers at this level to commission and possibly undertake audits of the design management process, and also of the product, communication or environmental design process.

Programmes and procedures

*Level 3: Design Activity Management/Design Function
Responsibilities*

- Organise office management
- Organise design job management and progress
- Undertake audits

At the design activity or operational level, the design manager is responsible for setting up all procedures related to management and control of design jobs, whether they are to be undertaken in-house or out-sourced. This should include:

1   Criteria for the selection of designers.
2   Requirements for each stage of the design job, e.g. briefs, project plans, models, visuals, reports etc.
3   Stages of the design projects and points at which they are to be reviewed, including level of review and personnel to be involved.
4   The criteria for decisions to be taken in the review.
5   The criteria for the choice of suppliers and types of contract.
6   The methods used for ordering, recording and monitoring of work.

These procedures, once established, must be communicated to all involved, and methods established for documenting the design activity. The design managers at this operational level should also undertake design skill and process audits, and specific product, communication and environmental audits to inform not only their own work but the overall development of goals, strategies and plans.

Organising for Design

Much management research into corporate success emphasises the importance of achieving the right corporate climate, culture and structure. This is important not only for design but also for the success and well-being of all work undertaken within the organisation.

The culture[13] of an organisation is dependent on a number of factors, including the size, history and tradition, technology, environment, leadership and management style. Often the most obvious display of culture is the organisational structure and the management style that operates within that structure. In addition, the function that has the controlling influence can significantly affect the culture. For example, an organisation dominated by the finance function might tend to be formal, analytical and mechanistic.

A number of years ago, researchers[14] found that mechanistic (very formal, hierarchical, bureaucratic and inflexible) systems work satisfactory only where conditions are stable (e.g. flow production departments), or in other situations where close control of highly specialised work is essential. Mechanistic forms of organisation do not prove as satisfactory when applied to innovative development projects, which need flexibility. Here, organic structures are much more likely to be successful. Typical features of organic systems have been defined by Bennett et al.,[15] where:

1   The unifying theme is the "common task", each individual contributes special knowledge and skills, and tasks are constantly refined as the total situation changes.

2   Hierarchy does not predominate, problems are tackled on a team basis rather than being referred up or down the line.

3   There is flexibility, jobs are not rigidly or precisely defined.

4   Control is through the "common" goal, rather than by institutions, rules and regulations.

5   Expertise and knowledge are located throughout the organisation, not just at the top.

6   Communications consist of information and advice rather than instructions and decisions.

Peters and Waterman[16] argue that a characteristic of the best performing organisations is that they are simultaneously able to retain central control while maximising the degree of flexibility, innovation and control at lower levels. These organisations have simultaneous loose–tight properties of structure and control. This is less related to structure than to management style.

Successful innovation and design have been linked repeatedly to a creative and design sympathetic climate, which involves informal and lateral interaction, and communications between design and all other functions. Creating this is relatively simple for a smaller company; a larger one may be more cumbersome and bureaucratic in its operation and will require considerable change. When organising for design, senior managers must audit their organisation to determine how receptive it is to the value of and use of design, and develop strategies for changing the structure and culture where necessary.

Structure is related to the strategy, and, as Johnson and Scholes[17] point out, different structures are appropriate for different strategies. Structures that encourage organic management style, teamwork and frequent communication between design and all other functions and levels have been identified as the best for supporting and maximising the use of design.

People, structures, culture and climate

Level 1: Board/Top Management Responsibilities

- Create innovation and design-supportive structure and climate
- Choose design advisors, external consultants, design directors
- Set clear hierarchy of design responsibility

The first responsibility of senior management is to support and value the contribution design makes to the organisation's activities, and to communicate this philosophy throughout. One visible sign of support for design is the clear definition of the function of design, and the appointment of a director responsible for design. According to Topalian,[18] to be responsible for design means being accountable for all design work undertaken by or on behalf of the company. It is the design director, along with the chief executive and other senior level managers, who provides the leadership and backs the quality of the designs produced. It is the design director who must ensure that design strategy and policies are translated into reality throughout the organisation, and that the Board is fully aware of the breadth of design activity within the organisation. Topalian recommends that a non-executive director be appointed from the design profession to guide decision making. This can be impractical for small organisations. However, there should be senior level responsibility for all aspects of design in the organisation.

A first task in terms of developing a structure which promotes effective design management and encourages innovation involves assessing the current structure, management style and culture, to determine to what degree it may need to change. In terms of structure and management style, for instance, Quinn points out that, "if there are five layers between the designers and the decision makers, you need five 'yesses' to go forward but one 'no' will stop you.[19] Also, it is important to avoid what Quinn calls the tyranny of paper plans. There is, however, no single successful approach; the most common denominators in successful companies are setting goals, selecting the right people, and establishing a few critical limits and decision points.[20]

To ensure that design is not a subdivision of marketing or production or any other function, but contributes equally with these functions, design must be given its own identity under the leadership of the design director. However, this does not mean that departmentalism and hierarchical structures should necessarily evolve from that. Pilditch[21] makes a convincing case for the "new organisation which is less hierarchical and much flatter, where communications whiz across functions. Ideas flow from side to side at least as much as up and down. People work in teams. Where all the departments that are necessary work together all the time". Working in groups and allowing individual autonomy and entrepreneurship, bringing functions together – these have all been identified as success factors in both product and organisation achievement. Senior managers have to address their own structure and develop a structure and climate that uses such techniques in order to achieve value from the use of design.

Olins,[22] in his paper to the Royal Society of Arts, "Mysteries of design management revealed", made his suggestion for a design management structure:

1   On the Board there has to be a responsible director – a champion for design.

2   There must be overt and continuing support from the rest of the Board.

3   A person or persons must be responsible for design in middle management, and must operate at the centre and throughout the various units.

4   There should be a series of task forces to make it work.

5   There should be some kind of codification or manual.

6   There should be a rolling programme which can be checked, monitored, modified and, where appropriate, amended.

7   There must be a commitment to all of these things by way of financial resource, which must of course, be properly accountable.

In addition to structuring design management in such a manner, there should be recognition of effort, by introducing reward systems for achieving goals. This will aid an organisational climate and particularly encourage the creative aspects of designers.

To establish design directions and inform policy, mechanisms such as *design advisory panels* can be introduced. These may be composed of designers alongside other functions and could also include external design advisors. Boots, the large pharmaceutical company,[23] operates a Design Policy Group, a fortnightly forum attended by Boot's directors responsible for merchandise and marketing together with an external design consultant. The formation of this group acted as a catalyst for a radical shift in design management thinking within the company. The group was used to sanction concepts "from a technical point of view and also from the point of view of whether it met the overall vision of where they wanted the business to go". Such a design advisory panel should not be used to confine design, but to ensure that it is consistent with the strategic goals, and to provide design vision and leadership.

Finally, once the design leadership is determined through design directors and advisory panels, a clear hierarchy of design responsibility must be in place. Topalian[24] suggests that:

"Success requires that executive responsibility for design is assigned formally to a senior manager who is given adequate access to and backing by the Board. Day-to-day responsibility for individual projects should be assigned at appropriate levels in the management hierarchy to ensure sufficient authority without wasting senior management time. All those with responsibility for design should have that fact fleshed out in their job descriptions – not merely stated – and the substance of this responsibility reviewed regularly."

The location of design within the organisation must also be addressed by senior management. Many alternatives can be examined, and a number of large organisations (e.g. Toshiba, Philips, Sony) have considered alternatives for the location of design within the corporate structure (Figure 7.3). It appears that a key issue in deciding the location of design is the ability of design to cross functions, and to gain direct access to key decision makers i.e. the chief executive or Board.

It is clear then, that the Board or top management level responsibility must be to ensure that a supportive structure and culture is in place, and that the right people are chosen to promote and manage design inside and outside the organisation. However, this must be achieved with the minimum bureaucracy and constraints, to allow lateral and vertical communication and co-operation among all functions.

Figure 7.3 – Examples of structures for design
(reproduced with permission)

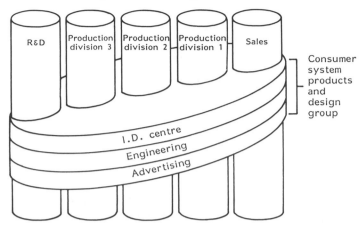

Source: Sony ID centre in Pilditch, J. *Winning Ways* (1987).
Design at the centre and close to the board: how it has evolved at Toshiba.

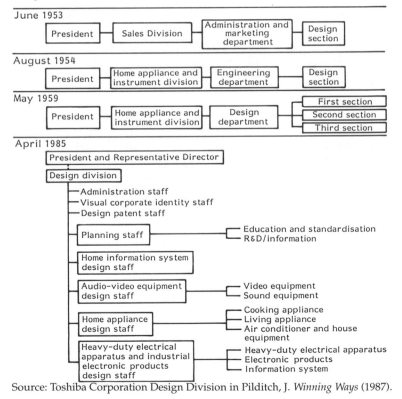

Source: Toshiba Corporation Design Division in Pilditch, J. *Winning Ways* (1987).

People, structures, culture and climate

Level 2: Middle/Functional Management Responsibilities

- Create cross-functional teams
- Create a design manager role
- Provide resources for designers

At this level, the responsibility is to ensure that the functional barriers are broken, to create teams that will work together effectively and towards a common purpose. For example, teams on a new product development project might involve functions from marketing, R&D, design and manufacturing; on corporate identity development and implementation, teams from marketing, internal and external design and operation managers might be involved. Colin Clipson[25] found, in his study of design in United States companies, that all the important decisions are made at the point of overlap between one function and another. Often smaller companies find it easier to form teams, to maintain the momentum and co-operation needed to pursue a project, and also to access the Board or executive decision making. Larger organisations also form teams, but all too often such teams become submerged in the depths of hierarchy and bureaucracy, and progress become unreasonably slow. Often in such situations the only way a project leader progresses is by escalation (i.e. getting access to a senior decision maker). Many larger organisations have attempted to avoid this by introducing techniques such as "skunk works", that is, small teams working very quickly and in close conjunction with the Board or chief executives.

Team formulation and the choice of a project leader is an important management skill, which has been addressed by Tjosvold[26] and others. All contributors to a team are important; however, the design contribution has traditionally been left out or not considered early enough. The team leader should understand the importance of design to any project and ensure the inclusion of appropriate expertise, that is, a design manager or designer from the design function, who also understands the contribution that design, in

---

collaboration with the other functions, is making to the activity being undertaken.

Walton[27] highlights, in a review of design teams, critical issues in their creation:

- **Structure/designing the design team:** simply bringing people with a variety of skills to work together does little to assure the success of the design team. On the one hand, it is important that communication is open, with numerous opportunities for informal exchange, and that hierarchy and bureaucratic procedures are minimised. At the same time, leadership, organisation and a sense of people's roles and expertise are critical. Fujimoto[28] found in the international automobile industry that the "designer as integrator" served as a cross-functional co-ordinator with responsibilities that included acting as a champion and advocate, and being an articulate liaison between disciplines ranging from engineering and production to marketing and sales. Keeley[29] suggests that is important to integrate the working styles of the various functions. For instance, designers may have a high tolerance for ambiguity while marketers have none; designers tend to work more quickly towards a deadline, while marketing tend to prefer a routine procedure.

- **Focus/identify the design problem:** given the interdisciplinary and democratic nature of teams, Walton suggests that there may be a tendency for the need to reach consensus or on the other hand failure to reach consensus, given the group's diversity. He suggests that failure to identify the focus clearly can lead to difficulty later in that members find they are not moving in a similar direction.

- **Learn a common language:** again, Walton suggests that in addition to a common focus the team must develop a common language: "to a marketing manager, a quality design may mean a distinctive package; to a mechanical engineer it may signify ease of fabrication; and to an industrial design it may translate into ease of use". Teams must develop a common language by defining these ambiguous terms. They must also understand the process each member uses to undertake their contribution to the work involved.

- **Empower the team:** the team must move away from being a group of individuals looking for their own rewards. Emphasis must be placed on shared responsibility and decision making. An atmosphere of openness and trust must be engendered between the team and those external to the team, i.e. corporate executives, consultants and suppliers.

- **Rotate leadership:** traditionally, one project manager is chosen who champions the project through to the end. However, Texas Instruments[30] have found rotating the leadership according to the stage of the project to be more effective. For instance, in the development of the Learning Path™, "During the first phase, marketing set the pace as the needs and users were identified. Engineering took over when technology was paramount and industrial design was handed the baton as human factors, positioning and packaging became the groups focus". Other studies[31] have identified the overriding characteristic of project organisation in best practice companies as the high status of the project manager: "they have significant spending authority, budget control and approve the membership of the team – key symbols of authority. They also have significant input or conduct performance reviews, thereby motivating the team members to work for the project's success, rather than purely for the achievement of functional goals".

The above advice considers the teams in which design is making a contribution, There is, however, another decision to be made by functional managers, that of using internal or external design teams. Recently there has been a trend towards out-sourcing design work rather than continuing it as an in-house overhead. There are admittedly cost benefits that may be achieved by out-sourcing, and also benefits of choosing the most appropriate design skills for the job, and of maintaining freshness of ideas. However, there may also be a cost, in terms of the designers' lack of understanding of the company and its culture, and the creation of barriers to effective communications. Often there is resistance and some internal resentment related to the use of external consultants, particularly if they are employed to undertake the most innovative and creative aspects of the design work, while other internal designers are left to implement the design or do the minor design servicing work.

When using external design consultants, a design manager must be employed to negotiate and monitor the external consultants' role in any project, carefully directing the external designers' exposure to company culture and knowledge, relative to the needs of the project. For instance, a design group employed to develop a new corporate image may need to be exposed to the entirety of the organisation climate and culture, in order to understand it and reflect the values of the company appropriately through the new identity. However, a company looking for a completely innovative range of packaging may find it more effective to have the external designers work in isolation, to achieve a new and novel approach.

Once the team structure and the design manager, project leaders and design team are in place, this functional level of middle managers must ensure that resources are available, not only for individual projects, in terms of approving overall programme/project costs, but also for the appropriate resources in terms of design facilities and environment to work in. Designers must have access, if necessary, to appropriate equipment (e.g. computers, workshops, cameras etc.), to appropriate specialists in R&D and to external advisors and specialists. If external consultants are involved, they too must have an agreed budget, as well as access to the appropriate personal and facilities within the organisation, to enable them to undertake the work they have been contracted to do.

People, structures, culture and climate

Level 3: Design Activity Management/Design Function Responsibilities

- Ensure the necessary skills are available
- Direct policy for the selection of designers

The design manager at the operational level must ensure that the necessary skills for undertaking design work of any nature are available to the organisation, whether this involves buying it in or developing an in-house design team. It is also important to ensure that where, for instance, external consultants are employed, the design manager responsible for contracting and managing the relationships fully understands the project and can therefore develop appropriate selection and evaluation criteria. For instance, an inexperienced design manager working with a marketing group on the development of packaging, might have a "pet" consultancy he/she enjoys working with. However, that design consultancy may not have the skills (either technical or aesthetic) necessary to interpret correctly that specific packaging brief. This causes relationship and credibility problems for the inexperienced design manager working with senior marketing personal. It can also result in numerous and expensive changes in concept design to get it right.

Choosing the design manager for a team and the necessary design skills, requires at least a checklist of skills, developed by the senior managers under the guidance of a design manager with experience in selection. In the area of product design, an outline checklist already exists in BS7000.[32] Under the heading of "Planning the design resource to meet corporate objectives", it recommends that when planning to provide appropriately trained and qualified staff, design managers should consider the following points:

1   Total number of staff required

2   Category breakdown of the staff requirement

3   Number of staff to be directly employed by the company

4   Number of consultant, freelance or contract staff required

5   Need for new skills to meet planned business

More details, in terms of the practical skills requirements of good designers, are offered by the Open University,[33] particularly the ability to:

- read design trends
- give attention to things
- see prestige through outward products
- have a general catalyst effect
- have a tendency to leaps of innovation, novelty and lateral thinking

- vivid conceptualising, rapid turnover of ideas
- visual modelling, targeting specific problems
- produce detailed mock-ups or prototypes for evaluation
- produce models with increasing precision for costing and so on
- achieve control of craftsmanship, detail and finish

Work undertaken on behalf of NEDO[34] identified a competency cluster for effective designers in the garment and textile industry. Many of the findings could be translated to competencies for other fields of design (Table 7.3).

Table 7.3 – Competency model for designers

"Driving the process" competencies
• Commitment, enthusiasm, self-confidence
• Results orientation
• Team orientation
• High standards*
"Design" competencies
• "Objective" creativity
• Technical
• Colour and conceptual ability*
"Business orientation" competencies
• Organisational, planning, problem solving
• Commercial skills
"Perspective and framework" competencies
• Gathering and using information
• Strategic thinking
• Consumer/customer focus
"Interpersonal" competencies
• Builds relationships
• Influence*
• Presentation skills
• Flexible

* Competencies that discriminate outstanding designers.

NEDO Garment and Textile Sector Group (1993) Best practice in design and development, PE International

This report also recommends that in applying a competency model objective, assessment of individuals against competency factors needs to be undertaken by professionals experienced in such a process, to ensure that individual careers and competencies are not undermined or damaged. Such a programme could be followed by the development of a process of competency enhancement for those designers selected, to improve and update their skills.

Once the necessary skills have been defined, the selection of in-house designers can take place. However, if external design groups are to be used, a policy must also be established for their selection. Some organisations develop a relationship with a selection of consultancies, rotating their use depending on the needs of the project. In this way, the design group becomes familiar with the company strategy and policies, and also with its design management process. Such companies believe that the rotation ensures a degree of freshness in approach to the design problem, without loss of consistency with the overall corporate philosophy.

Other companies engage design consultancies on an "as and when" basis, but there is a danger here, unless a policy for selection is established. For example, choosing a friend of a friend or basing choice of design consultancy on a colleague's recommendation may not always result in success. The designers may not have the appropriate skills or facilities to undertake the particular project. The design skills necessary must be identified; use of a selection service and a selection panel, with presentations and discussion with the targeted design consultants, is advised before proceeding.

Investment and finance

Level 1: Board/Top Management Responsibilities

- Evaluate major design strategy decisions
- Ensure funding is available to implement strategy

When establishing a design strategy, the Board or senior executive must evaluate it in terms of the resources necessary to enable the work to be undertaken. A continuing resource commitment will be required, as such strategic programmes may last for several years.

When calculating the funds necessary, an organisation must make predictions on costs, sales, profits and investment available, not only from the organisation's own resources but also from external bodies, i.e. their ability to raise loans from banks or cash from shareholders. In some industries – for instance, those where the development of a product involves highly complex processes and considerable expense in R&D and design – there is a trend towards forming strategic alliances to pool resources to fund projects. Companies must consider when they are looking for a return on investment, how long they can afford to defer a return, or indeed whether they are looking for a return in the short term, looking instead for an increase in brand awareness or attempting to open up new markets, and expecting a return over a much longer time-scale. Companies do use various funding strategies. In every case the financial goals must be clear.

Therefore, as part of strategic planning, the senior and top level managers must consider the degree of change required, and how this will affect the resource allocation. Johnson and Scholes[35] discuss three approaches:

1 Few changes in overall resources or the deployment of resources, i.e. where few changes are likely to occur with new strategies, resource allocation tends to proceed along largely historical lines. In design terms, this would be a situation where the value of design was established: where it was already part of the "value chain" and would continue to be so in the future.

2 Growth in the overall resource base, i.e. when growth occurs resources can be reallocated, by directing new resources selectively across the organisation. In this situation, design may be used as one of the tools for growth and therefore allocation of new resources would be considered in the light of design strategies and new design programmes, for example, in a new range of products, a new chain of outlets needing refurbishment, or in a corporate identity revision.

3   Allocating resources in static or declining situations, i.e. reallocation of resources must occur to maintain areas or support new developments. In such situations, funding an in-house design facility may not be economical. However, investment in selective design projects may help growth. Resources might then be reallocated to selected programmes and the design work out-sourced to reduce costs.

Once design is resourced, the second tier of management can allocate specific budgets to functions and project teams. Senior executives should expect from their managers an ability to provide design estimates, to enable the funding to be adequately planned and resourced.

Investment and finance

Level 2: Middle/Functional Management Responsibilities

- Define programme budgets
- Ensure approved list of designers and suppliers
- Provide design function with required resources to allow implementation of programme

This level of management provides the costing to the Board to enable them to develop a funding policy. They must also define the budgets for the programmes and projects, providing the design function with the resources to enable the design work to be undertaken. This is a crucial role in terms of controlling costs, but also in enabling design innovation and the implementation of strategy.

In addition, all functions must work together to consider the resource and budgeting implications for the entire project and programmes, i.e. the relationships between functions, the shared resources and the implications of actions on each other. For example, Burton and Next[36] were successful during the 1980s through a strategy of product/market differentiation, which was sustained by careful resource planning through the value chain. The procurement of merchandise, the hiring of shop staff, and the shop design and layout were as important as the product range, pricing and promotion strategies.

Many texts on management and strategy, when referring to resource allocation and budgeting, fail to mention specifically resource allocation to design. Design is often subsumed under the marketing or the R&D function. If an organisation is to use design to its full potential, it must see it as a discrete element, yet part of the chain.

Budgeting methodology depends on the conventions of the organisation. Managers will need to consider contingencies and change, referring to accurate past records for costs and overheads. As Heap[37] suggests, "Whatever the planning and budgeting methodology or techniques, the important factor is to clearly identify anticipated activity with anticipated results".

Investment and finance

Level 3: Design Activity Management/Design Function Responsibilities

- Manage design budget
- Estimate design costs

At the operational level, the design manager's contribution to budgeting and planning is to maintain and control both time and cost records. All design work must be monitored in terms of man hours, material costs and equipment costs, using job sheets and time sheets. Once a management information system is developed for this, it can be used for forecasting, for future estimation and for providing middle and senior management with the data on which future resource allocation decisions can be made.

Training and Learning

A training and development strategy for each level of the organisation is required, to create an organisation that understands the contribution of design to its success and the role that design plays within the organisation, and also develops the skills needed to use design effectively.

Training and learning

Level 1: Board/Top Management Responsibilities

- Build up understanding of the value of design and the design activity
- Develop a design-appreciative climate

The corporate or Board level of a company must understand the valuable contribution design makes to all corporate activity. Approaches to achieving this understanding must evolve from an analysis of the current situation, the needs of the individuals and of what is to be achieved. Such awareness-building may be achieved by a programme of seminars, or by inviting an experienced designer to act as consultant to the Board.

Often a radical change occurs when an outside consultant is asked to undertake a design audit or a benchmarking study and present findings to the Board. Frequently, the value of design is only understood when it affects the "bottom line". A study by the Design Innovation Group[38] looked at the benefits and costs of investment in design. It found that "Design influences commercial success by adding value to the product and can make the difference between a workable idea and a marketable product. Investment in design improves financial performance, retains and regains market share, enhances exports and affects the competitiveness of industry". The British Design Council use this message to promote the use of design to industry.

However, once the core message is understood, more specific development must address the effect that design has on the whole corporate image, through products, communications and environments, to its various publics. David Bernstein[39] identified nine publics (Figure 7.4) where design acts as an intermediary to influence their of perceptions of the company. The Board and all levels of the company need to build up an understanding of this design influence and how it can be used to good effect. The Board should also understand the design activity and the critical nature of the interface between design and other functions, in terms of overall corporate success.

Figure 7.4 – The nine publics of a company image.
Source: Bernstein, D. (1984) *Corporate Image and Reality*,
Holt, Rinehart and Winston (Cassell), Eastbourne

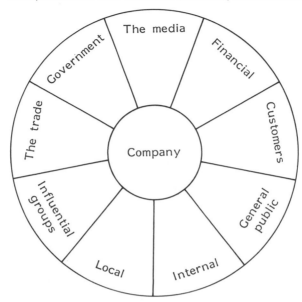

It is important that consciousness raising activities in design
are planned and subsequently evaluated. Such programmes
for building up corporate level awareness must:

1 Determine the development objectives
2 Consider the methods available
3 Plan a programme
4 Implement the programme
5 Monitor and evaluate the programme
6 Make recommendations for change or further training
   and development where necessary

Training and learning

Level 2: Middle/Functional Management Responsibilities

• Build up level of design awareness
• Create good design project teams
• Integrate design with other functions

Design managers at this level will understand design, but "Design" as a function must achieve respect from other functional managers. Important as it is for Board/senior management to value and understand design, it is critical for middle or functional managers, not only to understand design's contribution, but also see how it impacts their own functions.

There are therefore two training issues to consider here. The first is the development of design managers, in terms of their own management skills; that is, building good design teams, motivating and managing them, and also working with other functions on projects or programmes. The second is the development of other functions to increase design understanding and appreciation, and the ability to work in a team which includes or integrates the design. Design management and design awareness programmes have never been easily available in Britain; indeed, few business or design schools offer them as a matter of course. However, the British Design Council and the Department of Trade and Industry, and the Design Management Institute in the United States offer advice in locating and developing programmes. It is important when developing awareness programmes that designers are not merely used to proliferate the importance of design, but include training on how it should be used, and for what strategic purpose.

Team development and general management skill training are more easily identified, by using internal training functions or, indeed, the many outside agencies which offer such services. Of particular relevance for design managers at this level is training in project management skills and project leader skills.

As with senior management training, programmes must be planned, which will entail the following procedures:

1 Analyse training and development needs; this may involve skills and competency audit

2 Define training objectives

3 Identify appropriate training methods

4   Implement training programmes

5   Monitor and evaluate programmes

6   Make recommendations for changes or further training
     and development

Training and learning

*Level 3: Design Activity Management/Design Function
Responsibilities*

- Develop business awareness among designers
- Team building between designers and with other functions
- Design skills

A frequent criticism of designers is their lack of understanding of business. When the relationship between design
and other functions has been seen to be most effective,[40] it is
where the designer understands the underlying principles
of the business and the roles of the functions of that business. Indeed, it is appropriate, in some instances, for a
design manager to have qualifications in both design and
management or marketing.

Designers are trained to be original in their thinking, which
often makes them individualists in their approach to work.
This can lead to problems when there is a need for them to
work in teams. Although design education is addressing
this issue, it is still appropriate to use training and development to strengthen teamwork, both within a design team
and between designers and other functions on project
teams. Research[41] indicates that an audit of perceptions and
attitudes between functional groups can identify particular
areas of conflict, miscommunication and misunderstanding. If identified prior to a project, such problems can then
be addressed in a training workshop before the project
begins, preventing problems later in the project.

At an operational level, it is fundamentally important that
the designers maintain and increase their core skills and
competencies. Here, competency assessment should be
addressed. There are a number of methods for such assess-

ment: the use of appraisal/performance reviews, self-assessment and peer assessment, psychometric testing. Trained assessors can be used to establish an assessment centre, where all the above techniques are used, in addition to observed exercises. Once the assessment has taken place, the priorities and goals can be defined and the most appropriate means of achieving them established. For instance, skill development may include both design skill development (e.g. training in the use of new software packages for design) and market awareness (e.g. development of a broader knowledge of the market-place, by sending the designer to a number of trade shows or exhibitions or to work with a sales executive for a period of time).

Whatever the training need at this level, the same process of identifying the need, determining the training objectives and the resources available, designing the training programme, and implementing, monitoring and evaluating it are necessary to achieve effective use of training and development initiatives.

Implementing and Monitoring Design

Having created an environment in which the value of design to the core business is appreciated, developed the appropriate structures for making the best use of design, and planned the corporate design strategy, a critical stage is to implement and monitor those strategies, changes and programmes. In the management, and now design management, literature, a key element to success is *communication*: from how well the corporate strategy is communicated to all stakeholders, to how well a small design brief is communicated from marketer to designer, effective communication and co-operation at all levels is essential to corporate success.

Communication and documentation

Level 1: Board/Top Management Responsibilities

• Communicate statement of mission/objective

The key communication issue at Board/corporate level is the communication of the vision. It often seems very clear to those near the top, but fog builds up in many medium to large organisations, and it becomes very difficult for the operational level to know which line to follow. They frequently get lost or go their own way. Management at a senior level must provide direction, communicating the objectives clearly to enable the other levels to develop operational plans.

In design terms, this means giving a clear commitment to the value of design, identifying "design" goals, benchmarking the company against competitors and defining a design target to be achieved: for example, using design to improve the ergonomic, usability and aesthetic quality of products or using design to increase market awareness of the corporate name. These objectives should be defined and documented so that both the design function or design management function and all other functions are aware of what is to be achieved.

Communication and documentation

Level 2: Middle/Functional Management Responsibilities

- Write programme plans for marketing, design and production
- Create phase checklists

Once corporate goals have been set and communicated, functional managers are responsible for producing plans to achieve them. Design managers may have to consider, for instance, how to achieve greater corporate name awareness, possibly through a new corporate identity policy or the strengthening of the name through a revised branding and packaging design policy. Such design plans cannot be written in isolation but must be developed in conjunction with marketing and other functions.

In addition, the process by which the programmes or projects are conducted should be determined and communicated to all company participants. This involves documenting a process of phase or stage reviews, along the life of a project, and identifying a checklist of issues that must be addressed at each phase review and communicating them to all personnel involved. One example of such a communication system is the lifecycle management guides produced for all personnel in the British company GPT. These not only define product lifecycle phase reviews, but also the issues to address prior to and during a project (Figure 7.5).

Figure 7.5 – Sample of GPT guide to phase reviews.
Source: GPT (1992) Life cycle management: Your guide to phase reviews (reproduced with permission)

Before phase review meeting

- define detailed design and development tasks including simulation and costs

Deliverables

- marketing plan
- product plan

- market requirements spec

PHASE 3

Product development
Planning and design

- systems and product specs

- test and verification specs

- business case/NPIA
- capital spend identified

- project management plan
- key success criteria/measures
- concurrent engineering plan

- engineering plans
- design review results

- manufacturing and procurement plan

- customer services plan

- test and verification plan
- systems integration
- product proving
- manufacturing process proving
- field trial

- risk analysis

Communication of plans and processes are critical to the effective implementation of projects. However, the level of bureaucracy must not be allowed to impede the ability to implement projects quickly and efficiently. Therefore, whatever documentation is produced must be clear, simple and quick to read, and the process set up should enable effective and rapid decision making.

Communication and documentation

Level 3: Design Activity Management/Design Function Responsibilities

- Project documentation and control
- Learning from mistakes

The design function must be able to estimate and plan projects accurately. They must also learn from previous mistakes. In order to do this effectively, documentation of project plans, project briefs, costing, time schedules, people and processes, and project concepts, details and drawings must be maintained.

There are effective off-the-shelf computer programs and management information systems that will help in managing and communicating such project management information. In addition, designers must develop a system of maintaining and filing project "visual material" for future reference, in terms of product/project modification (as well as copyright, design right and other legal issues). This data is also useful as a reference when undertaking a company design audit.

Documentation for Design

The following list is indicative of the design documentation needs for an organisation:

1 **Corporate mission**

- Corporate design objectives
- Strategy for design

2 **Corporate design policy**

- Guidelines on legal, environmental and other design policy issues

3 **Corporate identity manual**

- Products

- Environments

- Communications (including literature, advertising, signage, uniforms etc.)

4 **The corporate design management process**

- Design management process

- Risk analysis procedure

5 **Design management documents**

- Time sheets, job sheets, scheduling and costing forms

- Guides to writing design briefs and design evaluation

- Project records

Programmes and projects

Level 1: Board/Top Management Responsibilities

- Chair major phase review

- Determine priorities for programmes

In terms of actually conducting programmes and projects, senior management is generally responsible for determining programme or project priorities. If projects, for instance, are initiated in an ad hoc manner throughout the organisation, however innovative or valuable they are, effort may be dissipated or frustration may occur as the result of an unclear line of authority for "go-ahead" or resources for allocation. Those projects that succeed in such circumstances are frequently those that are elevated to corporate level awareness and develop Board level patronage (often without being assessed in terms of compatibility with the overall strategy). To avoid this, corporate level managers must set priorities based on the overall corporate objectives.

Design should be clearly evident in the project priorities. There is little point in trying to promote a vision that includes a clear stance on design, for all operations of a company, if all of the programmes and projects given priority proceed to pay lip service to design. For example, calling in the designer at the end of the project to "tart up" the product or to provide some packaging and sales literature is not using design effectively. This is not a frequent occurrence in today's large multinational operations; however, there remain a large number of small and medium sized companies that do not understand the role of design, and do not incorporate it effectively in setting project priorities.

Corporate management involvement in monitoring programmes and major projects will obviously vary depending on the size of the organisation. Involvement may range from reviewing monthly reports and attending and chairing major phase reviews, to informal meetings with the project team or, more specifically, with the designers involved. However monitoring is achieved, it should be consistent and purposeful, that is, it should inform decision making on the project (e.g. authorisation for proceeding or resource allocation). Such monitoring procedures not only keep top management appraised of what is going on, they also ensure that functional managers and project leaders are focusing on the right direction and understand what is achieved, and what needs to be done.

Senior managers must also decide when written reports are appropriate and when their presence and involvement is necessary. This latter eventuality is often necessary to expedite or enforce project deadlines. Written reports, on the other hand, are more viable when a lag in project development time can be allocated to the report writing stage. At both this and the functional level, the use of "management by walking around" (MBWA)[42] not only keeps management informed of project progress and problems, but also signals the importance and urgency of the work. Designers who see management interest will realise the value placed on design by the organisation.

Programmes and projects

Level 2: Middle/Functional Management Responsibilities

- Develop brief
- Manage reviews
- Ensure functional involvement
- Allocate resources, accommodation, technical backup and customer information

Having developed project proposals and plans earlier in the management process, at the implementation stage managers must develop the design brief. The design brief's role in the satisfactory progress of a design project is crucial. Indeed, without a design brief that is clearly communicated and understood by all personnel, problems usually result during the design and development process. For instance, a designer's misunderstanding of the marketing department's view of the customer needs can result in frequent redesigning or modification of concepts. This, in itself, is not a problem if the process is designed to withstand the time and costs involved in modification. However, if it is expected that the process will move forward with alacrity and resources have been allocated accordingly, then the resulting budgetary adjustments for frequent revision may make the project wholly unprofitable.

There is not a specific way in which a design brief should be developed and written. However, experience indicates that the functional managers (including design/design managers) must work together to achieve a common understanding.

The Design Brief

There are also no rules governing the content of design briefs, except possibly in architecture and engineering. In communications, design and product design the form of the brief is very dependent on the client (internal or external) and the designer (Table 7.3).

The form the brief takes also depends on when designers are brought into the new product development process. If, for instance, they are brought in at the "idea generation" stage, they will be working with the team (i.e. marketing, production, or operations, finance etc.) to discuss the whole development, and specific design briefs will be written when alternative concepts are required. These briefs arise from joint discussion among the team, and are probably drafted by the designers themselves.

Table 7.3 – Summary of design brief content

Background to the company
The design problem
Design specification, product attributes
Consumer and market information
Costs, budgets
Time-scales

On the other hand, where a product concept has been developed and the marketing strategy formulated, the brief may have been constructed by management and communicated to the designers. In this case, designers often question the brief in detail to establish that they and the client have the same understanding of the problem, and the client has considered alternative strategies to the design brief given.

The most effective way of generating a design brief is by bringing in the designers at the onset of the project, at the idea generation stage, so they can contribute to the process as well as understand the demands made of the design process.

A design brief should:

- Outline the aims and objectives in relation to the corporate strategy, including marketing strategy, i.e. where the company sees itself going, how it hopes to achieve it and how this particular design brief fits into the picture.

- Convey competitor information

- Provide the answer as to "who, what, why, where and when". The brief will therefore need to assess questions about cost and time-scale, consumer and other relevant information; also materials and manufacturing facilities as appropriate (e.g. if it was literature or publicity material, the designer would make recommendations about the printer; whereas for a consumer product, the firm would outline its manufacturing capabilities).

The well-trained designer will carefully question all aspects of the brief, to establish the reasoning and validity behind the project, and look at the alternatives.

Once the design brief has been communicated and the project set in place, the functional managers must manage the review progress. The design manager will be most concerned with the stages of the design process, particularly at the conceptual and detailed design stages. Design managers should not only be involved at these phases, along with other functions, but also need to be at all reviews from project onset to conclusion.

Project managers at this level must also ensure that resources and technical support are adequately flowing to the operating team, and that the interfaces between the functions are working effectively and simultaneously. Monitoring, through the phase reviews and personal involvement, should be continued, not only of the projects but also of the effectiveness of functional co-operation.

Programmes and projects

Level 3: Design Activity Management/Design Function Responsibilities

- Brief
- Research
- Concept
- Detail design
- Implementation and costs

The implementation and monitoring actions needed of designers or design managers at an operational level are very much concerned with the phases of the design process. Initially the brief must be established and a common understanding achieved between design and other functions as to the requirements in design terms and the "deliverables". The design requirements can be determined by a number of methods, such as discussion and conversation about current design and competitors' design or the use of mood-boards (Figure 7.6) to establish a common agreement over the design direction or the use of semantic differentials. Semantic differentials (Table 7.4) use descriptors at the ends of a scale (eg. flamboyant to subdued), to identify the degree to which that design attribute is required. Other tools such as "scenarios" describe the customer or consumer and their lifestyle. All of these methods aid common understanding of the design requirements. Functional, technical, production, distribution and other requirements must also be determined and understood by all parties.

Figure 7.6 – Mood-boards for Stirling Cooper shop interior originated by David Quigley Associates, Architects

Once the design brief has been agreed upon and understood, the designer/design manager must ensure that the design research needs are fulfilled. For instance, the designer may need to research the lifestyle of those for whom he/she is designing, or consider competitors' designs. Indeed, the designer will also need information

Table 7.4 – Example of semantic differential for use in a design brief, here describing the consumer of a product

	Very much	Somewhat	Neither	Somewhat	Very much	
Young						Mature
Up-to-date						Old fashioned
Extrovert						Introvert
Leader						Follower

on the materials, technology and processes necessary to produce and deliver the end product.

During the conceptual design stage, it is the design function's responsibility to conduct brainstorming/experimental discussion, and also to undertake risk analysis and consider technical and commercial feasibility. During refinement, further risk analysis should take place in conjunction with other functions.

Detailed design reviews must involve not only the designers, but also any functional or operational manager or group concerned with bringing the design into reality. For example, in interior design, this may involve lighting contractors and installation contractors; in literature design, the printers, photographers and illustrators etc. This ensures that once the design moves forward into production, it can do so with confidence that major changes in design will not be necessary as a result of one function's late intervention in the design decision making.

Finally, monitoring and control must be achieved by the design manager, maintaining job/project records, costing and time sheets, and also supervising the efficiency of the design progress. Any deviation from the plans and schedule must be assessed, and the implications reported to all other functions.

Evaluating Design

For any area of evaluation, a process of defining appropriate evaluation criteria, prioritising those criteria and developing an evaluation procedure must be established. The evaluation process must also be communicated to all involved in the programmes or projects.

Evaluating design

Level 1: Board/Top Management Responsibilities

- Achievement of targets
- Comparison of design performance against design strategy

Having set targets or design objectives in the planning process, corporate level managers must use these targets to develop criteria against which the company and the design outcomes can be assessed. These could include financial, legal, technical, operational, administration and control criteria, and also design attribute criteria – for example, improved innovation, increased quality, increased consumer awareness of the brand, improved storage, packaging and display, improved sales, or improved customer satisfaction with the aesthetics, function and presentation of the product.

Evaluating design

Level 2: Middle/Functional Management Responsibilities

- Evaluation of the design process and product
- Evaluation of return on investment

The functional managers should evaluate the whole design process against the plans, to assess whether the objectives set were achieved, both in terms of process and products. The product will be evaluated internally, but also externally by customers and consumers. This evaluation should be collected and should inform the development process. The design process will be evaluated internally; it may also be relevant to assess external contributions to the process – for instance, the use of suppliers or sub-contractors. Once again, the results should contribute to the overall planning procedures. In both cases, maintaining the loop of evaluation, planning and development is important.

Another critical evaluation is to assess the return on investment for the design programme or projects. Again, establishing criteria against objectives is important here, because, as stated before, the return in the short term may not always be financial. It may be related to entering a new market successfully or developing greater brand awareness.

Evaluating design

Level 3: Design Activity Management/Design Function Responsibilities

- Evaluate design outcome against brief objectives
- Evaluate use in the market
- Evaluate effectiveness

At the functional level, evaluation becomes much more specific, for instance using the design brief to establish criteria to evaluate the outcome. Semantic differentials (Table 7.5) can often be of value here, in judging to what extent the product attributes coincide with the desired attributes set out in the brief semantic differential. Such evaluation may be conducted not only by designers or other functions on the design team, but also by objective outsiders and consumers.

Table 7.5 – Semantic differential for use in a design brief

Product attribute semantic at briefing						
	Very much	Somewhat	Neither	Somewhat	Very much	
Delicate	x					Tough
Up-to-date		x				Old fashioned
Simple	x					Complex
Leader		x				Follower

Table 7.5 shows how the attributes were identified at briefing; once the concept is assessed, the evaluation tends to veer towards a more complex and traditional design than envisaged at the briefing (Table 7.6).

Once the product is in use, whether it is a corporate image, a product or environment, evaluation by users is valuable in establishing the design effectiveness and in informing the whole development process.

Table 7.6 – Semantic differential for use in a product concept evaluation

Product attribute semantic at concept evaluation

	Very much	Somewhat	Neither	Somewhat	Very much	
Delicate	x					Tough
Up-to-date				x		Old fashioned
Simple			x			Complex
Leader				x		Follower

All evaluation is evolutionary; it can form part of the ongoing "audit process" used to inform and plan corporate design strategy, design policy, design management and design activity. Systems for evaluation must necessarily be specific to the organisation. They need not necessarily become burdensome: merely establishing checklists of issues to consider post-project, identifying the personnel responsible and ensuring it this understood and accepted by all participants will enable evaluation to take place.

Conclusion

This chapter has set out an agenda for managing design from the corporate and strategic level through to the design activity level, which is summarised in Table 7.7. Managing design is an integral part of management itself. However, it is frequently forgotten in the "chaos" which ensues. This agenda has attempted to put it back into context, and remind managers what they must consider to use design effectively. In many ways, much of the guidance given in the literature is full of contradictions; provide policies, define strategies and goals yet allow for innovation and creativity within organic structures – and inexhaustible. Each organisation must use whatever tools are appropriate for their own situation. It must always be borne in mind that if design is to be valued and used effectively, it must be understood, appreciated, and communicated, and should always be on the agenda.

Table 7.7 – Agenda and actions for design

	Planning design			Organising design			Implementation and monitoring		Evaluation
	Strategy	Policy	Process planning	People and structures	Investment and finance	Training and Learning	Documentation Communication	Projects	
Level 1: Board top	1.1	2.1	3.1	4.1	5.1	6.1	7.1	8.1	9.1
	• Define corporate strategic objectives incorporating corporate design objectives • Approve design strategy linked to marketing strategy • Ensuring design strategy covers products, communications and environment	• Define the meaning of design within the organisation • Approve policies standards or guidelines on design and also on related factors such as quality, legal and environmental issues • Approve financial systems and cost controls related to design	• Define programmes • Define targets	• Create innovation and design supportive structure and climate • Choose design advisors, external consultants, design directors • Set clear hierarchy of design responsibility	• Evaluate major design strategy decisions • Ensure funding is available to implement strategy	• Build up understanding of the value of design and the design activity • Develop design-appreciative climate	• Communicate statement of mission/ objective	• Chair major phase review • Determine priorities for programmes	• Achievement of targets • Comparison of design performance against design strategy
Level 2: Middle/ business/ function	1.2	2.2	3.2	4.2	5.2	6.2	7.2	8.2	9.2
	• Use design audits to inform strategy • Define design strategy to achieve corporate objectives • Coordinate detailed strategy with market-	• Define design policy • Define design performance standards • Define quality, legal and environmental standards relating to design (including materials,	• Set preferred programme/ project procedures • Define project proposal contents • Commission and undertake audits	• Create cross-functional teams • Create design manager role • Provide resources for designers	• Define programme budgets • Ensure approved list of designers and suppliers • Provide design function with required resources to	• Build up level of design awareness • Create good design project teams • Integrate design with other functions	• Write programme plans for marketing, design and production • Create phase checklists	• Develop brief • Manage reviews • Ensure functional involvement • Allocate resources accommodation, technical backup, cus-	• Evaluation of the design process and product • Evaluation of return on investment

Table 7.7 – *Continued*

	Planning design			Organising design			Implementation and monitoring		Evaluation
	Strategy	Policy	Process planning	People and structures	Investment and finance	Training and Learning	Documentation Communication	Projects	
	ing and other functions	safety, service and design) • Ensure consistency of policy across products, communications, and environments			allow implementation of programme			tomer information	
Level 3: Design activity/ function	1.3 • Maintain awareness of design trends • Contribute to design objectives and strategy	2.3 • Inform policy and define design specifics e.g. colours, shapes, sizes, corporate identity	3.3 • Organise office management • Organise design job management and progress • Undertake audits	4.3 • Ensure the necessary skills are available • Direct policy for the selection of designers	5.3 • Manage design budget • Estimate design costs	6.3 • Develop business awareness among designers • Team building between designers and with other functions • Design skills	7.3 • Project documentation and control • Learning from mistakes	8.3 • Brief • Research • Concept • Detail design • Implementation and costs	9.3 • Evaluate design outcome against brief objectives • Evaluate use in the market • Evaluate effectiveness

References

1 Olins, W. (1985) The mysteries of design management revealed, *Journal of the Royal Society of Arts*, January, 103–114.
2 Quinn, J B. (1992) Strategies for change: Logical incrementalism, in Mercer, D. (ed.) *Marketing*, Basil Blackwell, Oxford.
3 Thackara, J. (ed.) (1986) *New British Design*, Thames and Hudson, London.
4 Dumas, A. and Minztberg, H. (1990) Managing design, design management, *Journal of Design Management*.
5 Topalian, A. (1989) Organisational features that nurture design success in business enterprises, Proceedings of the Second International Conference on Engineering Management, Toronto.
6 Lorenz, C. (1987) *The new design dimension of corporate strategy*, paper presented at Fullbright and CNAA Managing Design Conference, Windsor.
7 Marks and Spencer (1990) *Annual report and financial statements*.
8 Marks and Spencer, internal document.
9 Dumas, A. and Minztberg, H. (1990) Managing design, designing management, *Journal of Design Management*.
10 Heap, J. (1989) *The Management of Innovation and Design*, Cassell, London.
11 Quinn, J.B. (1980) *Strategies for Change: Logical Incrementalism*, Richard D. Irwin, Illinois.
12 Lawrence, P. (ed.) (1986) *Views on Design*, Corporate Design Foundation and Design Management Institute, Boston, Mass.
13 Heap, J. (1989) *op cit.*
14 Burns, T. and Stalker, G.M. (1966) *The Management of Innovation*, 2nd edn, Tavistock, London.
15 Bennett, D., Lewis, C. and Oakley, M. (1988) Planning for products services and systems, *Operations Management*, 18–45.
16 Peters, T.J. and Waterman, R.H. (1982) *In Search of Excellence: Lessons from America's Best Run Companies*, Harper and Row, New York.
17 Johnson, G. and Scholes, K. (1989) *Exploring Corporate Strategy: Text and Cases*, Prentice Hall, Hemel Hempstead.
18 Topalian, A. (1980) Designers as directors, *Designer*, February, 8.
19 Quinn, J.B. (1980) *op cit.*
20 Pilditch, J. (1987) *Winning Ways*, Harper and Row, London.
21 Ibid.
22 Olins, W. (1985) *op cit.*
23 CBI (1989) *Issues, Business Success by Design*, no.1, CBI, London.
24 Topalian, A. (1989) *op cit.*
25 Clipson, C. (1984) *Competitive Edge Business Survey*, University of Michigan, Ann Arbor.
26 Tjosvold, D. (1991) *Team Organisation: An Enduring Competitive Advantage*, John Wiley, Chichester.

27 Walton, T. (1991) The hallmarks of successful design teams, *Design Management Journal*, pp 5–10.
28 Fujimoto, T. (1991) Product integrity and the role of the "designer-as-integrator", *Design Management Journal*, **2**(2), pp 29–35.
29 Keeley, L. (1991) Taking the D-team out of the minor leagues, *Design Management Journal*, **2**(2), pp 35–39.
30 Rice, T. (1991) Teaming strategic marketing with design, *Design Management Journal* **2**(2), pp 59–64.
31 Jackson, S. and Romeri, M. (1992) World class product development, *Manufacturing Breakthrough*, July/August.
32 British Standards Institute (1989) *Managing Product Design*, BS7000, BSI, London.
33 Walker, D. (1989) *Managing Design: Overview, Issues*, Open University Open Business School, Milton Keynes.
34 NEDO Garment and Textile Sector Group (1993) *Best practice in design and development*, PE International.
35 Johnson, G. and Scholes, K. (1989) *op cit*.
36 *The Guardian* (1985) Next, 25 March.
37 Heap, J. (1989) *op cit*.
38 Potter, S., Roy, R., Capon, C.H., Bruce, M., Walsh, V. and Lewis, J. (1991) *The Benefits and Costs of Investment in Design: Using Professional Design Expertise in Product, Engineering and Graphics Projects*, Open University/UMIST Design Innovation Group, Report DIG-O3, July.
39 Bernstein, D. (1984) *Company Image and Reality*, Holt, Rinehart and Winston, Eastbourne.
40 Jones, T. and Cooper, R. (1993) *The functional interfaces in new product development*, Proceedings of the International Engineering Conference, The Hague.
41 Cooper, R. and Jones, T. (1993) *The interface between design and other key functions in new product development*, The New Product Development Workshop, University of Groningen, The Netherlands, May.
42 McDonough, E.F. (1986) Matching management control systems to product strategies, *R&D Management*, **16**(2), pp 141–149.

Resource Guide

The study and practice of design management is evolving rapidly. There is a growing literature and new educational, industrial and research initiatives to promote the discipline further. To assist the reader in pursuing their studies or activities further, we provide here a guide to the resources – published and organisational – that will prove useful. The resources detailed comprise:

- Selected annotated bibliography
- Periodicals and journals
- Organisations
- Design management research and education
- Internet

Selected Annotated Bibliography

The references at the end of every chapter detail specific sources on material drawn upon in the main text. Rather than reproduce these in a bibliography, we have listed key texts, organised by broad subject area, with a brief summary of their content. Highly recommended publications are marked with an asterisk.

Design – general

*Pye, D. (1978) *The Nature and Aesthetics of Design*, The Herbert Press.

A highly readable, principled and inspiring exposition of what constitutes good design and the nature of the design process, arguing that art and problem solving are inseparable within design.

Potter, N. (1980) *What is Design?* Hyphen Press.

A well-written introduction to the role of the designer, design education and design methods. Although it is principally aimed at design students it is generally accessible to individuals without prior knowledge of design.

Design management – general introductions

Lorenz, C. (1986) *The Design Dimension*, Basil Blackwell, Oxford.

A readable account of industrial design's competitive power, developed from articles published in The Financial Times. Case studies include Olivetti, Sony, Ford and Philips.

*Pilditch, J. (1989) *Winning Ways*, Mercury Books.

Designer James Pilditch explains how winning companies use design. Drawing upon a range of examples, especially from Japan, the book is a highly readable, well-illustrated summary of best practice in innovation and design management.

Design management – textbooks and study guides

Heap, J. (1989) *The Management of Innovation and Design*, Cassell.

A brief introductory textbook for business students.

Hollins, G. and Hollins, B. (1991) *Total Design: Managing the Design Process in the Service Sector*, Pitman.

An introduction to design management as applied to the service sector, drawing from research findings to provide a prescriptive approach to the management of design.

*Walker, D. et al. (1989) *Managing Design*, P791, Open University Press, Milton Keynes.

The material for the Open University's course in design management represents the most wide ranging, accessible and stimulating introduction to the subject available. Twelve case studies are provided, using video, audio cassette and documentary material. The course guides are excellently presented and include assignments. The package is of use to students and managers in industry.

*Walsh, V. et al. (1992) *Winning by Design*, Basil Blackwell, Oxford.

Written by a team from the Open University and UMIST, this book draws upon the considerable research conducted by the authors on design's contribution to competitiveness. A more academic approach than others, it provides useful overviews and analysis of much of the literature in design management and innovation.

Design management and innovation – anthologies and readings

Gorb, P. (ed.) (1988) *Design Talks!* Design Council, London.

A collection of papers from design management seminars held at the London Business School, including contributions from Sir Terence Conran, Wally Olins and Rodney Fitch. Design managers provide material on various case studies, including Philips, Olivetti, 3M, London Underground, British Rail, Ford and others.

Gorb, P. (ed.) (1990) *Design Management*, Architecture, Design and Technology Press.

A second collection of London Business School seminar papers. Case studies include London Regional Transport, Clarks Shoes, Tootal Textiles, Richard Shops, Prudential and the Burton Group.

Henry, J. and Walker, D. (eds) (1991) *Managing Innovation*, Sage Publications, London.

A useful anthology of readings covering a range of issues in the management of innovation. Organisational and strategic commentaries are complemented by varied case study material, which includes Xerox, Rover, 3M and Harley-Davidson.

*Oakley, M. (ed.) (1990) *Design Management: A Handbook of Issues and Methods*, Basil Blackwell, Oxford.

Over 40 contributors provide a comprehensive introduction and overview to some critical issues in design management, ranging from the economic and business context of design to project management.

Academic researchers, designers, managers and others provide a range of perspectives on the field, including summaries of research, case studies and guidelines of best practice. Contributors include Robin Roy and David Walker from the Open University, Christopher Lorenz, Colin Clipson, Wally Olins and James Woudhuysen. Also includes an essay by Bill Evans on Japanese design management.

Roy, R. and Wield, D (eds) (1986) *Product Design and Technological Innovation: A Reader*, Open University Press, Milton Keynes.

A slightly dated, but nevertheless valuable anthology that provides various perspectives on design's role within innovation processes.

Corporate identity

Olins, W. (1990) *The Wolff Olins Guide to Corporate Identity*, Design Council, London.

A concise introduction to the subject written by one of Britain's leading practitioners in the field, this is consequently more prescriptive than analytical. Examples cited include Prudential, Akzo and ICI.

Bernstein, D. (1984) *Company Image and Reality*, Holt, Rinehart and Winston, Eastbourne.

An excellent discussion of the company image, corporate identity and design.

Case studies

Blaich, R. (1993) *Product Design and Corporate Strategy: Managing the Connection for Competitive Advantage*, McGraw-Hill.

The former design chief at Philips presents his case for design. Beginning with a discussion of general issues, most of the book comprises two detailed case studies of design management in Herman Miller and Philips.

Design Management Institute and The Design Council (1989) *Designing for Product Success: Essays and Case Studies from the TRIAD Design Project*.

Thirteen international case studies, including Braun, Canon, DEC, Sharp, Sony and Yamaha, which all illustrate the design process and its contribution to competitiveness. The DMI TRIAD project, this is a catalogue of an exhibition that includes essays on design management and the project's research methodology.

Heskett, J. (1989) *Philips: A Study of the Corporate Management of Design*, Trefoil Publications.

A detailed history and analysis of design management in the Dutch electronics company, with some diverse product case studies.

Kicherer, S. (1990) *Olivetti: A Study of the Corporate Management of Design*, Trefoil Publications.

A companion volume to the study of Philips, this examination of a company in similar markets provides interesting contrasts in terms of the design culture within the company.

Key reports and research

Corfield, K.G. (1979) *Product Design*, National Economic Development Office, London.

The historically significant report that first drew the issue of design to the attention of British government policy makers.

Cotton and Allied Textiles EDC (1984) *Designing for Success: Approaches to Managing Textile Design*, National Economic Development Office, London.

A comparative study of British and foreign textile manufacturers, analysing the place of design in management structures and design processes, together with management and education issues.

The Design Council (1983) *Report to The Design Council on the Design of British Consumer Goods by a Committee under the chairmanship of David Mellor OBE, RDI*.

A report on the state of design and design management in key British industries: ceramics, domestic appliances, furniture and textiles. Analyses the failure to integrate design within manufacturing, and thus does not make for uplifting reading.

*Fairhead, J. (1987) *Design for a Corporate Culture*, National Economic Development Office, London.

Developed from a working paper on international best practice on design management for an NEDC enquiry, the Fairhead report examines strategic aspects of product design, how an innovation culture can be developed and provides case study material on Black & Decker, Sony, Matsushita and Hewlett-Packard.

Potter, S., Roy, R., Capon, C.H., Bruce, M., Walsh, V. and Lewis, J. (1991) *The Benefits and Costs of Investment in Design: Using Professional Design Expertise in Product, Engineering and Graphics Projects*, Open University/UMIST Design Innovation Group.

Report on a major research project that examined the effectiveness of the DTI's grant scheme to promote the use of design consultancy. Provides empirical evidence on the benefits of design investment.

*Roy, R. and Potter, S. (1990) *Design and the Economy*, The Design Council, London.

A concise and readable introduction to the role played by design in Britain's economic performance, drawing on research and product examples.

Service, L.M., Hart, S.J. and Baker, M.J. (1989) *Profit by Design*, The Design Council, Scotland.

Based upon a survey of 369 companies, this research analyses the relationship between design management and competitiveness.

NEDO, Garment and Textile Sector Group (1993) *Best Practice in Design and Development*, PE International.

This report illustrates a method of competencies analysis and identifies good skills for design management in textile design.

Design in Britain

*Huygen, F. (1989) *British Design: Image and Identity*, Thames and Hudson, London.

A well-illustrated history that seeks to identify the distinctiveness of British design. Drawing upon examples from industrial, retail and popular culture design, Huygen's provocative and readable account includes the development of Britain's design consultancy industry.

Sparke, P. (ed.) (1986) *Did Britain Make It? British Design in Context 1946–1986*, The Design Council, London.

A collection of essays examining the post-war development of design in British industry and culture. Themes include the textiles and consumer electronics industries, design promotion and the retail industry.

Stewart, R. (1987) *Design and British Industry*, John Murray, Edinburgh.

A history of industrial design in Britain, which focuses on the development of state institutional support, promotion and design education.

Thackara, J. (ed.) (1986) *New British Design*, Thames and Hudson, London.

A snapshot of British experimental design in the mid-1980s. Although dated, it provides non-designers with a view of the possibilities in contemporary design, and John Thackara's introduction draws out some implications for industry.

International design

*Aldersey-Williams, H. (1992) *World Design: Nationalism and Globalism in Design*, Rizzoli.

A well-illustrated survey of design trends and approaches in 19 countries, together with case studies of global design strategies in IBM, Philips and Sony. An introduction analyses design in terms of the apparent conflict between national styles and global marketing.

Sparke, P. (1987) *Japanese Design*, Michael Joseph, London.

A readable and well-presented book that explains the nature and development of design in Japan with examples from a range of industries.

Design and environment issues

Burall, P. (1991) *Green Design*, The Design Council, London.

An introduction to environmental issues in design, including checklists of relevant design criteria and sources of further information.

*Mackenzie, D. (1991) *Green Design: Design for the Environment*, Laurence King.

A comprehensive identification of issues and survey of best practice in environmentally responsible design. Well-illustrated, there are many case studies covering product, packaging, graphic and textile design.

Papanek, V. (1984) *Design for the Real World*, Thames and Hudson, London.

A classic radical critique of industrial design including a useful summary of idea generating techniques.

Cultural and historical context

Attfield, J. and Kirkham, P. (eds) (1989) *A View from the Interior: Feminism, Women and Design*, The Women's Press.

A reader of feminist perspectives of design history, providing insights neglected by most design histories.

Bayley, S. (1991) *Taste: The Secret Meaning of Things*, Faber and Faber, London.

Criticised for its occasional sweeping assertions, Bayley's lively discussion is a thought-provoking introduction to the issues that determine what products people buy.

*Featherstone, M. (1991) *Consumer Culture and Postmodernism*, Sage Publications.

Critically reviews differing perspectives of postmodernism and addresses a range of issues, including the role of lifestyle, global culture and the changing nature of consumer society.

Forty, A. (1986) *Objects of Desire: Design and Society 1750–1980*, Thames and Hudson, London.

A history of design placed in the context of changing social and economic conditions.

McDermott, C. (1992) *Essential Design*, Bloomsbury, London.

A dictionary on design history issues and movements prefaced by a useful critical essay and including a well-organised bibliography.

*Sparke, P. (1986) *An Introduction to Design and Culture in the Twentieth Century*, Unwin Hyman, London.

A readable history which accounts for design's development in different countries, with one chapter focusing on design's changing relationship with manufacturing industry. Includes a good bibliography and glossary.

Tomlinson, A. (ed.) (1990) *Consumption, Identity and Style: Marketing, Meanings, and the Packaging of Pleasure*, Routledge, London.

A series of readings on aspects of consumer culture, with a useful introduction by the editor that considers the meaning of commodities.

*Walker, J. A. (1989) *Design History and the History of Design*, Pluto Press.

A summary and critique of design history literature, with useful chapters on lifestyle and consumption which provide a readable theoretical introduction to historical and cultural perspectives.

Periodicals and Journals

The following specialist journals provide news and analysis in the fields of design and design management.

Axis

Japanese design journal, including English language translations of major features. International topics are covered, with particular coverage of Japan.

Blueprint

Architecture and design.

Co-Design

Quarterly journal covering design and design management issues.

Design

Monthly journal published by the Design Council.

Design Management Journal

American academic journal published by the Harvard Design Management Institute.

Design Review

Journal of the Chartered Society of Designers, with a range of news and features on design.

Design Studies

British academic journal of the Design Research Society, including articles on design management research.

Design Week

Trade paper of the British design industry, featuring regular surveys on the use of design and the structure of the consultancy industry.

EcoDesign

Journal of the Ecological Design Association, with occasional articles on product design.

ID

American journal with good coverage of design and design management in the USA.

Journal of Product Innovation Management

American academic journal which covers international research on product development and design

Organisations

The following organisations play distinctive roles in the promotion of design and the provision of information on it.

Chartered Society of Designers

29 Bedford Square, London WC1B 3EG, tel: 071 631 1510

Represents the professional interests of designers, with membership open to design managers. Offers a range of legal and information services to members.

Department of Trade and Industry

Innovation Enquiry Line, tel: 0800 44 2001

Through its Enterprise Initiative, the DTI promotes innovation and design in British industry. Up-to-date information on its services and free literature on design and innovation is available by contacting its Innovation Enquiry line.

Design Business Association

29 Bedford Square, London WC1B 3EG, tel: 071 631 1510

An offshoot of the Chartered Society, the DBA represents the commercial interests of design consultancies through the promotion of design and the establishment of professional training programmes for designers. Provides a free directory of members to design buyers.

Design Council

28 Haymarket, London SW1Y 4SU, tel: 071 839 8000

State-funded body to promote design in British industry and support design education.

Design and Industries Association (DIA)

17 Lawn Crescent, Kew Gardens, Surrey TW9 3NR, tel: 081 940 4925

Founded in 1915, the DIA brings together industrialists and designers to promote more effective use of design in industry. The Association organises various events, including conferences and study tours for corporate and individual members.

Design Museum

Butlers Wharf, Shad Thames, London SE1 2YD, tel: 071 403 6933

Provides permanent historical collection of design, a changing showcase of new design, major exhibition and lecture programme on design issues and design research library.

Ecological Design Association

20 High Street, Stroud, Gloucestershire GL5 1AS, tel: 0453 765575

Promotes environmental approaches in design, providing educational events and information for companies and designers.

Royal Society for the Encouragement of Arts, Manufactures and Commerce (RSA)

8 John Adam Street, London WC2N 6EZ, tel: 071 930 5115

Established in 1754, the RSA seeks to promote design through a range of activities, including an annual bursary competition for young designers sponsored by industry.

Design Management Research and Education

Various university and other educational bodies undertake research or provide education in design management. Below is a selective listing of such bodies.

CODE Consortium of Design Educationalists

2 Mount Hill Cottages, Stratford Road, Wicken, Milton Keynes, MK19 6DG, tel: 0908 567842

A consortium of leading institutions in the field of design research and Sponsors of the *Co-Design Journal*.

Design Management Institute

107 South Street, Suite 502, Boston, MA 02111-2811, USA, tel: +1 617 338 6380

Publisher of the *Design Management Journal*, the Institute promotes design management through education, research and publications.

Design Research Society

Institute of Advanced Studies, Manchester Metropolitan University, All Saints, Manchester M15 6BH

A forum of academic researchers in design and design management, organising a regular series of meetings and seminars. Publishes the *Design Studies* journal.

Domus Academy

Edificio C/2, Milanofiori, 20090 Assago (Mi), Italy, tel: +39 2 8244017

A postgraduate school of industrial design, fashion design and design management based in Milan. During the summer the school offers intensive summer schools in design management for managers, designers and others.

European Academy of Design

CDMT, University College Salford, Frederick Road, Salford, M6 6PU, tel: 061 834 6633, ext: 484

An organisation to promote the publication and dissemination of research in design through the establishment of a bi-annual conference and the publication of proceedings.

London Business School, Centre for Design Management

Sussex Place, Regents Park, London NW1 4SA, tel: 071 262 5050

Design management is offered on the MBA programme, along with bespoke courses for industry and a seminar programmes. The centre has regular visiting researchers in design management from Japan.

De Montfort University

Department of Design Management, School of Design and Manufacture, De Montfort University, The Gateway, Leicester L31 9BH, tel: 0533 551551

De Montfort offer a BA Hons and an MA (full- and part-time) in design management; they also offer short courses and bespoke courses for industry.

Open University

Design Innovation Group, Faculty of Technology (Design), Walton Hall, Milton Keynes MK7 6AA, tel: 0908 653556

The Design Innovation Group – run jointly with UMIST – is responsible for Britain's largest programme of research in the fields of design and design management. The group also provides teaching materials for the OU's range of design courses including "Managing Design", cited above.

Royal College of Art

Design Age, Kensington Gore, London SW7 2EU, tel: 071 584 5020

The Design Age programme undertakes research and promotes awareness on the implications of demographic change for design disciplines.

Staffordshire University

Design Research Centre, School of Design and Ceramics, College Road, Stoke-on-Trent ST4 2DE, tel: 0782 744531 ext. 3303 (contact: Mike Press)

The centre undertakes continuing research projects in design management and environmental issues in design. Also provides an MA and short course programme in design management.

University College Salford

The Research Unit, Centre for Design, Manufacture and Technology, Frederick Road, Salford M6 6PU, tel: 061 834 6633 ext. 484 (contact: Rachel Cooper)

Varied research programmes in design management and co-ordination of "North West Design Talks", a series of seminars for industrialists and designers on design management issues.

University of Manchester Institute of Science and Technology

Manchester School of Management, PO Box 88, Manchester M60 1QD, tel: 061 236 3311

Design management is taught as part of an MSc in marketing, along with other short courses in effective design management.

Internet

The Internet is an international network of computers offering users access to databases, electronic mail facilities and networking on a vast array of subjects. Most universities provide their staff and students with free access to the Internet. The following two interest groups are particularly relevant to design.

Design-Research

Design-Research forum covers the discussion of theory, practice, policy, methods, IT, management and training likely to be of interest to researchers, teachers and practitioners in design. It also includes information on events, conferences, courses, etc. Send an E-mail message to **mailbase@uk.ac.mailbase** with the one line message: **subscribe design-research your name.**

IDFORUM

Loosely concerned with industrial design, the subjects covered by IDFORUM are broad. A monthly 'newsletter' is sent out. Send an E-mail message to **listerv@vm1.yorku.ca** with the one line message: **subscribe IDFORUM your name.**

Gophers

Easy to access 'gopher' serves provide menus of information and access top computer sources worldwide. These are constantly evolving with new ones being established. The authors have found that the gopher at the following locations provides an excellent starting point for design-related searching: **coombs.anu.edu.au.**

The Design Agenda

Readers of this book are welcome to engage in discussion with its authors. Please E-mail your comments to **dctmp@staffs.ac.uk.**

Index